THE GOSPEL ACCORDING TO ST. JOHN

NEW TESTAMENT FOR SPIRITUAL READING

VOLUME 8

Edited by

John L. McKenzie, S.J.

THE GOSPEL
ACCORDING TO ST. JOHN

Volume 2

Josef Blank

CROSSROAD · NEW YORK

1981
The Crossroad Publishing Company
575 Lexington Avenue, New York, NY 10022

Originally published as *Das Evangelium nach Johannes 2*
© 1977 by Patmos-Verlag
from the series *Geistliche Schriftlesung*
edited by Wolfgang Trilling
with Karl Hermann Schelke and Heinz Schürmann

English translation © 1981 by The Crossroad Publishing Company
Translated by Matthew J. O'Connell

Library of Congress Catalog Card Number: 81-68180
ISBN: 0-8245-0117-9

OUTLINE

PREFACE   1

EXEGETICAL AND THEOLOGICAL
INTRODUCTION   9

 I. The Last Supper and the Washing of the
    Feet (13:1-30)   22

    1. The Washing of the Feet (13:1-11)   22

    2. Instructions to the Disciples (13:12-20)   27

    3. Identification of the Traitor (13:21-30)   33

 II. THE FIRST FAREWELL DISCOURSE
     (13:31–14:31)   39

    1. The New Commandment (13:31-35)   39

    2. Prediction of Peter's Denial (13:36-38)   48

    3. Exhortation to Faith; Jesus the Revealer
       of God (14:1-11)   51

    4. Promise of "Greater Works"; Certainty
       That Prayer Will Be Heard (14:12-14)   69

    5. Love for Jesus; Promise of the "Supporter"
       and of "Seeing Jesus Again" (14:15-24)   76

    6. Second Statement about the "Supporter"
       (14:25-26)   92

    7. "Peace" as the Farewell Gift of Jesus;
       Conclusion of the First Farewell
       Discourse (14:27-31)   97

 III. THE SECOND FAREWELL DISCOURSE
      (15:1–16:33)   106

    1. The True Vine (15:1-10)   106

2. The Friends of Jesus (15:11-17)   115

3. The Community of Jesus' Disciples and
the Hatred of the World (15:18–16:4a)   122
   a) The Community of Disciples and the
Hatred of the World (15:18-25)   123
   b) The Paraclete and the Disciples as
Witnesses to Jesus (15:26-27)   126
   c) Persecution by the Synagogue
(16:1-4a)   128

4. The Activity of the Spirit-Supporter
(16:4b-15)   133
   a) The Departure of Jesus (16:4b-7)   134
   b) The Judgment on the World
(16:8-11)   135
   c) The Spirit Teaches the Community
(16:12-15)   139

5. The Promise of Jesus' Return (16:16-22)   151

6. The Clarity of the Day of the Lord
(16:23-28)   159

7. Conclusion of the Second
Farewell Discourse (16:29-33)   176

IV. THE FAREWELL PRAYER OR
HIGHPRIESTLY PRAYER OF JESUS
(17:1–26)   191

1. The Revelation of Jesus (17:1-5)   194

2. Prayer for the Disciples Left Behind
in the World (17:6-19)   203

3. Prayer for the Community (17:20-24)   211

4. Conclusion of the Prayer (17:25-26)   218

NOTES   231

PREFACE

Readers of this series may be surprised to find that the volumes on the Gospel according to John begin not with chapters 1-12, as might have been expected, but with chapters 13-21, which contain the account of the last supper, the farewell discourses, and the final prayer of Jesus, as well as the account of his passion and resurrection. In addition, the method followed will be different in many respects from that of the earlier volumes in the series.*

The first and more important of these two differences is closely connected with the question of how we may enter into the theological "angle of vision," problematic, and intention of the last of the canonical gospels. This question is not easily answered. In my book *Krisis*, which investigated the christology and eschatology of John, I dealt extensively with the fourth gospel. Yet I must admit that I still find it extremely difficult to approach this text. There is great danger of taking this seemingly simple document all too lightly. In fact, the text is like a smooth wall: you are constantly slipping on it or else you cannot get even an initial foothold. I understand Ernst Käsemann quite well when he writes of himself: "I shall be discussing a subject which, in the last analysis, I do not understand;"[1] I find myself in the same position. But his book also confirmed me in thinking that one must tackle this text with more perseverance and especially that one must take greater account of its context in the history of theology and of the Church than I did at one time.

The reader should not think that these reflections are out of place

*See the Publisher's Note in volume 1, p. viii.

1

in a commentary which is chiefly meant for meditation! For the fourth gospel is by its nature an extensive *meditation on Jesus* and *reflection on Jesus*. Each of these two elements, meditation and reflection, is constantly passing over into the other, and the two are very closely linked. An exploration of this gospel for purposes of meditation must emphasize precisely the meditative character of the book itself. The principles and presuppositions of this meditation are, however, nowhere more clearly expressed than in the farewell discourses. It is for this reason that I regard myself as justified in beginning the commentary as I do.

As regards introductory questions about the origin of the fourth gospel, the history of its tradition, the identity of its author, and its relations with the synoptic gospels,[2] I shall say only what is required for the understanding of the commentary that will follow. The name *John* is kept as being traditional. It is of little importance whether or not we take the name as referring to a witness who belonged to the circle of Jesus' disciples; for, if that is who John is, then John is obviously not the literary author of the gospel, but rather the guarantor of the Johannine tradition concerning Jesus. Nor does it make much difference whether we take John as referring to a Johannine circle, a kind of school, or even to a later editor who pulled together the tradition he had before him and revised its theology. The language, style, and theology all show a good deal of unity, a fact which suggests to me that at the end of the chain of tradition stood an evangelist-personality, a very early Christian theologian who was highly gifted and set his mark on the entire work. It is to this man, whom I cannot further identify, that I give the traditional name John.

This man certainly does not belong to the apostolic generation. Rather, he sees it as his task to take in hand and reflect on the questions of a period that is already considerably removed from the early period of Jesus and the original community. For this John, in fact, the very distance from the primitive period of Jesus and the apostles becomes a special problem to which he is far more sensitive than are the synoptic writers, and—even more important—to which he expressly calls his readers' attention. We may state the same problem in the language of Søren Kierkegaard who saw this point very clearly and on whose conception of it Rudolf Bultmann is dependent in his commentary on John. Is the "disciple at second hand" (a term that includes all who were not direct disciples of the historical Jesus, or what Kierkegaard calls "immediate disciples") at a disadvantage in principle when compared with the "immediate disciple"? What is the situation of Christians who live at an ever greater historical distance from Jesus? What kind of relationship can they have to him? What is Christianity in the period after Jesus and the first apostles?[3]

We touch here on a problem that contemporary theology treats rather like an unwelcome stepchild. In current reflection on the historical Jesus, the gospel of John is understandably pushed somewhat into the background; it has long been agreed in critical scholarship that in the historical inquiry about Jesus this gospel has no particularly valuable contribution to make. The discourses of Jesus as delivered in this gospel do not, at least in their present form, go back to Jesus himself but are the creation of the evangelist or his school. They belong rather in the area of meditation on Jesus. No one can deny that Jesus is the central object of John's interest, but just as undeniably his interest is not that of a historian but that of a believing Christian and a theologian.

Perhaps John is to be counted among the prophets of the early Church, so that in his writing prophecy and theological teaching have fused in a unique manner. Early Christian prophecy has frequently been understood to be a means whereby the exalted Christ spoke to his own (in this view, no doubt is being cast on the identity of the exalted Christ with the earthly Jesus). From the viewpoint, then, of a purely or even primarily historical interest, the neglect of the fourth gospel is to some extent understandable. Whether or not such neglect is also objectively justified is another question entirely; in fact, the answer to it must probably be no. John was clear in his own mind, of course, that any naive search back to the historical Jesus was impossible. To a certain extent even the synoptic writers were aware of this. It is well known that we interpret them wrongly if we regard their gospels as historical reports about Jesus; this is true even for the gospel of Mark and the Q source of the discourses. The theological purpose of the synoptics is not historical reconstruction but to make Jesus present to the Church of their

3

day. At the same time, however, they are essentially closer than is John to the older tradition about Jesus. What distinguishes John from the synoptics is that he feels and reflects the growing distance from the historical Jesus much more intensely than they do.

In addition, John is concerned to give this basic experience a positive meaning. The question he is bent on answering is, what does it mean to believe in Jesus Christ at the end of the first century or the beginning of the second? Why is the link with Jesus of Nazareth not only very important but even indispensable for this faith? Could we not interpret the Christian understanding of salvation much more effectively with new and current categories, especially those of gnostic thought? Would not the gnostic myth of salvation and the redeemer, which promises man a purely spiritual, other-worldly, supratemporal, and nonhistorical redemption from the present wretched world, be adequate? Why, then, the continual linking of Christianity back to Jesus from the obscure town of Nazareth?

In addition, is not such a linking with the past a questionable business, unless it is accompanied by a thrust in an entirely different direction that might be expressed this way: Christianity can be true to Jesus and thus to its own origin only if it accepts the risk of a new linguistic and conceptual formulation of the *cause* and *person* of Jesus. In his gospel, this John of ours has embarked on a bold theological adventure. In so doing, he looks like a tightrope walker for whom a false step to right or left could plunge into the abyss. The hermeneutical problem of Christian theology, which no reflection on Jesus of Nazareth can avoid, is met by John in a way from which all later generations can learn. John stands on a boundary line. The relation back to Jesus of Nazareth is just as important to him as the question of a new formulation of Jesus' message for John's own age, world, and society. In the mind of this theologian and evangelist there is no Christianity without the historical Jesus, whose historical and geographical context he endeavors to recreate with all the means at his disposal. At the same time, however, the message about Jesus, the *kerygma*, will remain a closed book and bear no fruit unless it is communicated and interpreted in language intelligible to the hearers in John's own society, whose range of ideas is determined by their intellectual and cultural milieu and whose

4

language is hellenistic or gnosticizing. John probably feels that this is the society and thought-world to which he himself belongs. The missionary nature of the good news urges him onward, as it were. Now, if these considerations correctly gauge, at least to some extent, the theological aim of John, then this gospel becomes highly relevant to our own age and to our reflections and efforts.

In this context, we must also pay attention to the situation of the Johannine community. Johannine dualism, that sharp division between the community of believers and the unbelieving world or cosmos (the latter being very often represented by "the Jews"), has in my opinion a background not only in theological doctrine, the history of religion, and an intellectual world-view. In all probability, it also has a sociological background to which little attention has hitherto been paid.

Christian communities at the end of the first century were largely urban. Unfortunately, we know only too little of the origins of their members, but it may be taken as fairly certain that at this period the communities still had few members from the upper classes. The lower and middle classes provided the majority of the recruits. The understanding of salvation and faith was not oriented to political and social activity, except insofar as this was inseparable from the preaching of the faith and the recruitment based on it. Christians at this period regarded themselves primarily as aliens and sojourners, as the First Letter of Peter phrases it (2:11), in a largely unconcerned or even hostile world. The feeling of being an alien was widespread. There was still a profound division between pagan society and the Christian faith-community. Anyone who converted to the Christian faith was made an expatriate, as it were; was cut off radically from established ways and from traditional pagan society with its religiously based conceptions and values.

Such seems to me to be the sociological background of Johannine dualism, and it must be given greater weight alongside factors based on the history of religion and of ideas. But since Christians were convinced—and John is no exception here—that faith in Jesus Christ had to do with the salvation of the world and society in their entirety, this dualism was constantly being breached and overcome. It was not absolutized as a cosmic dualism, as in gnosticism, nor was it even taken over as a world view that underlay everything else.

5

Consequently, in interpreting John's statements we must allow for the historical situation of the community, and at the same time bear in mind our own situation which is historically quite different by comparison.

In the light of all these preliminary considerations, a different kind of biblical meditation also suggests itself. Since this series began (1961, and therefore before Vatican II), there have been many changes on the ideological and ecclesiological scene, and these could not fail to make their influence felt, even if only on my own view of things. Therefore I would like to explain briefly my conception of the task I have undertaken in this book. I said earlier that the meditation form is basic to the fourth gospel. It is therefore important to highlight the meditative structure of the text itself; doing so leads us directly to meditation. Although it is not my intention to deal with detailed questions of exegesis that are better explored in the major commentaries, it is nonetheless important to deal as clearly as possible with theological questions that are directly connected with the meditative structure of the text. The more or less lengthy introductions at the beginning of the various main sections are the primary place for handling these. These introductions also contain the indispensable exegetical information without which a solidly based meditation is impossible, in my opinion.

Here too, is the place for attempts to discuss the theological questions in such a way that they will shed light on our situation with its own problems. As far as possible, it will be made clear why the problems of John and his community are still of some concern to us; the question must also be asked whether these problems are in fact still ours, and why they are or are not. The ideal reader, after all, is not one who sits numbly before the text in pious reverence, but one who is called upon to think along with the text and even to think further where it leaves off. In other words, a reader who wants not only to gain a better understanding of the evangelist and what he is trying to say, but also to gain, with John's help, a better understanding of self and of the central problems of Christianity as it existed in John's day and as it exists today is needed. Admittedly, this means that we are setting our sights high. But even if we were to come only a few steps closer to this goal, the result would perhaps be to set in motion the kind of meditation we find in the gospel itself. Meditation, properly understood, can never serve solely for one's own edification. It is rather a way of participating in the universal event of the word of God that willed to become flesh in Jesus Christ. For the word to become flesh also means that it takes concrete form in the historical world of any given moment.

JOSEF BLANK

EXEGETICAL AND THEOLOGICAL
INTRODUCTION

1. The Johannine tradition, like the Markan (14:1–16:8), had at its disposal a continuous account of the passion and resurrection of Jesus. To this report a narration of the last meal Jesus took with his disciples seems to have been added at a very early date. According to Paul (1 Cor. 11:23-26) and the synoptic writers (Mark 14:22-25; Matt. 26:26-29; Luke 22:15-20) Jesus instituted the symbolic action of the Eucharist, the Lord's Supper, at this last supper. In addition, the last supper was, in the view of the synoptics, a passover meal at which the passover lamb was eaten in accordance with Jewish custom (cf. Mark 14:12-17 par.).

Here we have an important difference between John and the synoptics. John knows a tradition regarding the last supper, but for him, unlike the synoptics, this final meal is not a passover meal but purely and simply a farewell meal. More importantly, John reports nothing about Jesus instituting the Eucharist during this final meal.

This state of affairs has caused scholars very great difficulties down to our own day. John and the synoptics are in agreement that Jesus was condemned to death by Pontius Pilate, the Roman procurator, and executed on the cross, on a Friday, "the day of preparation before the sabbath." But according to the synoptics this Friday was the day of the passover feast, that is, the most important Jewish festival of the entire year, whereas for John this Friday was the day *before* the feast (cf. 18:28). We can transpose this into dates: According to the synoptics, Jesus died on Friday, the fifteenth of Nisan, but according to John he died on Friday, the fourteenth of Nisan, and at the very hour when the ritual slaughter of the passover lambs was taking place in the temple at Jerusalem. According to John, Jesus is the true passover lamb, no bone of which may be broken (cf. 19:31-36).

We shall see that John uses a whole series of theological motifs in his presentation of the last supper and his story of the passion. Indeed we must speak of a *symbolic presentation* or at least of an *interest in symbols* on the part of the fourth evangelist. At the same time, however, we may not overlook the fact that the synoptics cannot be said to be more objective than John. They too make use of theological motifs when they depict the last supper as a passover meal and connect the institution of the Eucharist with the passover meal. All attempts to harmonize these two divergent traditions have thus far failed. Even the Qumran texts with their variant calendar for the feasts have not helped matters; we must choose one or the other tradition.

As far as the Eucharist is concerned, the gospel of John speaks of it in chapter 6 in connection with the great discourse on the bread of life, which at its end passes over into a discourse on the Eucharist (6:51-59). My own view is that the eucharistic discourse was part of the original and not added only later by an ecclesiastical editor. This would mean, of course, that it is to this discourse that we must look for what John has to say about the Eucharist. In his tradition the Eucharist was thus an independent unit of tradition that had no fixed link with the tradition concerning the supper. The other possibility is that John himself separated this unit from the tradition concerning the supper and made it independent. For our understanding of the supper, however, the decisive point is the use John made of the tradition concerning it. To this tradition he linked the account of the washing of the feet, which has a theological significance that can hardly be overestimated.

As for the date of Jesus' death, we should point out that in the view of a considerable number of scholars John is here to be preferred to the synoptic writers. For it is highly unlikely that the trial and execution of Jesus took place on the most important feast day of the year. Even if the Romans might be thought capable of such an action, there are major reasons for doubting the Jews would have done the same. To me this argument is convincing. Accordingly, Jesus died on the fourteenth of Nisan. When did the fourteenth of

Nisan fall on a Friday? With the help of astronomical calculations, scholars have determined that April 7 in the year A.D. 30 is the likeliest date. If we follow John, then of course the last supper cannot have been a passover meal. Furthermore, the theological symbolism of the fourth evangelist then has a historical basis.

In addition, John has integrated into his presentation various other traditions that have parallels in the synoptics. To these we will refer at the proper time and place. We shall go into the special problems of the Johannine account of the passion and Easter in the introduction to that section.

2. A striking peculiarity of the fourth gospel is the lengthy farewell discourses that begin in 13:31 and close with the great prayer of Jesus (the "highpriestly prayer," as it is also called). How shall we evaluate these farewell discourses? What is their meaning?

2.1. In connection with his account of the last supper and the institution of the Eucharist Luke in his gospel already has a series of other sayings of Jesus that are added as a kind of farewell conversation. In them a number of parallels to John can be found (cf. Luke 22:24-30, 31-34, 35-38). It is fairly easy to see the point of these words in Luke: they are instructions of Jesus to his disciples and are formulated with a view to the time when Jesus will no longer be present in their midst. It is likewise fairly easy to show that these instructions were not originally given in the context in which they now stand. Luke evidently wanted to emphasize instructions meant for the time when Jesus would be absent and therefore he introduced them at this point. In this connection H. Schürmann writes, "All regulations for the community have their ground here in the Eucharist and are ordered to it. For a life of faith and brotherly love among the disciples of Jesus is a life in the brotherhood of a community that celebrates the Lord's Supper."[4] When viewed in this light, John is seen to be continuing a tradition that arose before him and independently of him. At the same time, however, the farewell discourses of John have a different theological orientation than those of Luke.

2.2. How did these farewell discourses come into being? At first sight, they seem to supply something like a testament of Jesus, a collection of last words that are especially authoritative precisely because they are his last words. But here again we must avoid attempts to give a historical or psychological interpretation. In fact, the Old Testament and Judaism contain a broad tradition of such testament-like farewell discourses. These provide *literary models* belonging to a specific *literary genre*, the genre of farewell discourses.

The chief models to be mentioned from the Old Testament are the farewell discourse of the patriarch Jacob to his twelve sons (Gen. 49:1-27) and the entire Book of Deuteronomy (the fifth Book of Moses), the literary framework of which takes the form of a farewell address of Moses to the Israelites shortly before his death and the ensuing conquest.[5] In its present form the book of Deuteronomy claims to be a farewell address of Moses to the Israelites. The framework (Deut. 1–4 and 31–34) heightens the farewell or departure aspect of the situation by a backward look at the period Israel had spent in the wilderness and, at the end, by a concluding blessing that is accompanied by earnest exhortations regarding the imminent new period of settlement in the promised land. Into this framework are introduced separate instructions, some older, some more recent.[6] The farewell address thus turns out to be a *literary fiction*. G. von Rad is right in saying: "The sermons in Deuteronomy are addressed to Israel in the form of words of Moses, now near his death, when they arrived in the land of Moab after their wanderings. This fiction is maintained consistently throughout the whole of Deuteronomy. But it is really a fiction. In fact, these sermons are addressed to the Israel of the later period of the monarchy."[7]

What is the point of this literary fiction? The whole is given the form of a farewell discourse by Moses in order, first of all, to emphasize the importance and urgency of the exhortations given. The description of the book as a *testament* also underscores its importance. The authority of Moses here is not understood as something belonging to the historical past, but as an ongoing authority that obliges the people even of later times; this view was still maintained in postexilic Judaism. New formulations and commandments are integrated into the old Mosaic tradition; expression is thus given to the continuity of tradition.

Finally, the literary schema is meant as a help in making the original situation of decision a present reality: All Israel is once again confronted with the choice between life and death. This element of re-present-ation is so important to the book of Deuteronomy that the latter even invented a classic formulation of it: "He, our God, concluded a covenant with us at Horeb; not with our fathers did he conclude this covenant, no, but with us ourselves, those here today, all of us who are alive" (Deut. 5:2-3; Martin Buber's version). The idea that the covenant on Sinai is not a great event of the past, but a present event and one that binds here and now, affecting each generation in its turn, is here expressed with all clarity.

2.3. The situation is similar when we come to the Johannine farewell discourses. Here again we are dealing with a literary fiction. The formulation should not evoke resistance, even though initially it sounds somewhat disenchanting. For various reasons I would maintain that John even took the form consciously from Deuteronomy; one thing that points to this is the concluding prayer of Jesus, which is a kind of parallel to the blessing given by Moses. As in Deuteronomy, the literary genre is pressed into the service of a new message that is linked with the older Jesus-tradition. As a matter of fact, the words we quoted just above from G. von Rad can be applied without qualification to the Johannine farewell discourses. As thus applied they would read: The farewell discourses of John's gospel are spoken to the community of Jesus' disciples who have come with him to the point of parting which is his imminent death, and are put on the lips of Jesus just before his death. The fiction is faithfully adhered to throughout the farewell discourses, but it is nonetheless truly a fiction, since the Christian community being addressed is in fact that of about 100 A.D., a community that is already aware of being considerably distant from the historical Jesus.

It is on the basis of this understanding that we can best approach the problem of the farewell discourses. We will therefore renounce any attempt to assign these discourses in any form to the historical Jesus. But we must immediately add that just as in Deuteronomy Moses is not regarded as a figure of the historical past but as an authority decisive for the present moment, so too the authority of Jesus is decisive for the life of the Jesus-community. In fact, the farewell discourses are at the center of the Johannine "theology of re-present-ation"[8] and are even to some extent the key to it. In them it is not the historical Jesus who speaks directly, but the present, exalted Lord who speaks through the mouth of the authorized man of the Spirit (the spiritual man, cf. 1 Cor. 2:15). It is a matter of indifference whether we call him prophet or evangelist, for in the last analysis both figures are united in the person of John.

At the same time, however, this spiritual man does not regard himself as cut off from or unrelated to history and tradition; on the contrary, he knows that he is tied to Jesus and bound by his authority, which is superior to his own in every respect. The reference to Jesus is taken for granted by the spiritual man and his community; both are intelligible to themselves only in the light of Jesus. On the other hand, the evangelist sees himself faced with the need to answer new questions. Usually we do not realize with sufficient clarity how deep a change took place in the early Church when the first, apostolic generation of eyewitnesses had left the stage of history, when the separation from Judaism became definitive after A.D. 70, and when expectation of the Lord's imminent return (the *parousia*) grew weak and people had to prepare themselves for a long journey through history. It is evident that at such a moment wholly new problems must have arisen. John, therefore, must on his own express new answers *in the name of Jesus*, answers that can appeal to Jesus' authority. In this critical situation he cannot leave the community of Jesus to grapple with its questions alone. It is precisely the faith which binds him to Jesus and his message that gives John the courage to venture on a new interpretation of the Christian witness of faith, along the lines of his own Johannine theology.

2.4. Can these new problems be specified in greater detail?

2.41. First, a word about the structure of the farewell discourses. We shall divide chapters 13-17 into four major units: (1) last supper and washing of the feet (13:1–30); (2) first farewell discourse (13:31–14:31); (3) second farewell discourse (14–16); (4) the last prayer of Jesus (17).

It is easy to see that we are confronted here with two originally independent farewell discourses, since a first part evidently ends in 14:31b with the remark, "Rise, let us go hence." It is probable that this invitation was originally followed by the account of the short journey to the Mount of Olives, which is introduced in 18:1: "When Jesus had spoken these words, he went with his disciples across the brook Kidron." We may surmise that the older literary presentation contained a continuous account of the last supper (including the washing of the feet and a farewell discourse) and a sequel along the lines of 18:1ff., and that the other two units—the second farewell discourse and the final prayer of Jesus—were inserted later.

On the other hand, these two later units are not at all distinct in language and theology from what we think of as the Johannine style, and they probably had the same editor as the rest of the gospel. It is no longer possible to say with any certainty why these two sections were added. In fact, in some respects the two farewell discourses can be described as a first and second version of the same discourse, since the two texts have a series of themes in common, and they overlap in various ways.

2.42. From the theological standpoint the farewell discourses are dominated by the theme of *the departure of Jesus*. This is clear from 13:1, a programmatic verse: "Before the feast of the Passover, since Jesus knew that his hour had come to pass over from this world to the Father, and since he had loved his own who were in the world, he loved them to the end." The motif of Jesus' departure is sounded repeatedly; it even determines the emotional mood of the entire scene. At the same time, however, the evangelist intends to make it clear to his readers and hearers that his departure does not mean an end pure and simple, at which time everything would be over and done with. Rather, to the eyes of faith, the departure of Jesus can only be a passing over to the Father, an entry into the dimension of God or the divine glory.

Admittedly, as far as the world is concerned, Jesus is no longer present; but in John's view, this simply illustrates the manner in which unbelief sees things. Similarly, if believers were to argue, "What meaning does this Jesus have for us any longer? We never knew him ourselves, and we cannot even any longer question those who did know him!" their thoughts and questions would resemble those of the world. They would not yet have understood that faith grounds a new and different kind of relationship with Jesus, a relationship whose ultimate meaning cannot be obscured even by the absence of Jesus from the visible world.

Misunderstandings by the disciples are a favorite stylistic device of John; he deliberately uses it to stimulate his hearers to a broader and deeper reflection. In the farewell discourses he makes abundant use of this method. This is not mere accident. For the question of the present significance of Jesus is precisely the one that kindles the interest of believers and at the same time causes special difficulties for the community. John regards the problem of "not seeing and yet believing" (20:29) as the central problem of Christian existence in the period after Jesus' departure. The evangelist intends the misunderstandings to be a help in grappling with this problem. I speak expressly of *grappling* because believers cannot evade this problem except at the price of removing themselves from history as the human locus of faith; only death or the return of Christ can eliminate this basic tension from faith. The believer who remains in the world must be brought to realize that the departure and resultant absence of Jesus not only are not a decisive objection to faith but are characteristic of and give structure to Christian faith in the midst of the world and history.

Moreover, the way of Jesus as involving a departure *to the Father* is, as such, also the way the believer must travel in the world. The farewell situation is therefore to be understood as a typical situation of passing over. For this reason it is very well chosen, since this passing over makes it possible to give a very precise portrayal of the special situation in which faith and the community of Jesus find themselves as they continue to exist in the world. The special dialectic of faith becomes manifest here, a dialectic that in John is grounded in the Christ-event, that is, in the exaltation and glorification of Jesus or the unity of cross and resurrection.

2.43. In this context, the shift of emphasis that marks Johannine eschatology also becomes clear. In full consonance with the primitive Christian tradition John understands the cross and resurrection of Jesus as the divinely caused "eschatological turning point"[9] that has occurred once and for all and now definitively determines the situation of faith. There is widespread agreement in the New Testament writings that the primitive Church regarded the coming of Jesus and especially his death on the cross and his resurrection as having an *eschatological* significance (significance for the end time or final age). The only question is how various Christians interpreted this eschatological meaning.

The enthusiastic and apocalyptic interpretation was evidently dominant in the expectation, on the part of the very first Christians, of an imminent parousia; there were certainly groups that expected Jesus to come soon in the form of the heavenly Son of man. Paul's writings already show a shift of emphasis, but the expectation of an imminent cosmic parousia still plays an important role. John is evidently familiar with such traditions and comes to terms with them. He radically transforms the Son of man christology,[10] chiefly with the help of the idea of exaltation. In the Johannine concept of exaltation the crucified Jesus is seen as simultaneously the glorified Jesus who is to be given the honor due to God. In other words, the *phases* which were originally distinct are combined to give a unified but paradoxical total picture; one thinks spontaneously of the forms used in expressionist paintings.

In addition, John has not simply dropped the idea of the parousia, although he has disengaged it from the apocalyptic mode of presentation that is familiar to us, especially from the synoptic apocalypse (Mark 13; Matt. 24–25; Luke 21:5-36). The return of Christ already coincides with the resurrection or Easter and continues subsequently in the community. The Christian hope for the future is thus by no means eliminated; rather, it is now shaped entirely by the Christ-event, since the way of Jesus through death to the glory of the Father becomes the model of the believer's way. Thus hope for the future is radically fused with the idea of following Christ.

2.44. We have already spoken of the rupture between the world (the cosmos) and the community of disciples. The global Johannine concept of the world as a designation for the world of humanity which is opposed to God and whose hostility is manifested in the rejection of Jesus and of his disciples as well, is already a source of numerous difficulties for the modern mind; its affective tone is thoroughly negative. In our day, world means the space in which we live our lives; it means the totality of things. When we speak of the cosmos, we mean the universe as understood by the natural sciences, which in recent centuries have studied it with such striking success. The emphasis is quite different in the Johannine concept of the world.

It is clear that there is in John no radical devaluation of the world in the sense of God's good creation as depicted in Genesis 1 or in John's own prologue where it is a creation produced by the divine word (1:3). John does not share the (gnostic) view that the world as such is evil, much less the fullness of evil. Such a materialization of evil would in fact contradict the biblical idea of creation.

What John has in mind is a historical conception of the cosmos that is manifested above all in the rejection of Jesus. In John the concept, "this world," includes the problem of evil. But evil, in John's view, always finds concrete expression in some evil action of humanity and is defined chiefly by means of the two concepts of *lie* and *hatred*. It would be an unhistorical way of approaching the subject and would in addition contradict the text, were we simply to explain away this viewpoint of John. On the other hand, it is also clear that we may not turn it into a hard and fast dogma.

Neither may we overlook the fact that John's community, which was a small group, faced a society which had little but mockery and contempt for the message and the community, and that the first persecutions had meanwhile occurred. It is in this historical context that the life of the community at this period must be seen. The community understood itself to be the community of Jesus in the midst of a hostile world which it had to face unprotected and without recognition by civil law. It is understandable that this situation should also have influenced the way in which the Christian community interpreted its own internal existence, since aggression from without would strengthen the internal cohesion of the group. In its internal life the group regarded itself as the community of Jesus' friends and as brothers and sisters. Much that at first sight seems like a withdrawal into pure inwardness has its basis in this fact. The same point emerges from the fact that when it comes to the internal life of the community the commandment of love is always put forward as the central directive Jesus left his followers.

Exclusive union with Jesus is thus seen as the most important

18

bond holding the community together and as the foundation that supports it. We may take the frequent mention of "prayer in the name of Jesus," that is, prayer in which Jesus is invoked, as a reference to the community's worship. Modern man, hearing this phrase, would think rather of individual personal prayer, but for primitive Christianity the worship of the community, and this precisely in the form of a cult of Christ, was extremely important. The assembly and its activity took place in the name of Jesus. From this we can also understand how the idea of the *unity of the community of Jesus* gained in importance. Probably there were heretical groups, early Christians sects (of a gnostic type, in all likelihood), which by reason of their doctrines as well as their practice endangered the cohesion of the community and thus its unity as well.

The First Letter of John suggests that this is what in fact happened. In John, of course, the unity of the community, the Church, is still understood and grounded in a completely christological and theological way. A little later, in the letters of Bishop Ignatius of Antioch (who died a martyr at Rome in about A.D. 110), tied with the bishop of the community as a new institutional factor of unity have already acquired great importance. In John, the bishop has as yet no role in establishing unity; John's conviction is that unity is both created and assured by living faith in Jesus and by the Holy Spirit.

2.45. A further special group of statements must be mentioned here since they play a significant role in the farewell discourses. I am referring to the various statements about the supporter, the Holy Spirit, or the spirit of truth. In the technical terminology of the exegetes these statements are called "paraclete sayings"; there are five of them in all (14:15-17, 25-26; 15:26-27; 16:4b-11, 12-15).

The Greek word *paraklētos*, which occurs five times in the New Testament, and only in the Johannine literature (14:16, 26; 15:26; 16:7; and once with reference to Jesus himself, in 1 John 2:1), frequently means a person who comes forward in behalf of another as a mediator or intercessor or as helper and supporter. In its application, the word is not limited to the legal counsel, the advocate in a court, although many of the Latin Church Fathers translated it thus (*advocatus*). Since their time, *paraklētos* has usually been translated as "helper" or "supporter."[11]

When we ask why the word *paraklētos* was chosen, we should probably think of the figure of the *intercessor*, which was a widespread phenomenon in antiquity, both in society at large, where in every possible circumstance people sought the help of an intercessor or mediator, and, closer at hand, in the Jewish faith which acknowledged heavenly intercessors with God on man's behalf, whether in the form of good works, almsgiving, etc., or in the form of the great holy men of the past, such as Moses or the prophet Jeremiah. Apocalyptic literature, too, was familiar with heavenly intercessors.

As far as early Christianity is concerned, it is significant that all the intercessory figures and mediating persons known to Judaism and Hellenism in the religious sphere were eliminated from the picture by Jesus and his unique mediatorial function. Thus we find the apostle Paul already saying, "Christ Jesus who died and was raised sits at the right hand of God and *intercedes* for us" (Rom. 8:34). There is a similar conception in 1 John 2:1. This theology of Christ's unique mediatorial role finds sublime expression in the Letter to the Hebrews. It is worth noting, however, that Paul already knows also of a mediatorial or intercessory function which is exercised by the Spirit; this function is expressed in the well-known statement that the Spirit comes to the aid of our weakness and acts as intercessor with God when we pray (Rom. 8:26-27). In the Johannine tradition the concept of supporter or paraclete was used to express this function; it was probably applied first to Jesus (as in 1 John 2:1; but cf. also John 14:16 where the phrase "another supporter" suggests this) and was then transferred to the Spirit.

In order to grasp the meaning of the term supporter, we must try to put our finger on the supporter's function as given by the immediate context of the paraclete sayings. The following points emerge. "Another supporter" takes the place of Jesus. The coming of the supporter-Spirit presupposes the departure of Jesus; in fact, the departure is precisely the condition required if the Spirit is to be able to come. The sayings about the supporter-Spirit acquire their precise meaning in John from their context in the farewell discourses. Here the Spirit is seen entirely in relation to the person and work of Jesus, and yet at the same time he exercises a special function of his own that is parallel to that of Jesus. We must keep both of these aspects in mind: what the Spirit and Jesus have in common, and the ways in which they are distinct. In the person of the supporter-Spirit Jesus remains with his disciples; he directs the community through the Spirit.[12] He exercises a function within the community and a function in relation to those outside it: as teacher of the Christian community and as witness to the world.

John knows the early ecclesial tradition of experience of the Spirit, or the phenomenon of Spirit-induced enthusiasm. As the community of the *last time* the early Church was aware that it had been endowed with the gift of the Spirit. In John, however, a unification has taken place, in comparison with the very varied manifestations which the earlier experience of the Spirit had taken (cf. especially 1 Cor. 12–14). John, in a thoroughgoing way, links the Christian community's experience of the Spirit to Jesus and thus to the Jesus-tradition. Jesus and his word are the permanent central content of the Spirit's teaching; the most important task of the Spirit is to make the word and work of Jesus present and operative.[13]

We will probably come closest to an accurate understanding of the supporter-Spirit in John if we understand him to be the dynamic, efficacious power that renders Jesus present and causes the ever new event of Jesus' presence in history, an event with which the event of faith in Jesus and the community of Jesus is inseparably connected. On the other hand, the situation in John is still so un-formalized that the support which the Spirit gives extends directly to all the disciples of Jesus, to the entire Church; John knows as yet of no group of office-holders who are singled out for a special gift of the Spirit. He maintains the universal gift of the Spirit to all the disciples of Jesus, to all believers. For John, the ultimate criterion for the Spirit is the abiding link with Jesus; this much at least is absolutely decisive.

THE LAST SUPPER AND THE
WASHING OF THE FEET (13:1–30)

The Washing of the Feet (13:1–11)

Exegesis

The story of the washing of the feet in John is the vestibule to the passion narrative; for this reason, if for no other, its importance can hardly be exaggerated. The story is not, of course, a historical account, nor would it become such even if an older tradition regarding it were to be found (none such can in fact be shown). We have here rather a *symbolic story* which gives concentrated expression to a certain understanding of Jesus and his death. The section is clearly structured: After an introductory observation (v. 1) comes the story of the symbolic action (vv. 2-5) and then a first interpretation (vv. 6-11).

Verse 1 with its indication of date ("before the feast of Passover") and its statement of a basic principle forms an introduction not only to the farewell discourses but to the entire account of the supper and the passion. The whole narrative stands under the sign of the "hour of Jesus," which has now come. The content of the "hour" is specified by the phrases "pass over from this world to the Father" and "loved them to the end" or "perfectly." In the Greek text this relation to the entire ensuing narrative is even clearer, since the phrase *eis telos* ("to the end" or "perfectly") is matched by the word *tetelestai* ("it is finished" or "it is done fully") in 19:30b. The passage of Jesus to the Father, which comprises his death on the cross and his resurrection (the hour includes both) is seen by John as the highest and most complete expression of Jesus' love for the disciples. The story that John will now go on to tell is not an ordinary story that happened to take place at some time or other, but *the story of love in its perfect form.*

Verses 2-5 refer succinctly to the last supper as known to John from the tradition. Even Judas Iscariot is brought in right at the beginning as the one who played a chief role in the handing over of Jesus. He comes on the scene as a tool of the devil. At the center of the picture, however, stands the symbolic action of washing the feet. In authentic Johannine fashion, verse 3 depicts Jesus as the divinely appointed representative who possesses complete authority—a power to save—and consequently also a freedom and an utter sovereignty that do not desert him even in the all-decisive moment of his hour.

In this interpretation, Jesus was not overtaken by blind destiny, but rather had full control of the entire sequence of events that were to affect him. The passion is seen much more as an action of Jesus than as a passion, that is, something he undergoes. The ground of this superiority is to be found in Jesus' union with God, with the Father, for this union takes what an onlooker might regard as incomprehensible and meaningless and lifts it into another, mysterious dimension in which love reigns. Even the episode of the washing of the feet presupposes Jesus' superiority. When he condescends to perform the lowliest of services for his disciples, his action is a sign of supreme freedom. (In an entirely different spirit it is told of Emperor Caligula that he deliberately humiliated prominent Roman senators by ordering them to wash his feet.[14]) At the same time, the washing of the feet is seen as a symbolic interpretation of the meaning of Jesus' death. Jesus performs the humblest task of a slave for his disciples whom he loves to the end.

Verses 6-11 comprise chiefly the dialogue between Peter and Jesus and provide a first interpretation of Jesus' symbolic action. Here the evangelist uses the *Johannine misunderstanding* as a stylistic device. Initially, Peter does not understand at all what Jesus is doing; in fact, he even rejects it. He regards it as impossible that Jesus, whom he knows and honors as his master, should wash his feet. Verse 7 is ambiguous and therefore leaves the situation still wide open: Peter (and the other disciples, whose spokesman he is) does not as yet grasp the meaning of the episode, but he will understand it later. The 'later' is left unspecified, but it is natural to think of it as referring to Jesus' death and resurrection. John is thus indicating to the reader the perspective in which he should view the story. Jesus is answering Peter's refusal by telling him that if a person is to have a share in him, Jesus, if he is to be in communion with him and belong to him, then he must accept the slave-service Jesus offers; in other words, he must accept the death of Jesus as a death that brings him salvation. Peter's violent reaction (v. 9), as he goes to the other extreme, is again based on a misunderstanding.

The sense of verse 10 is not entirely clear. Many expositors relate the words "he who has bathed" to baptism, and the subsequent words "does not need to wash, except for his feet" to the daily penance a Christian does. Others suggest a reference to the Eucharist. This last is very improbable. It is possible that the words "except for his feet" are a later addition, so that the text originally read, "does not need to wash, but is entirely clean."[15] If this be the case, then the reference to baptism would also be eliminated. For an understanding of the whole episode we must start with the fact that the symbolic action of washing the feet is *related to the salvific meaning of Jesus' death*. The washing of the feet symbolizes a complete, comprehensive cleansing and interprets the effect of Jesus' death along the lines of 1 John 1:7: "And the blood of Jesus his Son cleanses us from all sin."

If we attempt nonetheless to wrestle a meaning from the added words "except for his feet," it can be sought only in the continuation of the example given by Jesus. We would have here a first reference to the idea that in their dealings with one another the disciples are to take Jesus for their model. There is no reference to baptism or even to the word, but only to the saving death of Jesus which brings a total cleansing to all who allow themselves to be touched by it.

Our starting point, then, is the christological and soteriological meaning of the washing of the feet (soteriology is the doctrine of redemption). John understands the life of Jesus and especially his death on the cross as an incomparable service of love which Jesus renders to humankind. He sees the whole life and death of Jesus under the sign of existence in the service of others. In so doing, he is in agreement with what is said in the hymn to Christ in the Letter to the Philippians (2:5-11) as well as with the synoptic sayings on Jesus as servant (Mark 10:45; Matt. 20:28; Luke 22:27). Perfect love is to be seen at work when Jesus makes himself the servant of all; at the same time, this unreserved life for others is the highest expression of Jesus' relationship with God. Throughout his life Jesus interpreted God as love that liberates and rescues persons. The meaning of the symbolic action of washing the feet is clear when seen against the background of the revelation of God that Jesus brought us.

Verses 10b-11 modulate back into the historical situation which the account supposes, when they say that not all are clean and when this statement is justified by a reference to Judas the traitor. By his betrayal Judas excludes himself from the community with Jesus on which salvation depends. In principle, no one is excluded from profiting by the saving service and love of Jesus, but the dark possibility remains open that persons may bar themselves from thus profiting. Where and in what manner this happens can hardly be judged from outside.

Meditation

According to John, the person and life of Jesus are associated with the manifestation of the highest, freest, and truest love the world has ever known, a love that gives all humanity an inkling of what God really is, namely the God characterized by such love as this. It is precisely in his suffering and dying that Jesus fulfills his vocation, which is to reveal this God. For, when seen against the background of such an experience of God, even Jesus' journey to the cross cannot be regarded as a journey into nothingness, into utterly hopeless darkness, but must be judged rather to be a "passing over from this world to the Father." The God and Father of Jesus is the real "beyond" of human life, although the term beyond is already questionable, since this God of love is even now everywhere and always close to humans; this same love is already the foundation of human life. As John sees it, the union of Jesus with this love gives him an unprecedented freedom and authority in the decisive final hour.

This basic attitude of Jesus immediately gives rise to a further aspect: he who reveals divine love even to the point of accepting death must manifest this love in the form of union with his followers, in the form of a life lived for others. The commitment of Jesus to his disciples, or his love as directed to others, is not to be separated from the divine side of that love. This love is simply unlimited and inexhaustible, and the discussions about whether involvement with others may cause the love of God to be downplayed are at bottom too narrowly conceived and start with an entirely false premise. In practice, the question must rather be turned around: Are those who insist so stubbornly on the vertical ready to plunge into the bound-less world of relations with their fellow human beings? Anyone who lives under the sign of love and acts out of love is certainly living by the power of the central divine reality as disclosed to us by Jesus, and he will certainly not reach the end of his loving so soon.

Decisive, of course, is the criterion which Jesus establishes and which finds expression in the symbol of washing the feet: love shows itself in the humbling of self, the limiting of self, and in living and acting for others. Loving means helping the others to live their own lives, to be free, independent, and capable of living; it means cre-ating for others the human living space needed. For us today the symbolism of the washing of feet has lost much of its original ex-pressive power. In the slaveholding society of antiquity, in which the washing of feet had its real vital context, its message was un-mistakable. Jesus was identifying himself with those who were re-garded as of no account. Love, as he understood and practiced it, included a renunciation of power and domination, as well as a read-iness to perform even the most despised service. The washing of feet was considered at that time as work to be done by the dregs of society. Peter's refusal reveals the internal resistance which the minds of the privileged offered to such expectations. Yet if one wants to belong to Jesus, one must be ready for such a radical change of outlook, and this means that in the last analysis only love can effect the truly liberating change of outlook and the end of all domination by forces outside oneself.

To put the whole matter in other words: According to John, Jesus took the concept of God, which from time immemorial had included the ideas of omnipotence and domination, and completely recast it by showing that God is to be encountered at the point where one

26

renounces every form of power and domination and is open to others. "Where goodness and love reside, there God is," says an ancient hymn of the Church. There, too, people become free of themselves and free for others. The symbol of the washing of feet is, of course, not proof against misunderstanding, as, for example, when some turn it into a liturgical gesture and make it part of a system of domination, while failing to see that it is in fact a radical challenge to any and every system of domination. Even Peter must allow his certainties to be challenged. John realized that Jesus had brought into the world a radically new understanding of God and humanity, an understanding which struck at the very foundations of a slave-holding society and of relations involving domination, because it made the power of love the center of all things divine and human. The washing of feet was the most forceful symbol that even we can think of for giving expression to this new understanding.

Instructions to the Disciples (13:12–20)

Exegesis

The washing of the feet is followed by instructions to the disciples which include a second interpretation of the washing (vv. 12-15) as well as a series of loosely connected individual sayings that resemble the synoptic logia of Jesus (vv. 16-17, 18-19, 20).

The most important thing here is to assess correctly the character of this section. R. Bultmann says, "The explicit theme of the first section is the fellowship with Jesus; this is shown to be grounded . . . in the service rendered by Jesus . . . . The second section adds that this fellowship of the disciples with Jesus at the same time opens up a fellowship amongst themselves, and that for the former to exist, the latter must be made a reality through the disciples' action . . . . Thus 13.1-20 describes the founding of the community and the law of its being."[16]

The point, therefore, is not to interpret the normative example of Jesus in a moralistic way and thereby to underestimate its real significance, but rather to derive from it the law, the model, or even the basic structure of the community of Jesus which is the Church. The washing of feet and with it the farewell discourses will be misunderstood if they are taken as pious discourses aimed at interior edification. They are concerned rather with showing forth the theologico-ontological structure of the community of Jesus. We must recall once again the fictive character of the farewell discourses. What the Johannine Jesus says to his disciples in this final hour is aimed directly at the self-understanding of the Johannine community which is being addressed. The fourth gospel's understanding of Jesus and its understanding of the community (its *ecclesiology*) are intimately connected with one another.

The first section (vv. 12-15) makes a direct application of Jesus' symbolic action. It is in the nature of things that Jesus should himself make this application; as is expressly stated, he acts as "teacher" and "lord" of his disciples. The evangelist's acceptance of precisely these two titles of majesty shows that what is to come is not a nonobligatory communication but an authoritatively binding instruction. As teacher and lord, which is what the disciples rightly understand Jesus to be, he has made himself the slave of all; before their very eyes he has given a demonstration of what he regards as the right way to act. If the community of Jesus' disciples really acknowledges him to be their teacher and lord, they must also accept the consequences such an acknowledgment imposes and not be satisfied with a merely oral profession. They are bound by the example of Jesus, and this means by his commitment to love to the point of dying on the cross.

Verse 14 brings out this aspect of obligation. The Greek verb *opheilete* means literally "you are obliged, you must." It is not left, therefore, to the pleasure of the community whether or not they will imitate the exemplary action of Jesus; rather, their confession of Jesus as teacher and lord imposes, as a direct consequence, the obligation to take him as their model.

The key word "one another" is repeatedly to be heard from this point on. It characterizes that new partnership which Jesus has established and which, according to John, is to determine the overall nature of the community of Jesus. It is also in its light that the word "example" is to be properly understood. The symbol of the washing of feet is a symbol of Jesus' total commitment, of his laying his life on the line to the point of surrendering it in death. Consequently, this symbol is also to be applied in an authoritative and compre-

28

hensive way to the whole existence and activity of the community of Jesus. It is the hallmark that must be stamped on all Christian and ecclesial activity, showing it to be activity that has love for its root.

Verses 16-17 show that only such an uncompromising understanding of the text does justice to it. These verses have their prototypes in synoptic sayings (Luke 6:40; Matt. 10:24 [Q]). In addition, there is the solemnly emphatic introduction in the double "Amen"—"it is certainly so," "truly." The relation of slave and master or envoy (*apostolos*) and the one who commissions and sends is one of strict superiority and subordination. The slave and the envoy do not act of their own initiative but are bound to follow their instructions. In the thinking of antiquity there was a juridical element in this relationship. The meaning is clear: for his disciples Jesus is the man of unparalleled authority; for them, his instructions are authoritative and binding.

It is not to be forgotten, of course, that Jesus' authority is tied with his love and, in fact, is even identical with it. It is love as such that is the basis for the highest authority. If the community is to understand itself in the light of Jesus, it must also acknowledge the binding force of Jesus' love; then it will live under the continual claim of that love. But in that love the community will also find its entire blessedness, happiness, and salvation.

The third section of this passage (vv. 18-19) again returns to the historical context of the last supper. The tradition was familiar with Judas' betrayal. Mark the evangelist had already seen in the betrayal of Jesus by one of his friends a fulfillment of the Scriptures (Ps. 41:10). More generally, it was quite natural for the primitive Church to use the linguistic models given it in the Old Testament, or Scripture, in interpreting the death of Jesus. What is usually called the "proof from Scripture" should not be taken to mean a logical process of demonstration, but is more correctly to be conceived as a new application of old language. Christians took over familiar images and formulations in order to give expression to the meaning Jesus had for them. That is what is happening here.

According to the Hebrew text, on which John depends more heavily here, the Scripture passage reads, "Even the man who is my friend, whom I trusted, and who eats my bread, raises his heel against me" (Ps. 41:10). The meaning of the citation is this: even the closest friends have joined the ranks of the enemy. The "man of peace" (literal translation) is the close friend. The sign of the inviolable bond of trust with such a person is the shared meal; the sharing of a meal creates a *communio*. Yet these friends have broken all these hallowed bonds of trust, dependence, and friendship.[17]

It was in this light that the primitive Church viewed Judas the traitor. According to John, Jesus knows what his fate is; he knows that he must carry out the divine plan of salvation. This is a post-Easter understanding of Jesus, to whom the faith of the primitive Church ascribed superhuman status, even as far as his knowledge was concerned. At the same time, the evangelist gives a didactic indication of the purpose of this prior knowledge on the part of Jesus: the fulfillment of even this dark prediction will help the disciples to faith in Jesus; it will help them to believe that "I am he." The Johannine "I am" formula, which makes its appearance here again, is the most deeply significant of the self-expressions of the Johannine Christ; it designates Jesus as the revealer and savior sent by God.[18] Even the fulfillment of the Scripture passages connected with the tragedy, at first sight so utterly incomprehensible, of the betrayal and execution of Jesus, should help the disciples to see Jesus as the revealer of God and to believe in him. This motif recurs several times in the farewell discourses (14:29; 16:4).

The fourth section, consisting of verse 20, can be taken as the Johannine version of a saying of Jesus that occurs in the synoptic tradition as well (cf. Luke 10:16; Matt. 10:40; also Mark 9:37). In its original form the saying had early Christian missionary preaching for its context. In the missionary preaching activity of the envoys of Jesus Jesus himself is to be encountered, while in the message God comes to meet his own. Anyone who receives the messenger authoritatively sent by Jesus receives Jesus himself, and anyone who receives Jesus thereby, in the final reckoning, receives God. This view of things rests on the conviction that in the proclamation about Jesus Jesus himself is present. In its Johannine context, the saying once again emphasizes the point that the instructions of Jesus, which link the activity of the community to his own exemplary activity that is the source of meaning and salvation, are to be taken seriously. It also shows that the authority of the community is grounded in the fact that it is sent by Jesus and receives legitimation from him.

John seems to broaden the scope of this principle regarding those sent; that is, he seems no longer to be thinking in particular of apostles, missionaries, and evangelists. In any event, the text gives no basis for thus restricting it to a limited group of persons. This means that every disciple of Jesus and the community which is the sum-total of all the disciples of Jesus are sent; they are messengers of Jesus. Legitimation by Jesus is however not a purely formal matter but has a content: it is a commission to live and act according to the norm which is Jesus himself. Whenever this norm is disregarded, the community loses its authority, as do also the special representatives of the community, those holding ecclesial office.

Meditation

The words of the historical Jesus to his disciples in these moments of farewell are a testament to the community of Jesus in every age. The concern of the fourth evangelist is to make clear, by successive new approaches, the meaning of the person, words, and actions of Jesus. Because Jesus is the divinely sent savior and revealer, this meaning becomes exemplary in a radical and even absolute sense. In other words, for John Jesus, being teacher and lord, is also the basic law, the fundamental reality, and therefore also the unconditional norm for the community. Paul had already formulated the relationship in very similar terms: "For no other foundation can anyone lay than that which is laid, which is Jesus Christ" (1 Cor. 3:11).

By this foundation and according to this norm everything is to be measured that claims the name Christian or ecclesial. The person of Jesus is therefore also the "basic law" (*lex fundamentalis*) of his Church. Only when this fact has been forgotten can people get the idea that the community needs a further basic law. The early Christian faith in revelation, as attested by John, makes such a basic law of a juridical kind impossible. For the foundation of the Church and Christianity is determined by Jesus and by the disciples' relationship to him, and therefore by faith and love which are superior and prior to any human legal ordering of things and are therefore not to be grasped in juridical terms. No human authority, not even Church officials or a Church code of laws, can dispose at will of this realm of freedom which Jesus Christ has marked out in advance. All that people can do is to find ways of carrying out this basic instruction of Jesus. Such ways, even when they take the form of Church laws, are always relative, limited, liable to become outmoded, in need of improvement, and changeable. They must be constantly readapted to the historical needs of the community of Jesus. The criterion for such adaptation is set down for all ages in the foundation which is Jesus himself.

In concrete terms, the norm can be expressed thus: to be there for one another in the name of Jesus. It is no accident that the Johannine community thinks of itself first and foremost as the community of the friends, brothers and sisters of Jesus. So strongly felt is the unparalleled predominance of the person of Jesus that there really cannot be any other authorities alongside him and apart from him, any other teachers and lords (cf. also Matt. 23:8-11). Within this community there are no relations of dominating and dominated. Instead, the rule is "for one another" (*allēlous*): an unreserved mutuality, a communication in Jesus, a collaboration; everything, therefore, is to be grounded in love of Jesus.

In dealing with the Johannine community (or communities) we are undoubtedly dealing with small and relatively limited groups. The requirement of "for one another" can be put in practice only in a community in which people know each other and talk to each other. In the society formed by a universal Church these basic aspects of life necessarily take second place. As a result, the universal Church as an institution has, in the course of history, taken the place originally occupied by the community or congregation. It is not to be assumed without examination that this shift represents progress effected by the Holy Spirit, for in the process important incentives and possibilities present at the beginning have been eliminated. Then, too, the ecclesiastical apparatus now shares in the abstractness and coldness that mark similar apparatuses elsewhere; we would be well advised to admit how far that apparatus has moved from Christianity in its original form. When confronted with this development, the Johannine model exercises a critique of institutions.

There would probably be a greater sense of happiness and joy in

Christian communities if the people in them were more intensely concerned with the cause of Jesus; if they reflected more on how this cause is to be presented to the contemporary world. At first sight the model offered us by Jesus in the symbol of washing the feet cuts a poor figure. However, we must go back to the roots of this symbol, as we have endeavored to do here, and see the man whom the community believes to be and honors as lord, Son of God, and revealer of God, showing himself by his actions to be the slave of all; the "Son of God" subverting, by his practice, the relations of domination proper to a slaveholding society! Then we must say that what is being required is nothing less than a complete change of outlook.

The model given in Jesus has still never been matched, to say nothing of being outmoded. If the situation in the world were to change in the way in which John, in virtue of Jesus' authority, calls for it to change, not only would people's claims to domination be held within bounds, but the often disfigured features of the community of Jesus would once again be seen in their purity. People would again be able more easily to believe in such things as "I am he," that is, that this Jesus with his flawless humanity is the revealer of God. Then we would again see the kind of Christian authority that is based not on official appointment but on the inherent credibility with which the cause of Jesus is set forth.

The community of Jesus is bound permanently to follow the model described in 13:1-20. At the present juncture we can admittedly only confess that this model is not exercising its influence over wide areas of Christian life. At the same time, however, we can assert that many hopeful beginnings are being made. Beyond a doubt, there is a longing for this model abroad in today's world.

Identification of the Traitor (13:21–30)

Exegesis

Like the synoptic writers (Mark 14:18-21; Matt. 26:21-25; Luke 22:21-23), John includes a brief account of the identification of Judas as the traitor at the last supper.

The four evangelists agree in repeating that Jesus was to be betrayed by a disciple from the inner circle of the twelve. The name of this disciple is Judas Iscariot (according to Mark 3:19; 14:10, 43) or Judas Iscariot, son of Simon (according to John 6:71; 13:26). Although critical objections have been raised against this tradition, it is so well founded, as far as the fact as such is concerned, that it may be regarded as certain. We must, of course, distinguish here between the historical fact and the interpretation given it by the Christian community or the evangelists. It is obvious that from a very early date Christians were reflecting on the disheartening fact and that the person of Judas the traitor inevitably became a figure of legend.

The surname "Iscariot" is interpreted in two ways. (1) Iscariot means "man from Kerioth": Kerioth, a village thought to be located in southern Judea, south of Hebron, would then be the native place of this *"Jehuda-ish-keriot."*[19] (2) Another interpretation derives the word "Iscariot" from *sicarius* (dagger). According to Flavius Josephus, the *sicarii* (daggermen) were members of a terrorist group within the Jewish liberation movement; via the name, an attempt is made to link Judas with these terrorists—according to Mark 3:19, "Judas Iscariot, who betrayed him" was one of the twelve; he is always mentioned last in the lists of the twelve (Mark 3:16-19; Matt. 10:2-4; Luke 6:13-16). John 6:70-71 is familiar with this tradition.

Mark 14:10-11 (cf. Matt 26:14-16; Luke 22:3-6) recounts the betrayal by Judas. It is reported that the chief priests had been delighted with the idea and had promised him money for his act. The identification of the betrayer by Jesus (Mark 14:18-21 par.) was doubtless part of the primitive Christian explanation regarding Judas. In the account of the identification the language of Psalm 41:10[20] surely played an important role. The primitive Church understood even this act of betrayal to be a fulfillment of the Scriptures, for the Church was thereby able to make this incomprehensible action comprehensible. Another reason for this approach was that Jesus had foreseen his own destiny and therefore the betrayal of Judas as well. This does not mean, however, that only the proof from Scripture made possible the discovery of Judas' betrayal!

Also to be taken into consideration is the fact that legend seized upon the figure of Judas at a very early date. People looked for a motive for his action and lighted upon the greed or avarice of Judas (cf. also 12:4-6). Legendary, above all, are the stories of Judas' bad end (Matt. 27:3-10; Acts 1:15-20); these texts are meant to make the reader shudder rather than to present historical fact. Once all these presuppositions have been established, the question arises, how did John interpret the figure of Judas the traitor?

The announcement (v. 21) that Jesus knew in advance of Judas' betrayal fits in nicely with Johannine christology. Yet the traditional prediction, "one of you will betray me," is given special emphasis in John. Jesus is deeply troubled, and such trouble "in spirit" is always a sign in John that Jesus is confronting the evil powers in general or the greatest of the evil powers, death, in particular. Hearing his words, the disciples look at one another in puzzlement, for they do not know whom he means (v. 22). It is at this point that the "disciple whom Jesus loved" (v. 23) is introduced for the first time.[21] The gospel of John does not tell us the name of this singular figure, but the description of him as the "disciple whom Jesus loved" has always stirred the interest of interpreters and fascinated the minds of the pious.

The tradition of the early Church usually identified him with John the apostle, whom it also regarded as the author of the fourth gospel. But since the advent of critical scholarship this view has become questionable. If we review the passages in which this singular figure comes on the scene (13:23; 19:26; 21:7, 20), we will be inclined to see in him a historical person rather than a symbolic or purely literary personage. More precisely, he would be the authority whom the Johannine circle regarded as the guarantor of the authentic tradition about Jesus. We shall here accept this hypothesis, which has been argued especially by R. Schnackenburg. This disciple, therefore, is not to be identified with the evangelist. At the same time, however, it is to be assumed that the evangelist brings this witness on the scene at important points in order to lend weight to the tradition he is following. It seems advisable, then, that the exegete should interpret the figure of the "disciple whom Jesus loved" according to the context on each occasion, without inquiring too closely into the question of what the historical fact may have been. In verses 23-26 this disciple has surely acquired a place in the text only at a secondary stage.

The description of the scene presupposes the ancient custom of "reclining at table" or the symposium. The disciple is lying on the bosom of Jesus, that is, he has evidently laid his head on Jesus' side. He is introduced in this position so that he may solve the riddle of who the betrayer is (vv. 24-26). It is noteworthy that even Peter turns to him with the request that he would ask Jesus who was meant; this is what the disciple then does.

Jesus' answer—"It is he to whom I shall give this morsel when I have dipped it"—is a formulation influenced by Psalm 41:10; in fact, the whole description of the sequence of actions is likewise motivated by the psalm. John goes beyond the older tradition (Mark 14:18-21) when he says that along with the morsel the devil entered into Judas. Jesus' reaction to this—"What you are going to do, do soon," by which he means, "Act now, but do it quickly"—is again misinterpreted by the disciples. They think that Jesus has sent Judas to buy something or commissioned him to give something to the poor, as was the Jewish custom at the passover feast. This section ends with the lapidary statement, "So, after receiving the morsel, he immediately went out; and it was night" (v. 30). The powerful symbolism is unmistakable.

The significance of the Johannine description is certainly to be found in the way the evangelist has heightened the dramatic element in the tradition. What appears in Mark as a drastically simplified statement of fact is here heightened and presented in a very artistic manner. The interior and exterior dramas are connected, and the scene is described in such a way that the reader seems directly involved in it. This manner of presentation will be seen at its most effective in the Johannine account of the passion. Jesus knows exactly what is going on, and so does Judas, in his own fashion. Of the other disciples only the one whom Jesus loves shares this knowledge.

But in the midst of the human activity something far more profound is occurring. The real adversary of Jesus is not Judas, who is only a tool to be used in carrying out a plan. The real adversary is Satan, or the power of evil unqualified, into whose dark hands Judas has surrendered himself. The message of our text is to be found chiefly in the meditative, theologico-poetic manner of presentation. The aim is to shock the hearers or readers: This is how far things could go, that one of the intimate friends of Jesus should hand over the revealer of God to his enemies!

Meditation

The betrayal by Judas is one of those features of the passion narrative that mark the breakthrough of evil—evil in a mysterious incomprehensible form—into the course of human events. Betrayal among very intimate friends, a betrayal that causes the death of the person thus abandoned, has at all times been especially abhorrent to people. The poet Dante gave expression to this feeling when he placed traitors—Brutus, Cassius, and Judas—in the lowest circle of hell and in the immediate vicinity of Satan himself. If such a betrayal does not even result from a great idea, as when a person reaches new and superior convictions, but is done for the sake of contemptible gain, then even today we are inclined to despise as well as abhor such a traitor.

Again and again people have asked what motive could have led Judas to betray Jesus. Was he, for example, disillusioned with Jesus because the expected powerful attack upon the Romans never came and the messianic turning point did not arrive? We may reckon with such possibilities, but the New Testament gives us no sure information on the point. The New Testament writers do not regard personal motives as very important; their interest is in the fact that even a betrayer of Jesus had a place in the divine plan of salvation. Even the betrayal of love could not prevent the victory of love on the cross, but instead was forced to contribute to that victory. In its meditative approach to Jesus, faith glimpses the truth which no logic can take as a premise: divine love is greater than human evil, greater than any injustice and betrayal—and what human being is there who has not been a traitor in his or her own way?

It is noteworthy that according to the various New Testament witnesses Jesus nowhere behaves in a condemnatory way toward Judas. We do well to reflect on the fact that Christian tradition has not followed Jesus' example but has often played fast and loose with the figure of Judas. He has often been the occasion for kindling anti-Jewish feelings. Even in the dealings of Christians with one another Judas has been used as a scapegoat or a curse-word. In very recent years examples of such misuse have been given by even the highest ranking persons in the Church, when they have thrown the name "Judas" at priests who have married. Great care must be taken not to indulge in this kind of abusive rhetoric; no human being has the right to pass such judgments on others.

Betrayal among friends and among those who used to be joined by bonds of love hurts deeply. It inflicts wounds on men and women. If we look at things from this viewpoint, the question becomes an explosive one in the human world of each of us, since often enough a person will drop a friend or other good person for some shabby reason or simply because he or she is not up to the demands such a relationship makes—or for the sake of "higher motives."

It is possible that Judas was the kind of man who regarded identification with the then dominant system as more important than his ties with his friend Jesus; the kind of man who thought it dangerous to live in close proximity to such a person as Jesus. He could not handle the freedom and love that were demanded of him in this circle, and he grew unsure of himself. The reason for his insecurity would be that he had so internalized the system that he could not deal adequately with the problems and tensions imposed on him. If this be the case, he would be an example of the kind of betrayal that might be described as a weak person's betrayal, that is, betrayal by one so dependent on the social superego that his ego-weakness could only act as a tool of that superego, since there was not sufficient capability of real love. In any event, the New Testament says this much with unmistakable clarity: What was betrayed was not a truth or a mystery or a teaching but a man named Jesus.

THE FIRST FAREWELL DISCOURSE
(13:31–14:31)

The New Commandment (13:31–35)

Exegesis

The first farewell discourse begins after the departure of Judas the traitor. Now that a division has been effected in the inner circle of disciples, Jesus is in the presence only of those who are his truly faithful followers, his own in the full sense of the words. This fact determines the group to whom the discourse is addressed: It is not addressed, as was the entire first part of John's gospel (chap. 1-12), to outsiders, to the world, but only to those who have found their way to faith in Jesus. It is addressed to the internal community (or inside group) of believers.

We must remind ourselves that we are dealing here with a literary, fictitious situation. The evangelist uses the division among the disciples as a literary device in order to distinguish exoteric from esoteric teaching. This distinction is matched by a difference in content that is not to be sought at the level of the historical Jesus but at the level of the community, which experiences in its own life the difference between the unbelieving world and the community of faith. The themes treated in the discourse are to some extent paralleled in the first part of the gospel, but there are some new messages as well.

The whole passage to which we now turn can be divided into three distinct statements: (a) verses 31, 32, which have "glorification" as their key word and relate to the situation of Jesus himself; (b) verse 33 sheds light on the farewell character of the moment; (c) verses 34-35 contain the commandment of love as the all-important instruction of Jesus to the community.

Verses 31-32 speak of Jesus under the rubric of "the glorification of the Son of man." Any interpretation of this must take as its starting point John's own understanding of the words. Accordingly, it is not the earthly Jesus who is speaking, but the Johannine Jesus, that is, Jesus as seen and understood by the evangelist. But the evangelist is writing sixty to seventy years after the death of Jesus. If we do not bear this fact in mind, we will inevitably misunderstand the text.

We might apply here the concept of flashback that is used in films. Both the writer and his hearers are well aware that they are not contemporaries of Jesus. In addition, they have an exact knowledge of what faith says about Jesus, namely, that he is risen, exalted, and glorified; at the same time, they know that the glorified Jesus is identical with the earthly Jesus. This identity of the earthly Jesus with the glorified Jesus, of the historical Jesus with the Christ of faith, is the theological presupposition of our texts. Therefore we must accept and make our own the idea that it is the glorified Jesus who is presented as a man on earth and who speaks to the community. The result is a unique situation in which times overlap: flashback to the past, anticipation of the future. The linking of these two times, past and future, yields a special kind of present, into which the hearers are drawn.

This situation of overlap or inbetweenness with its linking of past and future in the present, or so as to form the present, is also identical with the time of faith. In this fact we can see the care and accuracy of the language John uses. For faith arises out of the history of Jesus and is directed toward the future of Jesus. It is a historical faith, situated in time and in the world, but at the same time it reaches beyond the present world-age into the divine future that has been revealed in Jesus and is already present in him. Thus the structure of faith corresponds exactly to the identity of the earthly with the glorified Jesus.

The words spoken are presented as the "words of the Son of man," and in their form (since Jesus speaks of the "Son of man" in the third person singular) they correspond to the Son of man sayings in the other gospels. John took over the Son of man designation from the primitive Christian (Palestinian) tradition regarding Jesus,[22] but he has given it an independent theological stamp,[23] of which we shall point out only the most important characteristics of this last:

John connects the idea of revelation with the title "Son of man." As Son of man Jesus is the revealer of God who brings the eschatological revelation, the definitive truth of God, and also communicates to men salvation or eternal life through faith. Another Johannine motif is that of the "descent and ascent" of the Son of man: he comes from the divine world into the earthly world, and then returns from the latter to the former. Finally, John speaks of the "lifting up" (elevation or exaltation) and "glorification" of the Son of man. He adopts this terminology when he formulates in his own way the primitive Christian proclamation of the cross and resurrection of Jesus.

In the Johannine treatment of the "Son of man" we have, then, a distinctive fusion of the (apocalyptic) title "Son of man" with the tradition regarding Jesus, with the primitive Christian kerygma, and with the idea of revelation (and perhaps with gnostic conceptions as well). The primary concern in all this is the abiding meaning of the revelation brought by Jesus.

"Glory" and "glorify" are words that have undergone the influence of the Bible. They represent the Greek word-group *doxa* and *doxazein* (the Hebrew *kabod*). The conceptual content of this group suggests various associations of ideas: divine light-glory, the splendor or radiance of God, the clarity and power of divine revelation, prestige or reputation. The verb *doxazein* means "to give splendor power, and prestige; to give a participation in the divine realm of being." "Glory" thus designates the divine sphere in contrast to the realm of this world and the earthly; consequently, "to glorify" means to raise someone into the divine sphere to become a participant in the divine world of light. Added to all this is the concept of revelation: for John, Jesus is the one who reveals the divine glory in the world, as is made clear, above all, in the Johannine miracle stories.[24]

The point being made in our text is that, according to the faith of the primitive Church, Jesus of Nazareth through his cross and resurrection has been taken up into the divine realm, and that as the glorified Jesus he continues to work in his community. The specification "now" (v. 31) indicates that the death and resurrection of Jesus is the decisive moment (*kairos*) in the history of salvation, the moment in which the "turning point of the ages (the eons)" takes place. At this moment in time Jesus is acknowledged and confirmed by God as revealer and savior, while God in turn receives from Jesus, especially through his obedience unto death on the cross, the recognition due him. This reciprocal glorification and recognition of Jesus by God and of God by Jesus brings to light the basic relationship which Christian faith will henceforth maintain and confess: that Jesus, as Messiah and Son of God, is the full and definitive revelation of God in the world. For the Christian believer God cannot henceforth be thought of apart from Jesus, nor can Jesus be understood apart from God.

The event of Jesus' glorification, however, is not something that is entirely past; rather, it already contains its own future. It is the foundation of a new era: the glorification of Jesus will take place throughout the future, first and foremost by reason of the fact that the cause of Jesus will continue to have its effect on history, especially within the space that is the community of Jesus. The glorification of Jesus by God will be realized in the faith and love of his own.

Verse 33 brings out the farewell character of the situation. Jesus will be with the disciples for only a short time longer; then he will depart for an unidentified destination, into a realm that is inaccessible to the disciples who are left behind. In the background, of course, is the thought that this departure of Jesus is a departure to the Father. This will be discussed in greater detail later. At this moment, the main point is to emphasize the decisive threshold that is to be crossed, the turning point: the period of Jesus' presence on earth is coming to an irrevocable end now that the moment of glorification is here. This gives rise not only to the question of where Jesus is going, but also to the further question of how the community will be linked to him and united with him after his departure.

In other words, John is not speaking here simply and unproblematically of a farewell and departure to an unidentified destination, as the reader might think at first glance. Rather, John is raising the fundamental question of the relation between the earthly, historical period of Jesus' life and the post-Easter period of faith in the Jesus who is no longer directly present. John raises this question, to begin with, in a negative form. To it is added the further idea that, according to John, the divine realm is in itself inaccessible to human beings and that only through Jesus do they gain access to it. If we thus interpret the function of verse 33, then its position between the statement about glorification (vv. 31-32) and the subsequent commandment of love becomes immediately intelligible.

Consequently, too, the "new commandment" of love takes on its full significance (vv. 34-35). In John, this commandment is the first and most important legacy of Jesus to his disciples, and the placing of it at the beginning of the first farewell discourse is doubtless intended to bring out its fundamental importance. If we compare the Johannine statement of the commandment of love with its counterpart in the synoptic gospels (Mark 12:28-34; Matt. 22:36-40; Luke 10:25-28), it is notable that in John there is no reference to the commandment of love for God and that the concept of "neighbor" does not appear. The Johannine formulation is rather, "Love one another." This "one another," each for the others, expresses in a comprehensive way the scope of the new commandment, which is certainly intended to be unlimited. It also shows that love means a reciprocal action or attitude.

A further point is that the commandment of love is motivated by knowledge of Christ: "Just as I have loved you, you must also love one another" (v. 34b). In this formulation, the conduct of Jesus, which is here summed up in the term love, is made normative and binding on the disciples; at the same time, the statement looks back to the symbolic action of washing the feet. Finally, there is also a missionary aspect to the commandment, a dimension of witness: by the mutual love in which the disciples embody the example of Jesus in their relations with one another, they will give "all people" a sign that they belong to Jesus. By their practice they will render visible

43

to the world the very heart of the revelation Jesus has brought.

When John calls the commandment of love a "new commandment," he shows that he understands this commandment, with its basis in Christ himself, to be the eschatological commandment; that is, the newness here is an eschatological newness. In love, the attitude of God to the world (3:16) becomes the motive that sustains people in their actions.

The Johannine formulation of the commandment of love can be properly understood only in the context of the entire Johannine theology of revelation and redemption. The best commentary we can turn to here is the First Letter of John (especially 3:11-18; 4:7-21). The gospel and the first letter agree in transmitting the commandment of "love for one another" as the unique, unparalleled, and decisive order given by Jesus. In contrast to the Matthean Sermon on the Mount (for example), the Johannine writings report no other commandments of Jesus. According to John, faith and love are the central, key concepts that control the entire Christian way of life. Both concepts are meant to be radical: they determine the nature of Christian existence from its very foundations; according to John, no further specifications are required.

In addition, both concepts are intended to be comprehensive or total: faith and love are to permeate and shape the whole Christian way of life in all its expressions. The motivation given, "Just as I have loved you," does not refer to some unchanged feeling that Jesus always had, but points concretely to the love-inspired death of Jesus on the cross: "By this you have come to understand love: that he laid down his life for us; so too we must lay down our lives for the brethren" (1 John 3:16). Such love has its origin in God (1 John 4:7ff.); it is a revelation of divine reality as such. The sentence, "God is love, and he who abides in love abides in God, and God in him" (1 John 4:16b), contains in concentrated form the entire Johannine theology of revelation. The basic ethical requirement of Christianity, the commandment of love, is here seen as having its ultimate ground in God: the one love, which is God, is made known to the world by Jesus, and this in a decisive manner by his death on the cross; that same love is at work in the mutual love of the disciples when their actions are determined by the norm embodied

44

in Jesus. In this sense, love is for John the fundamental concept of the entire revelation of Jesus; it is the content and essence of Christianity.

Meditation

Any reflection on the gospel of John that ventures to penetrate even a little way beneath the surface of the text very soon finds that it is tackling the central Christian problems. For the questions this gospel raises are not peripheral to Christianity; the issue is always Christianity in its entirety. If we wish to understand Christianity and its history not only in terms of the history of culture or ideas or religion but in the light of its center, then we must realize that since the days of the apostles and the postapostolic generation the main concern has always been to hold fast to the memory of Jesus and thereby to the cause of Jesus as well, and to grasp and formulate anew the meaning of Jesus for one's own time. The focus of attention, therefore, has been the presence of Jesus. Faith could never be satisfied with a purely historical Jesus who belongs to a distant past and whom scholars could, if need be, reconstruct with the tools of historical method. No, faith has always been looking for the Jesus of here and now, the "Jesus for us." The power of Christianity to influence people, especially in its more credible manifestations, has always been measured by its ability and power to bring the figure of Jesus into the present moment and make his voice heard. Faith in the resurrection of Jesus from the dead—that faith with its paradoxical character and its exorbitant demands upon normal thinking—is the most decisive expression of the fact that Christianity is not concerned with a dead Jesus who belongs to the past, but with a living Jesus who has something to say to us. John shows that he has grasped this problem in all its acuteness when he presents the earthly Jesus as at the same time the Jesus who is glorified by God, and has him speak to us as the historical Jesus.

The most important thing about the New Testament witness to Christ, especially as this witness is found in the gospels, is that it did not surrender the link with the historical Jesus of Nazareth, or

Jesus the "true man," as dogmatic theology calls him.[25] The link with the historical Jesus-event expresses the will to preserve historical continuity, and this is due in turn to the sure instinct that the specifically Christian element in Christianity will be lost if the earthly, human figure of Jesus disappears from sight. For this reason, Irenaeus of Lyons (ca. A. D. 205) regards the rejection of the incarnation as characteristic of every heresy: "Not a single heretic teaches that the Word of God was made flesh."[26] Christian faith insists that the history of Jesus with all its human relativity and limitations is the locus of the unparalleled and permanently valid eschatological revelation, or explication of the meaning of God. The Christian mystery of salvation is the mystery of God's presence in the history of Jesus.

As the gospel of John also shows us, the primitive Church was profoundly marked by the experience of the presence of Jesus, and this above all in its liturgy. Preaching, faith, prayer, and the communal celebration of the Lord's Supper were the media of participation in the salvation now present. This question of the presence of Jesus is undoubtedly a question for us as well. The Second Vatican Council emphasizes the importance of the liturgy for this experience, when in its Constitution on the Liturgy it speaks of the "presence of Jesus" in the sacrifice of the Mass, the sacraments, the words of sacred Scripture, and communal prayer (No. 7).

Admittedly, there is danger here of a one-sided cultic understanding of the presence of Jesus. It was already a step forward when people no longer connected the real presence of Jesus exclusively with the Eucharistic species. Such a limitation had earlier undoubtedly led people to think of that presence in terms of magic, and this frame of mind has exercised a baneful influence down to our own day. It is worth asking ourselves whether the exclusive connection in past centuries of the presence of Jesus with the sacrifice of the Mass and the worship of the host did not play a decisive role in causing people no longer to experience this presence in their lives, in the world around them, and in society, and whether the secularization of the world, about which we talk so much, has not been, in part, a direct consequence of this one-sided way of thinking. The restriction of the experience of salvation to the esoteric sphere of liturgy frequently served as an alibi: here, in the liturgy, salvation reigned, while out yonder the unholy world went its wicked way. Today, on the contrary, we are once again rightly putting emphasis on the presence of Jesus and his Spirit in everday life, in the activity of the Church, and in human society.

How are we to explain the fact that twentieth-century persons with their great burden of knowledge, with their anxieties, uncertainties, and doubts are seeking contact with Jesus? Perhaps it is "memory in a moment of danger" (W. Benjamin) that serves as the stimulus (the danger, in this case, of losing themselves and finding no way out of the confusion of our time), and, along with this, the desire to become true human beings. We today can experience the presence of Jesus in the experience of our humanness and our fellowship with other people.

The presence of Jesus as experienced in faith is the first aspect emphasized in our text. The second is closely connected with it: "love for one another" as the one unique "new commandment" of Jesus. John preserves the internal connection of faith and love. Our own plight is due to the fact that these two activities, which belong unconditionally together, have been separated again and again. As a result, living faith has been turned into an isolated adherence to true propositions that have been imposed on people whether or not they understand them. As we can see more clearly today, this kind of thinking conceals an anxiety about salvation that is shot through with magical thinking and has had as its direct consequence the exercise, right down to our own day, of all kinds of intimidation, ranging from physical to spiritual violence, in the name of orthodox belief.

Love, meanwhile, has been shunted aside into the sphere of private moral behavior; but in that area, where law and authority determine what is to be done, love is really given no role to play. And yet, according to the New Testament understanding of things, love has unconditional primacy over orthodoxy, however pure the latter may be. "By this all men will know that you are my disciples, if you have love for one another" (v. 35). We need only take this statement at face value and apply it as a standard of judgment to Church activity past and present. The non-Christians of our day are hardly likely to think of saying about the Christian churches, "See how they love one another"—except, perhaps, in irony. Here is where we are summoned to repent and change our way of thinking. The emphasis must be, above all, on the social practice of love. Without love faith degenerates into an impersonal force and must inevitably serve to mask or cover over an authoritarian system of spiritual domination. Love always has the great advantage that, even if perhaps unwittingly and perhaps often in problematic forms, it is on the road to truth, to the God of love.

In addition, we should be fully convinced that Jesus' commandment of love is being far more widely obeyed in our world than a narrow parochial kind of Christianity is frequently willing to admit. John XXIII realized this and acted accordingly. Just as the light shines everywhere and cannot be monopolized by anyone, so love belongs to all. If we look at the world through the eyes of Jesus, there is no reason for pessimism.

Prediction of Peter's Denial (13:36–38)

Exegesis

With Jesus' prediction of Peter's denial John is once again adopting a bit of tradition (cf. Mark 14:29-31; Matt. 26:33-35; Luke 22:31-34). The prediction of Peter's denial is a fixed element in the gospel accounts of the passion. It is of interest that Luke the evangelist incorporated this feature of the tradition into his short farewell discourse (Luke 22:21-38) and even expanded it by adding a promise to Peter (Luke 22:31-32). All four gospels likewise recount Peter's actual denial of Jesus (cf. Mark 14:66-72; Matt. 26:69-75; Luke 22:56-62; John 18:15-18, 25-27).

The tradition that Peter had denied his master was certainly not invented but is historically reliable. In fact, Jesus' prediction of it may be regarded as a sure sign that the denial actually occurred. Why is this? The reason is that what we have here is certainly not a historical pronouncement of Jesus but a prophecy after the event. The intention behind the prediction can easily be guessed: the fact that Peter, the very man who was the leader of the primitive community, should have failed Jesus, his master and friend, in such a discreditable way, was a great strain on the community, a scandalous failure with which it had to come to terms. It attempted to cope with the problem by saying that Jesus knew in advance of his disciple's failure and in fact had even predicted it. Even this bitter disappointment, then, did not catch Jesus by surprise. By reason of his higher knowledge he knew of this failure by his friend; it was part of the divine plan of salvation. Such an approach to the problem also fitted in nicely with the Johannine picture of Jesus as one who had complete knowledge of his own destiny and was totally free.

John, therefore, took over this element of the tradition and emphasized it, while at the same time giving it a typically Johannine impress. The latter may be seen in, for example, the following details. Peter's question, "Where are you going?" picks up Jesus' words about "going" and makes it possible for the prediction concerning Peter to be fitted neatly into the farewell or departure context. Peter here falls into a momentous misunderstanding when he believes that he can and must follow Jesus on the road he is to take. (This also brings the key word "follow" into the text.) Jesus' answer is once again unspecific and mysterious: Peter cannot follow Jesus now, but later he will indeed follow him. This answer probably contains a reference to the death of Peter, whose violent end seems to have been known in detail to the Johannine tradition (for this cf. also 21:18-19).

Peter's misunderstanding finds expression in a resolute counter-assertion (v. 37). He believes that he is capable, by his own will and strength, of following Jesus. But this exaggerated estimate of his own capabilities is a danger for him. Peter wants to follow Jesus right now; he even wants to lay down his life for Jesus. The distinctive Johannine idiom "to lay down (one's) life for" (*thēnai tēn psychēn hyper*) brings out the decisive point of the misunderstanding. Such a "laying down of one's life for others" is possible, in John's view, only because Jesus has first laid down his life for all, for the entire world. It is therefore possible only as an imitation of the radical commitment of love exemplified by Jesus. John is saying that Peter completely mistakes his own situation in relation to Jesus. Peter must have Jesus' own self-giving before him if he is to attain the attitude of love he so boldly anticipates. For this very reason, the first result of his misunderstanding will be his denial of Jesus, that is, the experience of his own human frailty and weakness, his own failure.

Meditation

For all his exaggerated estimate of himself, Peter, as we have presented him, was not a philistine or the calculating kind of person who carefully reckons up his own capabilities and undertakes something only after he has first doubly insured himself so that nothing can go wrong. No, Peter wants to give himself wholly for Jesus; he is even willing to risk his life. But he has to learn from experience that he trusts too much in himself; he has to fail miserably. Since the entire New Testament presents Peter as an ambiguous and divided man, that is, as on the one hand the most important of Jesus' disciples and later the leader of the primitive Church, and as on the other hand a man of undecided character who easily capitulates (cf. Gal. 2:11-17), this picture of him must surely have had a basis in the historical Peter as people saw him. It is a testimony to the credibility of the New Testament tradition that it did not turn Peter into a hero; that change was left for a later period.

This brings us to the question of the criteria to be applied in our approach to historical tradition. There are institutions which, in their concern to heighten their present importance, prefer to see their own history as one of harmonious and ultimately victorious progress. We often view our personal life-stories in the same way; the problematic and shady side is suppressed; it is not allowed to appear on the facade. An earlier age likewise preferred a triumphalistic portrayal of the history of the Church and the popes; the history of Christianity was seen as an uninterrupted triumphal march through the centuries. Not only private but often even institutional failure, human and political failure, was excused by an appeal to historical circumstances. But the enemies of the Church only busied themselves all the more with presenting these failures as a chronicle of scandals.

The Bible, Old and New Testaments alike, shows a disarming

honesty in the face of human history. For the Bible there are not heroes with haloes, but only people who succeed or fail. Both kinds make the Bible the utterly human document that it is. In addition, the Bible measures human life by the very highest standards, before which no standing among peers is of any significance. A Christian view of history should likewise be marked by a more critical attitude and especially by a more self-critical attitude. This applies even to the most venerable institution of the western Church, the papacy. For in the papacy, too, light and shadow, greatness and wretchedness, high calling and abuse of power stand side by side with nothing to soften the contrast. For the very reason that we acknowledge the unparalleled importance of Jesus, we should not be anxious about the sordidness the past contains. In fact, coming to terms with this is a condition for producing a better Christianity in the future.

Exhortation to Faith;
Jesus the Revealer of God (14:1–11)

Exegesis

In its literary form this section is quite in the style of the Johannine revelatory discourse. It is divisible into four smaller units, which however are loosely linked to one another by key words that carry the thought forward. It begins with an exhortation to faith (v. 1) and then speaks of the "many dwellings in the Father's house" (vv.2-4). The two following units (vv. 5-7 and 8-11) deal, from differing viewpoints, with the teaching about Jesus as the eschatological revealer of God.

Verse 1. The discourse begins with an emphatic exhortation to faith that is couched first in negative, then in positive terms. The negative statement! is "Let not your hearts be anxious!" This admonition recalls the exhortation that occurs elsewhere in the Bible: "Fear not!" Thus we read in Isaiah 7:2, which is describing the reaction of King Ahaz and the people of Jerusalem to the news of the approach of hostile armies: "His heart and the heart of his people shook as the trees of the forest shake before the wind." The disturbance or anxiety of heart, as described here, is thus the opposite of faith. The phrase as used by Jesus looks to the situation of the community of disciples. What is it that can be thus unsettling their hearts? Two things—the continuous hostility of the world and the absence of Jesus.

The attitude of the world to the community is a constant challenge to faith; it creates insecurity and temptation that can go so far as to strike at the heart, the innermost self. If the heart yields to this unsettling attack, there is danger that the person may abandon faith. The anxiety of heart does not arise "from human weakness, but from the collision of the world with the revelation."[27] There is, then, a temptation against faith that is not dependent on temporal conditions (as, for example, on the changed circumstances of society), but is related to the historical situation of faith as such.

The absence of Jesus likewise contributes in its own way to the sense of insecurity (since faith cannot make its object and ground directly evident) and must be constantly dealt with anew. But the disciples are not to let their course be determined by this experience. Rather they are to realize that the experience of doubt is a possibility, and not deceive themselves about the precariousness of their situation—precariousness as judged by the world. At the same time, however, they are not to lose heart, but must believe.

In Johannine language, the noun "faith" (*pistis*) is never used, but only the verb "believe" (*pisteuein*). This is the case in our passage. In agreement with primitive Christian tradition, John means by the word "believe" the basic human attitude that responds to the claim of revelation as communicated in Jesus. Faith is a response to the message of salvation, but it is at the same time a firm trust that stands in contrast to the anxiety of the heart, and thus signifies the inner peace and stability of heart by which the anxiety is overcome and removed. Note how in Jesus' exhortation here faith in God and faith in Jesus are paralleled!

For the Old Testament and Judaism faith is a person's self-grounding in the divine ground of life from which existence and life flow; it is a trustful, unconditional reliance on the promise, word, and fidelity of God. People cannot, in this sense of the term, believe in anything and everything; in fact, one cannot believe in anything at all that is part of this world, but only in God, since God alone can satisfy a person's longing for what is unconditionally dependable. It is probably in this sense that Jesus spoke of faith.

In John, the concept of faith already has a Christian history behind it and has therefore undergone a significant expansion. Faith is now directed not only to God but to Jesus as well. In the eyes of the first Christians Jesus Christ was so closely connected with God that he himself became the object of faith. Faith in God is seen as mediated by Jesus; Jesus has become the historical guarantor of faith. Faith in God, in turn, becomes the ground for faith in Jesus, so that faith in God and faith in Jesus form, in John's view, an indivisible unity; the precise reasons for this will be given in the following sections of the present discourse.

Verses 2-4. This section is an instruction not so much on the heavenly dwellings as on the truth that the way of Jesus is fundamental, binding, and normative for the disciples, and therefore also full of promise for them. It is an instruction, too, on the truth that the separation of Jesus from his followers will not be permanent. John has given a new profundity to the primitive Christian idea of following Jesus (an idea that originates with the earthly Jesus) and has made of it, so to speak, a christological formula: "If any one serves me, he must follow me; and where I am, there shall my servant be also" (12:26). The way that Jesus goes is, however, the way of the Son of man, a way that leads to the Father via cross and resurrection. It is precisely this way that is now binding on the disciples as well, for belonging to Jesus means sharing, through faith and love, a common destiny with him.

The idea of the heavenly dwellings[28] also occurs in other New Testament texts: in Luke's "eternal habitations" (16:9) and especially in Paul: "For we know that if the earthly tent we live in is destroyed, we have a building from God, a house not made with hands, eternal in the heavens" (2 Cor. 5:1). The images of "house" and "dwelling" evidently appeal to a profound human need which can be described as the need for a definitive security, a native place, for safety and peace of a radical kind. If we reflect in this context on the eternal house or everlasting home, we will have a sense that life in this world is life in exile or an earthly pilgrimage; this feeling emerges clearly in the passage from Paul with its distinction between the "earthly tent" and the "house . . . eternal in the heavens." These various images have become part of traditional Christian language and awaken many resonances in hearers.

John uses the image of a dwelling but without describing it more fully. The emphasis is on the fact that in the house of God, the house of the Father, there are "many dwellings." To put it in abstract terms, with God each person will have the opportunity for the complete life that meets individual needs, an eternal happiness designed for that person alone. No one need be concerned that there may be no opportunity, no fulfillment. There at least there will be no housing shortage. The expression, "Otherwise, would I have told you . . . ?" (v. 2b) is probably a reference to other passages (e.g., 12:26; 17:24).

The departure of Jesus, as John sees it, means that he will act as a kind of heavenly billeting officer and prepare a dwelling for his friends. But connected with this is the further idea that people have no other possibility of reaching God except through Jesus the revealer. His way is the way all must travel to God.

Into this complex of ideas the expression "return of Jesus" is now introduced. Jesus will come back in order to take his followers with him so that they can live with him in an eternal community. But the introduction of the return of Jesus also leads to an unparalleled transformation of the primitive Christian expectation of Christ's return.[29] Faith, which even now mediates salvation and grants people a participation in eternal life, also has a future which is opened to it via the way of Jesus. This future is "heaven" as the place of God. In the preaching of Jesus as recorded by the synoptics "my Father's house" and the "kingdom of God" do not mean precisely the same thing; they are not simply coextensive concepts. In John, however, the first expression may be taken as replacing the second. For him, what is to the fore is not the coming of God's reign but the passage from the earthly world to the divine realm of the Father. The evangelist keeps the expression "return of Jesus" but it is integrated into the other conception. That is to say, in his own mind John probably thought of Jesus as coming to the disciple at the latter's death, in order to take the disciple to "the Father's house." The collective statement, "I . . . will take you (plural) to myself" means, therefore, that the promise is given to all disciples.

The form which fulfillment takes is indicated in the last part of verse 3: "that where I am going you may be also." A similar idea is expressed in 17:24: "Father, whatever you have given me: I desire that where I am they also may be with me, so that they may behold my glory which you have given me—that you loved me before the creation of the world." The completion of salvation consists in eternal communion with Christ, in being with Jesus in God's presence. Verse 4, which ends this unit, serves to introduce the key word "way" and thus to elicit the next question.

Verses 5-7. The question about the way to the promised goal gives the evangelist an opportunity to explain what is meant by quoting an especially solemn self-description of Jesus. Thomas's question (v. 5) represents a new use of the stylistic device of misunderstanding and also serves once again to emphasize the key word "way." "How, then, can we know the way?" In other words, *the question of the way* provides the theme at this point.

In the primarily figurative and poetic (metaphorical, symbolical) language of the fourth evangelist it is important that we perceive the various overtones that accompany the basic concepts. Thus the image of way includes the idea that people seek direction and consequently that the whole of life can be described as a way and specifically as life's way. A further question concerns the right way, for one can miss the way and go astray. For the devout person of the Old Testament God's instruction, or law, is the way of true life that he wills humans to follow (cf. Ps. 119). Other religions, too, ask about the way, the right path, that leads to redemption and salvation. Similarly, "the way" was probably a designation primitive Christianity used to distinguish itself from a piety centered on the law.[30] Consequently, way is not to be understood in a transferred sense, but is meant in a strict sense as an expression of human self-understanding. When a person asks about the way in this sense of the word, the meaning and goal of existence are being questioned.

That is precisely the point of Jesus' answer, "I am the way, the truth, and the life; no one comes to the Father except through me" (v. 6).

We have already met the Johannine "I am" formula (*ego eimi*) in 13:19. This new occurrence furnishes an occasion for giving closer consideration to the problem of the Johannine christological formula of revelation.[31]

The reader of the gospel of John soon notes that in certain contexts, and especially in the great discourses, one formula keeps recurring in which the Johannine Christ gives especially solemn expression to himself and his significance. The formula usually begins with the words "I am." These are frequently, though not always, followed by specifying words, e.g. ". . . the good shepherd." We must therefore distinguish between "I am" sayings that contain a symbolic term and "I am" sayings without a predicate. The formulas with a symbolic term are more frequent: "I am" the bread of life (6:35, 48), the living bread (6:51), the bread that has come down from heaven (6:41), the light of the world (8:12; cf. 9:5), the door (for the sheep: 10:7, 9), the good shepherd (10:11, 14), the resurrection and the life (11:25), the way, the truth, and the life (14:6), the true vine (15:1, 5). We find the "I am" without a predicate ("I am," "that I am he," etc.) in 6:20; 8:24, 58; 13:19; 18:5, 6, 8.

To begin with, it has been recognized that this formula does not serve simply for self-presentation, but is connected with a type of discourse that was widespread in the religious language of antiquity, in which a divinity makes himself known to his worshiper and expresses his willingness to help the latter.

It has been found, in particular, that the Old Testament contains similarly structured self-expressions of Jahweh, such as the well-known "I am who I am" of Exodus 3:14; this is notably the case in the discourses of Second Isaiah, as, for example, " 'You are my witnesses,' says the LORD, 'and my servant whom I have chosen, that you may know and believe me and understand that *I am he*. Before me no god was formed, nor shall there be any after me. *I, I am the LORD*, and besides me there is no savior' " (43:10-11). In the Old Testament, the "I am" without a predicate is the highest form of divine self-expression and self-commitment, and in this sense it is the formula of revelation *pure and simple*. Jahweh is the "absolute I" who addresses people and can never become an "it" (M. Buber).

When John takes over this formula and applies it to Jesus, "there can be no doubt that in this application to Jesus the latter is assigned a dignity that is unparalled in Jewish experience." However, the

56

application does not imply an out-and-out identification with God himself. Rather, "Jesus is the eschatological revealer of God, the one in whom God speaks directly to men."[32] The formula therefore serves to express the highest claim made by Jesus as revealer. But perhaps this statement is still too abstract and extrinsic. We must also take into account the fact that in the gospel of John the exalted Christ speaks as the earthly Jesus. If we then go on to ask what the vital context is for such a revelation by the Christ now present with us, we will be led once more to the primitive Christian liturgy and, more specifically, to prophetic preaching.

The prophet and preacher who is moved by the Spirit knows that he or she is the voice of the exalted Christ and that Christ speaks as through a human earthly instrument; when thus moved by the Spirit, the prophet formulates the kinds of statements we are now considering.[33] In the context of the liturgy, such formulas have the function of rendering present; they are to be understood after the manner in which the account of institution functions in the celebration of the Eucharist. When they are voiced, the community becomes aware of Christ present in its midst. In addition, as is clear from its linkage with various symbolic terms, the "I am" formula has the function of disclosing meaning: these symbolic terms help to articulate the salvific significance of Jesus for humanity.

The images (see the list above) have a broad symbolic and, in part, mythical background in both the Jewish and the Hellenistic worlds. They are images which give expression to important essential values of people or to mythico-religious intelligible meanings which, in the cultural situation of the time, describe what people understood by salvation and redemption. They express people's expectations regarding salvation. This can be seen in the fact that many of the symbols, such as "bread of life" or "light" or "life" occur in very diverse and independent mythical traditions; they form part, as it were, of the religious language of universal humanity. Wherever people have used religious terms to express their understanding of salvation and their longing for redemption, they have used these and similar symbols.

We may perhaps regard the universal human longing for "eternal," "true," or "real" life as the common nucleus of all such symbolic statements. Or, to put it another way, the symbols give expression to an ultimate interpretation of human existence, to people's basic understanding of themselves. In them we discover the radical meaning of religion, insofar, that is, as the question of people about existential meaning, as raised in every age, or the longing for a meaningful interpretation of life is, in fact, the religious question humanity poses to itself. At the time the fourth evangelist lived, very diverse groups in the Hellenistic world were asking this question in various ways. One important current of this kind was the gnostic movement. *Sotēria* ("salvation," "liberation," "redemption") was one of the great catchwords of the day. When John takes over these images, he evidently intends to assert that for him Jesus Christ is the definitive answer to the question of meaning that was being raised in these religious symbols. Jesus is the fulfillment of humanity's religious longing: of the Jewish expectation of salvation, and of the religious yearnings of the pagans. Jesus embodies the supreme existential values and intelligible meanings. The central conceptual content that appears over and over in the symbols is that of "life" or "eternal life." Jesus is the revealer who brings true, eternal, divine life.

All this suggests a twofold relation between Christianity and the religions. We start with a fact: the presupposition of the Johannine and indeed the entire primitive Christian message of salvation is that Jesus of Nazareth is the human historical form taken by the revealer of God and eschatological savior. On the one hand, then, this principle is the norm by which all other expectations of salvation are critically judged; the latter cannot furnish the salvation they promise.[34] On the other hand, the principle also yields a positive view of the religions, which may be formulated as follows: The religions with their various ways of interpreting human existence are the most profound and powerful expressions of humankind's longing for salvation. This longing for salvation, this religious yearning, is not illusory; it is an existential human fact which everyone can experience. It finds its supreme fulfillment in Jesus Christ and in the God of universal love for all, whom Jesus calls his Father. Consequently, what is expressly said of the Old Testament, that it is to be understood as a promise of Christ, holds analogously for all religions. In faith in Christ the religions too are superseded (*auf-gehoben*) in the two senses Hegel gives this term: in this faith they are fulfilled and brought to a higher completion.

As we said in connection with verse 5, people ask about the way—the way of life or the way of salvation—and thus about the meaning and goal of their own existence. Religions, for their part, attempt to answer this question regarding the way. Here Jesus says of himself, "I am the way." This means, first of all, in relation to all other ways, that Jesus himself is humanity's way to God; for the believer neither the Jewish way of salvation through a piety centered on the law (the Torah) nor the gnostic way of a purely interior knowledge of salvation has any standing alongside the way which is Jesus.

But the words of Jesus say something more than this. R. Bultmann writes, "By describing himself as the way Jesus makes two things clear: (1) his case is different from that of the disciples; he does not need a way for himself, as the disciples do, rather he is the way for them; (2) the way and the goal are not to be separated as they are in mythological thinking."[35] Salvation comes through *encounter* with Jesus the revealer. As applied to Jesus the concept of way includes his entire history, that is, his earthly activity, his death, and his resurrection; it also includes his way from heavenly preexistence into the world and back again to the Father, or, in other words, his coming from God and his going to God. People now have a way to God because in Jesus God himself has come to them and thus opened the way. The revelation of God in Jesus has now given a transcendent answer to questions regarding the way.

At the same time, Jesus' words also contain an implication for faith. If Jesus himself is the way, then faith as our response to revelation is also to be understood as way. Faith too is something vital and dynamic, a movement that lays hold of one's life and turns it into a continuous being on the way. Faith includes, of course, union with Jesus, but it also includes an ever new seeking of Jesus. *He himself* never becomes superfluous as far as the direction taken by faith is concerned; he is never outdated.

It is not so easy for us today to understand what Jesus means by describing himself as "the truth." This is because we attach quite divergent ideas to the concept of truth. When we speak of truth, we may mean (a) that a person says what is intended and thought; in other words, a correspondence of thought, intention, and speech, as opposed to any kind of deception or lie; or (b) that a thought, statement, or teaching corresponds to reality, as opposed to error. Today especially (c) truth may be understood as guidance for correct practice; and finally (d) truth is often understood as meaning that a statement or theory follows the rules of reason, logic, or scientific method.

The statement of Jesus which we are considering here does not fit in with any of these views. This is an indication that the understanding of truth is quite different from that of everyday speech and of science. The point is not that Jesus spoke the truth or that in his case thought and speech or speech and action were in harmony with one another, that is, that he never lied. The point is probably the primordial human quest of truth in the sense of the experience of meaning and certainty. This, it seems, is the basic thrust of the Johannine statement.[36]

We must here take into consideration above all the Old Testament understanding of truth (Hebrew: *emet*). *Emet* in the theological sense means the unconditionally reliable fidelity of God in his action, revelation, and commandments. Truth means the absolute dependability of God in his dealings with his people, so they can rely without reservation on God's word, his promise, his fidelity. Human beings can live by this *reliability—fidelity—truth* of God; it is this that assures the fundamental constancy and stability of their lives. Those who depend on God's word and revelation and count on it in practice by *doing the truth* in faith participate in the truth of God. In this understanding of truth, insight and action (theory and practice) or knowledge and experience are closely connected.

The central message of the gospel of John is that this truth of God encounters humanity in Jesus; in Jesus "grace and truth have come to pass" (1:17). It is this truth which encounters, befalls, and addresses people that liberates them: "If you remain in my word, you are truly my disciples; you will know the truth, and the truth will make you free" (8:31-32). In coming to know Jesus and his message humanity encounters the liberating truth and reality of God; in Jesus is also experienced truth as salvation and love; one can now live his

60

life in the truth. It is decisive for faith that it experiences liberating truth only in encounter with Jesus and his word; this truth is something that must be bestowed as a gift. But as a matter of fact it is abidingly bestowed on us in Jesus. Therefore Jesus fulfills in an unsurpassable manner our longing for ultimate truth and meaning.

Let us turn finally to the concept of "life." The meaning of this word in Johannine theology is really inexhaustible.[37] In continuity with Old Testamental and Jewish thinking, life (or eternal life) is a key word for the understanding of salvation and thus for everything that revelation has to offer. For the synoptic tradition the key word in regard to salvation is "reign of God"; for John, it is "life."

In order correctly to grasp the meaning of the word, we may refer to the modern concept of the quality of life. This phrase says that it is not enough for people to have the bare essentials of life—in regard to food, clothing, and shelter, for example—but that more is required for a fully human life, for example, a participation in a certain standard of living or in cultural values. Faith goes further: it tells us that even these things are not enough and that human life attains to its complete fulfillment only in communion with God. We might characterize this view as focusing on the eschatological quality of life. This is precisely what the fourth evangelist is speaking of: the absence of God as an absence of meaning, happiness, and joy is responsible for the most profound problems of human life and for alienation in the fullest sense of the term. On the other hand, true life as communicated through revelation consists in this, that Jesus offers us communion with God. Jesus, the Son of man, is the giver of eschatological life. He makes possible for us a life that transcends all other forms of fulfillment.

A decisive factor in John is that this eternal life is understood as something which is not solely in the future, as something which we will not share only in the distant future or after death. Rather, faith is the beginning of this eternal life. By faith, the human being already attains here and now to the new eschatological quality of life. Faith is the decisive step by which we pass from death to life because it is our participation in the communion with God which Jesus has made accessible to us (on this cf. 1 John 1:1-4).

Way, *truth*, and *life* form an intrinsic unity and describe for us

61

the various aspects of the revelation that is present in Jesus. Faith discovers all of this in Jesus himself. John has used new concepts to express the significance of Jesus in a new way, by interpreting him as God's response to the central human quest for meaning. What we are calling the quest for meaning is in the last analysis our question about the right way, about the truth that is permanently valid for us, and about the life whose quality no longer depends solely on the available natural blessings and which we can accept as unquestionably good and full of promise because in its complete form it reaches beyond even the boundary of death and is *eternal* life in the true sense. All this a person can find in the encounter with Jesus of Nazareth because Jesus gives access to complete communion with God. The statement that "no one comes to the Father except through me" (v. 6b) becomes intelligible against this background. It gives expression to the fact that people's relation to God is established by Jesus; there is no longer any way to God except through the man Jesus.

As verse 7 makes clear, knowledge of Jesus and knowledge of God are also inseparable. "To know Jesus" means that through him and in him we know God the Father. As long as we look at and judge Jesus only according to his human or social function, we have not yet come to know him adequately; neither have we as yet grasped the full scope of our religious quest for salvation and meaning. The point is not that these functions of Jesus—the human and the social— are incidental or indifferent, but that neither are they the *ultimate* and decisive thing. The knowledge of God in Jesus gives the concepts human and social a final dimension of meaning; only then do they acquire their full significance.

This ultimate dimension of meaning is given to us "henceforth," that is, from the time of Jesus' appearance in the world. In him we can find ourselves. The words "but henceforth you know him and have seen him" (i.e. God) emphasize once again the definitive character of the revelation given by Jesus. With his coming the revelation of God in history has taken place *once and for all*, so that we can encounter the Father over and over again, especially in the words of Jesus. What Jesus has brought is indeed past from a purely historical point of view, but in the strict sense it is always newly present, as soon as by faith people allow Jesus' word to address them and determine their lives. As far as the question of God is concerned, the future too is included in the revelation Jesus has brought. As long as the word of Jesus remains alive in human history and as long as it touches people and finds faith, the question of God, in whatever form it may be asked, will not go unanswered, even if appearances so often seem to belie this fact.

Verses 8-11. The foregoing unit has made it clear that we come to the Father through Jesus and that we attain knowledge of God through Jesus. This is the point of reference for Philip's question, which, once again, takes the form of a Johannine misunderstanding. The question articulates, as it were, the subliminal yearning for clear and definitive knowlege of God, for the vision of God, and it does so as a question that arises with a certain inevitability in this discourse of Jesus. Here again the misunderstanding serves to carry faith-inspired reflection a step further in the effort to reach the *central message* of this revelatory discourse. In his failure to understand, Philip represents the person who has still not grasped the real point, the religious person who perhaps takes Jesus to be a teacher of a new religious knowledge, but who also thinks this knowledge can be obtained as objective teaching or a kind of dogma about God, and subsequently dispense with the teacher.

In its content the question expresses the longing for a vision of God. In this longing to see the godhead directly and in its fullness we have the quintessence of mankind's whole religious desire: the desire to discover the meaning of all reality in an encounter with God. The religions, despite the variety of their responses, are precisely expressions of this kind of ultimate, definitive, and unsurpassable meaning. The Bible, too, is familiar with this yearning of people to see God, but it keeps insisting on the limits set to such a desire.

When Moses asks Jahweh, "Let me see your face," the answer given him is, "My face you cannot see; for no human being who sees me continues to live." The most that can be granted to him is to see the back of the divine glory, nothing more (cf. Exod. 33:18-23). The gospel of John retains this view that no one has ever seen God and that none can see him (1:18; 6:46; cf. 1 John 4:12). The

63

principle of the invisibility of God is in fact a basic presupposition of the Johannine theology of revelation. It must be admitted that when people speak about God, they often give the impression that they have forgotten this fundamental principle; otherwise they would be more understanding toward those who cannot see their way to believing in God.

In the biblical view, God manifests himself primarily to the hearer of the word. This is precisely the background for Jesus' response to Philip. His reproachful words; "Have I been with you for so long, Philip, and you still have not known me?" refer the reader once more to association with the historical Jesus. To know Jesus means precisely to recognize in him the revealer of God. It is possible to say a good deal about Jesus, but if this decisive point has not been grasped, then the talk about Jesus has not yet found its proper focus; all statements are still provisional and approximate. Every kind of association with Jesus, whether theological or devout or secular, must face the question asked of Philip.

Now the positive side: "He who has seen me has seen the Father." In encounter with Jesus the quest for God reaches its goal. For it is precisely the meaning of faith in Jesus that we find in him the mystery we call God. The seeing of Jesus that is meant here is, of course, not a bodily seeing but a seeing by faith. Faith has its own manner of seeing, one that must be exercised over and over. What faith in Jesus ultimately succeeds in seeing is the presence of God in Jesus the revealer. This being so, it is clear that the petition, "Show us the Father!" is superfluous.

Jesus now gives the reason why one who believes in him can see the Father: "Or do you not believe that I am in the Father and the Father is in me?" Here we have a characteristic Johannine expression, the formula of reciprocal immanence.[38] This formula, which is not to be misunderstood as a spatial conception, expresses the intimate solidarity and communion of God and Jesus.[39] The statement that Jesus is "in the Father" means that his life and activity are determined by God, whom he understands to be his Father, and, conversely, that his activity reveals God, so that God is present "in Jesus." Evidently, the truth of these words is accessible only through faith and not through speculation about God that is separable from faith, for faith gives one a living relationship to Jesus and

64

thereby to God; it assures participation in and communion with God.

The immanence formula is not a statement of speculative theology about the nature of Jesus and the relation of Father and Son within the Trinity. It is rather a description of a mutuality, a relation, an encounter; the description, as an expression of revelation, discloses the open space to which faith wins access. We understand the formula correctly if we take it as a description of a relationship based on love. This point is further emphasized in the following sentences, in which Jesus says that he acts and speaks wholly on the basis of his communion with God, his dependence (which at bottom is his unparalleled freedom) on the Father. In fact, in him God himself speaks and acts (vv. 10b-11). In the works of Jesus (in the concept of "work" words and signs are united) God's works are manifested. Faith is the living experience of all this.

Here again we must recall that the gospel of John is not theological speculation but a theological meditation on Jesus, that is, an exploration of what the person of Jesus means for faith. The various statements we have been discussing are all related to the historical individual, Jesus of Nazareth. They interpret Jesus, of course, from a specific viewpoint when they understand him as the revealer of God, as the place where people encounter God and can discover, through faith, the meaning of their lives. In different ways, the synoptics, Paul, and indeed the entire New Testament say the same thing. But this one and the same thing must be said in various ways, in ever new language and concepts.

The variety of the New Testament testimonies calls our attention to the fact that human language, even in the service of revelation, can only achieve *approximations* in its efforts to circumscribe the mystery of Jesus. All theological language is approximative; it is never a fully adequate expression of the reality. It puts us on the track, opens paths, shows aspects but it never lays hold of the reality in its entirety. In addition, Jesus manifests himself here as the one who fulfills the religious yearning of humanity. That which the religions sense and express, finds in Jesus of Nazareth the central core of meaning they had not known. For he is "the light that enlightens every person" (1:9). The eschatological revealer of God is revealer and savior for all.

This section with its variety of statements and themes allows us to glimpse something of the spaciousness of Johannine theological thinking. In it the central questions of faith find repeated expression.

Verse 1. Faith is always a human faith and therefore never independent of the historical personal and social situation in which we are at any time; in that situation, moreover, faith is always faith under attack. We are helped in understanding faith when we learn from John that things have always been this way and that the attack upon faith by the entire complex called the world and therefore by opposition from unbelief and the many-faceted experience of meaninglessness, helplessness, frustration, and resignation, is part of faith's situation in the world and in history. Such an insight relativizes the talk about the special crisis of faith in which we now supposedly find ourselves. As a matter of fact, the accepted view of faith is probably false or at least questionable, that is, the view which claims that there should be no temptations and doubts against faith, no crisis of faith. The faith that is directed to Jesus does not subscribe to the illusion of a world that is upright and sound, a world in which there should be no conflicts.

Faith that in the midst of crisis looks—as it may and should—for a trustworthy basis, an unshakable foundation, can in the last analysis find no other foundation than the word or message of Jesus. This faith finds the meaning it seeks not in an external serenity nor in the increased order and discipline which some people today want as a corrective for disorder nor in some vague hope that things will get better again. Faith finds its meaning solely in itself and its object: Jesus and God. The world cannot provide it with this meaning, but neither can it take it away. Faith is therefore always correlative to the quest for meaning and not to a quest for external success or progress. If faith were once to accept this truth, it would once again be in touch with its true self and would be in a position to experience new certainty about itself. It is not possible to demonstrate to anyone the meaning which faith attains, but it is indeed possible to live by it and bear living witness to it; in the last analysis, this is what counts.

Verses 2-4. The question of the hereafter is also clarified. John gives a short and terse answer to this question that troubles many people: *In the last analysis,* anyone who takes Jesus for his guide and has found in him the one who leads to salvation need not worry any more about the hereafter, the heavenly dwellings. To the questions, "What happens after death? Is death the end of everything?" John answers: The God of love is more real than death. Anyone who trusts in God during this life should cling to this trust and will not fall into the abyss of emptiness. God is the love that embraces all people, all times, all history, and therefore our little lives as well; it is against the background of this love that our lives acquire their true significance. All the ways of humankind lead finally to God. On that foundation all can live and die (and perhaps we should put the emphasis here on live!). No other answer is needed, no geography of the hereafter.

Verses 5-7. The "I am" statement "I am the way, the truth, and the life" has led us to the heart of the Johannine theology of revelation. According to this statement, Jesus is the answer to the religious longings of humankind. By means of the "I am" statements John enables us to gain a positive understanding of our religions and of the phenomenon of religion as such. Only a christological answer based on these and similar New Testament statements can really come to grips with the problem of religion (the religions). It teaches us to approach the religions with seriousness and to detect the yearning that finds expression in them, the longing for true life and an all-fulfilling meaning. They too are genuine ways of salvation, and on them the light of revelation shines, even if in a manner hidden from us.

Since such is their character, the religions must not be brutally destroyed, as they have so often been in the past. It can even be a perversion to impose on them by authoritarian decree a type of rule proper to the Latin Church (for example, the entire Roman Canon Law with all its sanctions). Latin, and especially Roman-Latin, Christianity is undoubtedly being called upon today to reflect critically on itself and to repent. This repentance will consist chiefly in revising its own absolute claims. The Roman-Latin Church has been characterized by an all too unreflective self-understanding that

67

has identified a specific expression of Christianity—an expression which is not intelligible apart from its social and historical foundations—with Christianity as such, and has forced not only legitimate but also questionable forms on the poor heathen. The witness of Jesus to the God of unconditional love must be carefully distinguished from this indefensible absolutizing of Latin Christianity.

There is an element of truth in the view, so often condemned in the past, that the religions of humankind are various ways to the one goal. We need not concern ourselves with whether they reach this goal within history. Christian faith identifies this goal with the one divine love that embraces all humankind, with the divine life which Jesus embodies as revealer. From this fact one conclusion at least must be drawn: that methods of conversion which attempt to advance toward or attain this goal in a violent, loveless, and unsympathetic manner are certainly wrong. The point, of course, is not that we should cultivate a superficial tolerance that does not take seriously the question of religious truth. On the contrary, the point is to cultivate the kind of tolerance that, according to the witness of the New Testament, is consonant with the God of love. The faith of which we speak feels no need of constantly busying itself or thinking in triumphalistic terms (for example, in terms of success as measured by large numbers). It has the ability to wait and hope and to cooperate in the salvation of all through an active love, such as finds expression, for example, in social involvement with the Third World.

Verses 8-11. The God of Jesus, the God of revelation, is not a thing of the past as far as faith is concerned. We are not yet done with him. As long as Jesus' words continue to be heard and accepted, the hope always remains that this God is coming to meet us and that his voice is reaching us in order that our hearts may turn to him. Admittedly, the question of whether we encounter and see the Father in Jesus can no longer be answered with the same certainty as in earlier times. The living God, whom no ecclesiastical office and no theology can claim for its own, does not have to speak; he can also remain silent and hide himself, just as he can reveal himself in a new way and make himself heard.

There is a critical issue here for the Church and believers. The

Bible, and especially its assertions about God, is for us today no longer a textbook with infallible information and formulas that one need only repeat. It functions rather as a challenge to critical reflection on ourselves. Specifically, it is the Johannine statements about the presence of God in Jesus that raise a great number of questions for us, and we cannot act as though we had already come to grips, in even an approximative way, with the statements we have been discussing in these pages. We have certainly not come to grips with them, and must admit our inadequacy.

In reading these texts, then, we find ourselves on the side of the questioners: "How can *we* know the way? Show us the Father, and that is enough for us!" Who can deny that our questions, too, betray numerous misunderstandings? Once we admit our perplexity, that is, once we admit that when it comes to the question about God we often know no more than our contemporaries whom we like to regard as an unbelieving generation, then perhaps the Johannine texts will have something to say to us once again. Perhaps they will set us on the track of the hidden God by showing us the way of faith.

Promise of "Greater Works"; Certainty That Prayer Will Be Heard (14:12–14)

Exegesis

This short unit of text (vv. 12-14) is divided into two parts: verse 12, which contains a promise for believers, and verses 13-14, which are a statement about "prayer in the name of Jesus" as prayer that will certainly be granted. Once we inquire into the connection between faith and prayer, there proves to be an inner connection between these two parts.

Verse 12 begins with the formula of solemn affirmation, "Amen, amen . . . ," that occurs repeatedly in John and gives special emphasis to the ensuing statement. The statement is in the form of a promise for the future; the situation in mind is that of the community of disciples after the departure of Jesus. If we recall once again the actual situation in which the evangelist is speaking, and realize that he is addressing first and foremost the Johannine community, the promise takes on a noteworthy double aspect. On the one hand, it is a prophecy formulated after the fact (*vaticinium ex eventu*). On the other hand, it is a statement about the important role of the post-Easter community insofar as it is a community that lives by faith. In this respect, and in view of the subsequent saying about prayer, the text resembles to some extent the synoptic saying about the "faith that moves mountains" (Mark 11:23-24; Matt. 21:21-23), in which a statement about the effects of faith is likewise connected with a promise regarding prayer. The possibility may not be excluded, therefore, that what we have here in verses 12-14 is the Johannine version of the saying in Mark.

The promise says that one who believes in Jesus will do the same work as Jesus did, and in fact will accomplish even greater works.[40]

In Johannine usage the concepts "work" (singular) and "works" (plural) overlap, but it may be said that, broadly speaking, the singular places the emphasis more on the total work of salvation done by Jesus, whereas the plural can also include the miracles, which for John are signs of salvation and revelation and consequently must also be seen in their connection with the one inclusive work of salvation. The plural too, therefore, can refer to the total saving work of Jesus. A further point to be taken into consideration is the correlation of *words* and *works*, as a result of which the term works quite often includes, or also refers to, words. These peculiar overlappings in usage must be taken into account in dealing with verse 12.

The works of Jesus include not only his signs, "but also and above all his words, and therefore his entire action, his entire revelatory activity . . . . It is these works of Jesus that the disciples and Christians who truly believe in Jesus will also do. What is meant here . . . is not a repetition of the individual works of Jesus in word and deed, but simply the continuation and completion of the revelatory activity of Jesus in word and deed, in and through the post-Easter Church of the disciples."[41]

The reason Jesus gives, "because I am going to the Father," emphasizes the situation in which the community of disciples finds itself: this community is to continue the activity of Jesus during the time of his absence. At the same time, these words of Jesus also give the reason why the fulfillment of the promise is assured. It is the exalted Jesus, now with the Father, who acts through the community; the works which the faithful do are therefore by no means their own achievements and exploits, but are the actions of Jesus being continued in the community. Just as Jesus, when on earth, did only the work of God his Father, so the believing disciples do the work of Jesus. Since faith is the basis of the works and makes them possible, the words of Jesus here are in fact a promise that faith will be efficacious.

Exegetes are not in agreement about what precisely is meant by "greater works."[42] It does not seem possible to exclude a reference to the post-Easter mission. While the activity of Jesus was limited in time and space, the post-Easter Church expanded, both geographically and in numbers, far beyond the original Jewish and Palestinian scene. There is a similar reference in 4:36-38: "The reaper already receives his wage and gathers fruit for eternal life, so that sower and reaper may rejoice together. For in this the saying is true: One man sows and another reaps. I have sent you forth to reap what you did not work for; others worked and you have entered into their labor."

Jesus' words, then, shed light on the relation between the work of the historical Jesus and that of the post-Easter community, as well as on the astonishing experience of the primitive Church that the real impact of Jesus began only after his departure. According to John, there is a parallel or correspondence between the activity of Jesus and that of the community (this is a conception we will come across frequently). It asserts that there is no difference in principle, no essential difference, between the action of Jesus and that of the community. The activity of the community, including its experience in its dealings with the world, does not have a structure different from that proper to the activity of Jesus. The model of Jesus continues to be binding in this respect as well.

There is a further point to consider: the activity of Jesus and its completion (definitively given with his departure to the Father) not only mark an ending but are also nothing short of a *condition for a new beginning*. The activity of Jesus on earth provides the basis for his ongoing activity in and through the community; it is thus the basis for the future of the community. In its efforts in behalf of the cause of Jesus, the community is promised a greater future. In fact

71

it may even be said that in the future the significance of Jesus' work will emerge ever more fully; the future, including subsequent church history, is a necessity if the work of Jesus is to bear its full fruit.

The farewell discourses speak several times (cf. 15:7; 16:23) of prayer and, in particular, "prayer in the name of Jesus" (14:13-14); this is a sign that the fourth evangelist regards the theme as of special mediatorial function of Jesus in heaven, a conception also current elsewhere in the primitive Church (cf. Rom. 8:34; 1 John in which he is named or invoked. The thought is obviously of the special 'mediatorial function' of Jesus in heaven, a conception also current elsewhere in the primitive Church (cf. Rom. 8:34; 1 John 2:1-2). According to it, Jesus intercedes with God for the faithful. The formula used in liturgical prayer, "through Christ our Lord" (*per Christum Dominum nostrum*) is a strict consequence of prayer "in the name of Jesus." It indicates—and in this it is fully in line with the gospel of John—that not only our relation to God but all Christian liturgy or cultus has a christological stamp.

It is notable that in our text Jesus himself, instead of God, is the addressee of prayer in the name of Jesus. He is the one whom we ask to grant the petition. But the theocentric character of prayer is brought out in verse 13b, where it is said that the ultimate goal is the "glorification of the Father through the Son." In other words, there is no objective contradiction when Jesus appears here as the granter of petitions, while elsewhere it is the Father who answers prayers.

Verse 14 repeats the statement once again and generalizes it: No matter what the disciples ask for, their prayers will be answered.

Prayer, as found in all religions, is the vital expression of religion. It is undoubtedly essential to religious persons that they should pray, although, as is to be expected, the form and content of prayer will correspond to the spirit of each religion and to its stage of development. The Old Testament psalms display the entire world of ancient Israelite faith in all its breadth and depth; correspondingly, Christian prayer in its pure form is an expression of the Christian attitude of faith.

Martin Luther writes, "Prayer alone is faith's work . . . . What is faith if not prayer? For prayer expects divine graces without interruption. But if it expects them, then it longs for them with all its heart. And it is this longing that is true prayer."[43] What Luther rightly emphasizes here, *the inner connection between faith and prayer*, is important (cf. also Mark 11:23-24). We may see in this connection the decisive factor in the New Testamental and Christian understanding of prayer. Every other aspect of prayer is either directly bound up with faith or else belongs among the peripheral phenomena (such are also to be found, of course, in the Christian ecclesiastical tradition). Faith is aware that it is essentially a link to God and that humanity is utterly dependent on him. Faith is not simply one attitude among many, as it might appear to be were we to judge by the widespread kind of religious practice that regards religion as simply one particular sphere alongside others, to be given its due tribute from people on special occasions. No, the act of believing always calls upon the whole person; its dynamism embraces the totality of human life.

In authentic prayer faith finds expression; gratitude and joy find a voice, but so do the temptations, distress, and poverty that mark faith. If prayer is thus sustained by and embedded in faith, it is not magic, not an effort to influence God by magical practices. This absence of magic is belied neither by the promise of fulfillment nor by the instruction to ask for everything and anything. The fact that faith dares ask for everything possible is simply a sign that this faith is reaching down to and finding expression in the occupations and concerns of everyday life. It means further that correct prayer requires thought. Prayer does not, of course, consist solely of thought and reflection; it also comprises insistent desire and a readiness to act. But the decisive factor in prayer is its integration with faith and therefore its link with Jesus' understanding of God, which is characterized by love.

Meditation

Verse 12, as we have seen, speaks of the promise attached to faith in Jesus; it speaks therefore of the future of faith. In this future, which contains at the same time the future of the community of disciples, the cause of Jesus goes on and will manifest itself in "greater works." The history of primitive Christianity, which tells us that the historical Jesus failed but also that only after Good Friday and Easter did his effectiveness really begin and have the opportunity to spread, should set us thinking as well as give us confidence. Early Christians saw proof that God and the Spirit were at work, precisely in the fact that people came to believe in the exalted Jesus.

This situation also sheds a certain amount of light on the question, so urgently felt today, of the future of Christianity. In this matter, there is need not only of the widely used historical and sociological approaches to the question, but also and above all of reflection on the theological aspect. One sociologist has this to say:

> We do not know what the future of religion is in our society. Therefore if we think we can base our action on what passes for sure knowledge on the subject, we will be building on sand . . . . If we believe that we possess at least a fragment of religious truth, then in my opinion we must confess this truth, even if the chances of its success in society at large seem slim. And if we believe we know the imperatives for social action, in politics or any other area, which flow from our religious commitment, then I suggest we follow these imperatives, even if we do not clearly see the consequences for religion or the Church.[44]

This view refers the question back to faith and theology, and rightly so.

The primitive Church saw in Jesus and his message the eschatological saving event, that is, precisely what John is describing in the concept of works. Connected with this belief is the conviction that the saving event contains the germ of its own future and that at every moment it far outstrips the future as the world understands it. Consequently, alongside the formula the cause of Jesus goes on, which as such looks to the mere passage of time and has an almost fatalistic ring to it, there must be set another formula: The cause of Jesus has not yet been fully grasped, it has not yet gotten across to people, it has not yet reached its fulfillment! It could be regarded as finished, passé, only if its great promises of the reign of God, the coming of true justice and love, fully human relationships among people and definitive peace among the nations had already been fulfilled. But in fact every realization of Christianity in history (thus far) has been fragmentary and often even quite dubious in character. This holds even for the Church. God's promise is far from having been realized; we are only on the way to such fulfillment. The return of Jesus is still in the future, and this is true for every age.

Viewed in the light of the promise, then, the question of the future of Christianity is a problematic question, one prompted rather by faint-heartedness. The question must rather be turned around. Are we ready to focus our attention on the great future potentially present in the message of Jesus and to move into it boldly? From this viewpoint the greater works sound like a kind of pedagogue's promise, as when a grownup dealing with a child adopts the child's perspective and withdraws into the background so that the child will take courage and be active. The cause of Jesus points to this greater future, for the eschatological horizon is the broadest horizon possible.

As far as prayer is concerned, the preceding remarks supply us with a new reason for not having asked earlier whether it makes any sense to pray. Is prayer not simply a form of self-assurance or (to put it in less friendly terms) a form of pious self-deception? When people pray, are they not just talking to the wall or to themselves? Is prayer not from the outset an abandonment of practice, a consolation for the weak who are unable to act? So run the objections. But, important though these are in their proper place,[45] in the final analysis they can be answered only when we understand prayer in the light of its Christian root, and that root is faith. Faith must and always will find expression in language, and prayer is one of the most important of these expressions: "I believe and therefore I also speak" (Ps. 116:10; cf. 2 Cor. 4:13).

It follows that difficulties in praying are probably signs that the attitude of faith itself has become somehow distorted. It must also be noted, of course, that such a distortion is also present when people pray habitually indeed but their prayer has become a ritual formality, when language bears no relation to reality, when inherited formulas are still used without thinking, even though they no longer say anything to the user, when people think prayer can be properly ordered, even in the liturgy, merely by following regulations (thus removing every opportunity for the spontaneous language of faith to find expression), when prayer no longer makes any change in

75

anything. If prayer is essentially a vital expression of faith, it cannot be practiced without reference to God and humanity and the world, but will always be the start of an open-ended, comprehensive integration of all areas of life.

It is on this basis that the criteria for right and wrong prayer must be established. It should give us pause when we find people no longer able to pray because prayer would be equivalent to an abandonment of personal responsibility, to a comfortable escape from tasks that fall within their competency. It is no longer permissible for us today to cultivate a naive, uncritical, and unenlightened view of the world. When, for example, crises and catastrophes occur which have been caused by human beings and must be dealt with by human beings, right prayer can only mean that we acknowledge both our guilt and our responsibility and make ourselves capable of a new and different kind of thinking and acting.

There is thus a practice of prayer that we must describe as immature because it is no longer adapted to the level our understanding of reality has reached. In this light we can appreciate the criticism that prayer is something childish. We must strive to attain to a developed, adult, mature form of prayer or prayer-based meditation, a form of self-reflection before God, which at the same time translates into action our relation to others and the world. The central issue here, then, is the faith we need for our social and political activity. The phrase "in the name of Jesus" provides the proper direction for such prayer—"Whether I act or write my verses,/Give me direction for my way" (Goethe). In this case, the phrase "in the name of Jesus" sums up the correspondence between those who pray and the cause of Jesus, which is meant to have an effect on the world. The phrase thus points to the greater works which are promised to action based on faith.

Love for Jesus; Promise of the "Supporter" and of "Seeing Jesus Again" (14:15–24)

Exegesis

The best way to approach this entire section is under the rubric of "love for Jesus": "The love which is directed to the Revealer . . .

at this point becomes the explicit theme."[46] The theme is briefly introduced in verse 5. The first "Paraclete-saying" follows in verses 16-17, and a statement about the "return" of Jesus to his own in verses 18-20. The following passage (vv. 21-24) takes up the theme of love once again and brings to light its ultimate theological depths.

This section in its entirety represents an answer to the question of the relationship between the believing community and Jesus, a question which we said earlier is the central theme of the farewell discourses: What is the importance to the community of its links with Jesus? How is this bond of union to be understood?

Verse 15. The verse deals with love for Jesus and tells us of what it consists. To love Jesus is to keep his commandments or, as it is put elsewhere, his words. This is the first occurrence of the typically Johannine Greek word *terein* (to keep hold of, pay attention to, observe, keep). The word is frequent in the Old Testament, chiefly in the context of the careful observance of the Mosaic law, the Torah. In John the law is replaced by Jesus' own "word" or his "commandment," which is to be kept or observed.[47] The expression emphasizes the element of duration, of steady adherence. At issue is the permanent binding force of Jesus' word or commandment, but also the active character of such adherence, in the sense of "putting the faith into practice," especially through love. Faith and love are understood as forming a unity, a comprehensive living whole. For this reason singular and plural are interchangeable (i.e., word, commandment; words, commandments) without any change in the overall meaning. The "commandments of Jesus" do not therefore in any sense refer to the ten commandments but first and foremost to "love one another" in which the entirety of Christian practice is summed up according to John.

The idea of the love of the disciples or believers for Jesus is very rare in the New Testament; the synoptics and Paul do not contain the expression at all. Except for John,[48] it occurs only in a characteristic passage of the First Letter of Peter, where we read, " You love him without having seen him; you believe in him without seeing him now; you rejoice in him with an inexpressible and transfigured joy, for you are attaining the goal of your faith, the salvation of your souls" (1 Pet. 1:8-9). The formulation in this text of Peter is helpful because it puts its finger on the precise problem with which John is concerned: What does it mean to "love Jesus" when one has not seen him and therefore cannot enter into the kind of relationship with him that is possible among human beings who are contemporaries?

At this point, it becomes clear once again how the fictive character of the farewell discourses enables John to state a problem that is agitating his community. It is not merely a question of whether "the next generation . . . without having had a personal relationship to him" can love Jesus.[49] That is evidently possible; indeed a person can become enthusiastic about this Jesus, even emotionally, and "with all his heart," and can "love" him. The real question is what follows from this? Is an emotional enthusiasm enough, or is something more required? To this question the text gives an unambiguous answer: To "love" Jesus means to keep his commandments.

Expressed here is the idea that the word or the teaching of Jesus continues to be binding on the community of disciples. Union with Jesus, as characterized by love of him, always entails the obligation to keep his word. The other gospels too are proof of precisely this fact, for that is why they handed on the words of Jesus. Faith is not a noncommittal friendly acknowledgment of Jesus, as one might acknowledge other important historical personages and even be enthusiastic about them; it is the obligatory acceptance of his commandments as instructions for the living of one's life. There must be an acceptance of the "practice of Jesus"; precisely in this is one's love of him proved. The statement in verse 15 is therefore to be understood in the light of 1 John 4:20: "If anyone says 'I love God,' but hates his brother, he is a liar. For the man who does not love his brother whom he sees cannot love God whom he does not see." That is the sense here: Anyone who does not keep the commandment of Jesus cannot love Jesus.

Verses 16-17. Here we find the first "paraclete-saying." Jesus promises the disciples a supporter or helper, a paraclete. We cannot help noticing the formula "another paraclete," which implies that the first supporter, who is to be replaced or supplemented by another, is Jesus himself. As a matter of fact, the term paraclete is applied to Jesus in the First Letter of John. There we read, "My children, I am writing this to you in order that you may not sin. And if anyone of you does sin, then we have an advocate [or supporter: a paraclete] with the Father, namely, Jesus Christ, the just one. He is the expiation for our sins, and not only for our sins but for those of the entire world" (1 John 2:1-2). These words describe the role of heavenly intercessor or mediator which Jesus has with the Father, a role he receives as the one exalted at God's side.

It is clear, however, that the translation "advocate" does not suit the Spirit-Paraclete in the gospel of John and that consequently the interpretation is difficult. The usual explanation is along the lines that we find in Bultmann: " The Spirit will be for them [the disciples] what Jesus had been: . . . a helper."[50] If, however, we follow the logic of the view that in the fictive farewell discourses it is not the earthly Jesus who speaks but the Christ now present, then we will adopt a different interpretation. The first paraclete is indeed Jesus, but in his role as heavenly mediator with God, and the other paraclete is the Spirit who acts on earth in his community, the Church, as its supporter and helper.[51] Here the two paracletes are not related by temporal succession but are parallel to one another (any temporal succession here is secondary). This is the best way to explain the remarkable parallel function which the Spirit-Paraclete has in John. The Spirit is not so much the successor of Jesus, as he is the personage who makes Jesus present; he is thus the agent through whom the exalted Jesus acts in the community.

Spirit (Hebrew: *ruah*; Greek: *pneuma*) has a special meaning in the biblical linguistic tradition, and we must attend to this if we are to understand correctly the meaning of the statements about the Holy Spirit. The modern reader must avoid two misunderstandings in particular. First, Spirit in the biblical sense does not mean the intellectual faculty or intelligence of a person, the human spirit. But secondly, the characterization of the Spirit as the third person of the divine Trinity, understandable though it may be, almost inevitably leads to misunderstandings today. The most profitable course is to start with the basic meaning of the Hebrew word *ruah*, which denotes the restless wind, the invigorating air, and thus from the outset connotes something dynamic, something in motion. Also to be kept in mind is the elusive character of the wind, which is well expressed in the words, "The wind (*pneuma*) blows where it will;

you hear its sound but do not know whence it comes or whither it goes; so it is with everyone who is born of the Spirit (*pneuma*)" (John 3:8). In addition, the word *ruah* connotes openness, communication, and creativity.[52]

The Bible usually speaks of spirit when it has something to say about the *reciprocal relationship of God and his people*. The concept does not serve only to characterize the nature of the divine; it describes the manner in which God comes to meet people, in which he is present for their sake, and in which people experience God and God's effect on them, namely, as an incomprehensible reality. We might recall here the words of Hölderlin: "God is near/and hard to grasp." This basic religious experience is what spirit expresses.

The expression "Spirit of truth" has Jewish prototypes (Qumran); in John truth means the divine reality that encounters people in Jesus. It is clear, therefore, that when John speaks of the Spirit of truth, he wants to express the manner in which Jesus and the revelation of God which he brings are there for persons, the manner in which they are present. The term "supporter" expresses chiefly the special *function* of these present realities: they are there to be a help to the community of believers.

In verse 16 Jesus appears as intercessor with the Father, one who "asks" the Father to give the disciples the "supporter." The presence, through the Spirit, of Jesus' revelation is understood to be a gift of God that is never independent of the giver and therefore as such can never become one's possession. On the other hand, the gift is an unconditional and abiding gift. In this connection, the words "remain with you" or, more exactly, "be with you," show that revelation does not mean a system of truths or propositions but an abiding communion with God himself. When the supporter is promised to the community "forever," the meaning is that union with Jesus, and through Jesus with God, is available to the community, in faith, always and throughout the entire future. Because the Spirit will be present, the community of Jesus will never be ousted from communion with God.

Moreover, if the Spirit is the presence of God and Jesus in the community which is united by faith, then we can also understand its being said that the world cannot receive the Spirit of truth "because it does not see him or know him." This is not a definition by-negation of the essence of the "world that is hostile to God," but only a definition of its closed attitude to the claim of God that is made present in the Spirit. That is, the statement holds only to the extent that the world remains a prisoner of its own closed mind and heart. The moment it opens itself to the Spirit it has already ceased to be world. For Spirit means openness, communication, and space in which to encounter truth, while world means resistance, the closed mind and heart. The latter can however be at any time penetrated by the working of the Spirit. When that happens, we have the miracle of "rebirth," the turning from unbelief to faith.

The reverse is also true: If the community of believers is the community of Jesus and God the Father, it is such because of the presence of the Spirit. In a more profound theological sense, it is, to the very depths of its being, the open community in which, at every moment, truth, that is, encounter with Jesus and God, can occur. In this community all will know the spirit of truth, "because he remains with you and will be in you." Perhaps we might more accurately say, because he will be "among you, in your midst," for the point here is not simply the individual's possession of the Spirit, inasmuch as the Spirit is to be event, power or dynamism, that is, an event that is open to others and creates community. Only thus is the Spirit of truth present.

Verses 18-20. The presence of the Spirit entails the presence of God and Jesus. Through the Spirit Jesus continues to come to his community. Read in this light, the statement about the "coming back of Jesus" is only another aspect of the same event spoken of in the preceding passage. The present passage illustrates the shift of accent in Johannine eschatology of which we have spoken several times.[53] The expression "I do not leave you orphans" reminds the disciples once again of Jesus' departure, that is, of that fundamental experience of the absence of the historical Jesus which shapes the existence of the community of Jesus' disciples in the world. The image of the orphaned children who at their parents' death must remain behind in the world without help or support occurs frequently in literature when a beloved master is definitively separated from his or her disciples by death (for example, Socrates). The point of the comparison is abandonment and helplessness.

To this orphaned state is contrasted the joyous promise "I come to you again." This is to say that the abandonment will last only a short time. Verse 19 says expressly that the orphaned state of the disciples will be only an outward seeming. Within a short time indeed Jesus will actually have died and disappeared as far as the world is concerned. It will see him no more and will maintain that his cause has been defeated for good. Death is the definitive end as far as the world and its outlook are concerned; in the world's eyes there is nothing beyond death. Not so to the eyes of faith. As far as the community of disciples is concerned, "you will see me, for I live and you too shall live." Jesus is referring to their experience of Easter: "That the one who was given over to death is alive, and bound up with that, that the life of the believers is grounded in his resurrection life . . . . The special feature of this promise in John and in particular in this passage, is that the experience of Easter is seen as the fulfillment of the *Promise of the Parousia.*"[54]

If the statement "for I will live and you shall live" in fact gives expression to the experience of Easter, then not only must we understand the Johannine accounts of Easter (chaps. 20-21) in this light, but we also get a new insight into how John understands the Easter faith. "Life" here is the eschatological, eternal and divine life into which Jesus has entered. Faith shares in this divine life, so that the encounter in faith with Jesus the revealer can be understood as a participation in the life that Jesus himself possesses. This means that from the viewpoint of the world there can be simply no talk about Easter, since the latter is something that simply cannot be grasped in the concepts the world uses. As soon as one can make any real sense of Easter, one is already standing on the side of the risen and living Jesus; one has already been affected by his presence through the Spirit. For, to faith, Easter means precisely this: not that Jesus is alive somewhere, but that he bears witness to himself ever anew, through the word and the Spirit, as a power present among persons to give them life. The community of believers is the perduring testimony to the presence of the Risen One.

Given this understanding of Easter, John is also able to combine the primitive Christian expectation of Christ's return (*parousia*) with the experience of Easter. This, in fact, is his special theological contribution, and it enables him to answer an urgent question of the community. The question arose out of the delay of the parousia. The primitive community, Paul included, lived in the expectation of Christ's imminent return. We know from the New Testament (2 Thess., 2 Pet.) that the delay in its coming led to a profound crisis in many communities. The author of the Second Letter of Peter gives this answer to the problem: "Dear brothers, you must not overlook this one point: that for the Lord *a day is like a thousand years and a thousand years are like a day*. This Lord is not delaying in keeping his promises, as some think who speak of delay; he is only being patient with you, for he wants no one to be lost but for all to be converted" (2 Pet. 3:8-9). Here, God's eternity and his patience with people provide pastoral arguments.

By comparison, John's answer to the problem is more radical. It comes from the very heart of Johannine belief about Christ: Easter is already the beginning of the parousia; the Risen One himself is already present among his own through his Spirit and will not leave them again for all eternity. For faith the future has already begun in Jesus so that difficulties about the date of the last things are no longer a serious problem. The Spirit is the coming and the future of Jesus as already present, that future which knows no end. It is in this open-ended future that faith lives. As the phrase "on that day" indicates, this future is at the same time the dawning of the eschatological "day of the Lord" on which the openness and brightness of God will break into the world and on which full communion with God will begin. If the disciples are to know that "I am in the Father and you in me and I in you," then the use of the "immanence formula" shows that with the presence of Jesus in the Spirit God's communion with all has in fact already begun. That the community should know this through faith is the great gift which is entrusted to it and to which it must bear witness.

Verses 21-24. This passage picks up the key word in verse 15 and leads to its deeper understanding. Verse 21a begins by repeating the thought that only those who keep the commandments of Jesus and know that they are bound to follow the model given in the practice of Jesus (the precise form the model takes we know from the washing of the feet)—only such ones love Jesus not merely in words but "in deed and truth." Those who act thus will also be drawn into the relationship to God that Jesus has, and the Father will love them even as he loves his Son Jesus. Jesus too will love them, and "I will reveal myself to them."

Given John's idea of the oneness of Father and Son, this statement is understandable. Jesus opens up, to faith, the possibility of full communion with God. Anyone who enters this exemplary circle of divine love is drawn fully into it. Once again, it is clear that in the revelation of Jesus, as John presents it, the ultimate goal is true and complete communion with God or communication and specifically a communication in, with, and within the encompassing love in which the real nature of God is disclosed. The content of the message is intimately connected with revelation as a communicative event; the content is not primarily a "doctrine" but a *communication*, and this means not simply a sharing in new information but a sharing in the self-communication in which Jesus reveals himself and, through the word of Jesus, in the self-communication of God. That the man Jesus is the locus of the divine self-communication is what is being said in the statement "The Word became flesh" (1:14).

Against this background, it is also clear that the revelation of Jesus follows upon the practice of Jesus: "He who is prepared to do the will of God will know whether the teaching comes from God or whether I am speaking on my own" (7:17). The point here is not simply the right moral attitude as a condition for knowing or understanding the teaching of Jesus or revelation. Rather the general principle is being asserted that faith and love as an indivisible unity represent the beginning, the first step, in attaining to the knowledge of revelation.

It is in this way that John explains a noteworthy fact which constantly recurs in matters of faith and revelation: theoretical, logical knowledge is not enough by itself if one is to believe and to understand Jesus. There is, of course, a great deal in the Bible that can be understood without faith. In fact, it must be said, in opposition to a much too simplistic approach to the matter, that the Bible is a book whose texts in their entirety are open to critico-rational analysis; it is not a collection of esoteric doctrines. Nevertheless there is a deeper understanding which is accessible only through faith, and this faith depends on an existential opening, on a commitment that risks engaging in a personal experiment with the word, a practical experiment. This decision to undertake a training in Christianity is itself not something that can be made the object of a theory, and yet it is an indispensable condition for understanding the revelation of Jesus. *Da amantem et scit quod dico:* "Bring me a lover: he will understand what I am saying" (Augustine).

The misunderstanding in verse 22, with its negative reference to the world, highlights once more the unique nature of the revelation of Jesus: the fact that it is in the last analysis inaccessible to the world. The fact that the question as such is not accepted and answered shows that it is not a real question but a literary device for bringing out the distinction between the world, which continues on without the revelation of Jesus, and the sphere of believers. As a matter of fact, when seen from the viewpoint of faith, the unbelief of the world is the difficult, unresolved question that remains a constant gall to believers. Perhaps the question implies a familiar thought: By rights God must make himself known in such a way that even unbelievers will see the light! The question expresses the anxiety and distress of the little flock, and their query is not a harmless one. For it is but a short step from thinking this way to forcibly imposing the truth on the unbelieving world. If the question expects that kind of answer, then we are indeed not far from resentment (*ressentiment*) and the will to power. If our analysis is correct, then it is also objectively right for Jesus simply to bypass the question; no one should venture on this downward path.

Instead of giving an answer, Jesus takes up the various threads again and moves on. He tells the disciples that faith, love, and revelation carry with them their own certainty. They do not depend on external confirmation by the world. If they did, then they would also be subject to the standard of the world and would have no power to disturb and challenge society. They would then not be "God's victory" that overcomes the world and must be constantly attested anew. At the same time, however, faith is referred back to the word of Jesus. This is why faith has its binding character, but also why it inspires a superior hope and confidence. Jesus' words here lead the believer into what we have called the exemplary circle of divine love. This is precisely why the abiding link with the person and word of Jesus is, in principle, of such central importance for Christian faith.

The significance of this backward reference is thus not only historical, in the sense that Christian faith always acquires its identity only by its connection with this irreplaceable origin. It is also the case—and this must be repeated time and again—that what is indispensably and distinctively Christian cannot be determined in accordance with an objective criterion which is readily available for consultation, but only in accordance with the criterion which is Jesus himself. At the same time, when the question of Jesus as the abiding ground, the permanently valid, normative presupposition of all Christian identity, is addressed to the person of Jesus, it expands in a remarkable way into the question of "God" and of divine love as the indispensable background of meaning for the person of Jesus. It is precisely herein that the uniqueness and irreplaceableness of Jesus for faith consists.

The question is often asked today, "Why is this Jesus really needed? Can we not retain all Christian assertions or whatever is significant and essential in Christianity, and let Jesus go?" To this there can in fact be but one answer, "Because Jesus is the revealer of God." This answer is always a witness based on faith; in giving it, the believer confesses Jesus and invites the other to be open to the experience of faith. In this context it must also be said that as long as a person has not grasped the significance of Jesus as the sole and singular center of meaning for Christian faith, he or she has not understood Christianity but is still living in the Forecourt of the Pagans.

John emphasizes this point in his own way when he now attaches to faith the promise that "we will come to him and dwell with him." The question of the heavenly dwellings is raised once more and answered in an inverse way, as it were: The coming of Jesus to his followers signifies the coming of God as well! The word "dwell" points to the definitive and permanent character of God's presence and of the revelation. According to this statement of Jesus, the community of believers is the new eschatological dwelling place of God; it is the temple of God in the world.

The community is this, however, precisely as the community of believers that has found in Jesus the center and focus of its faith. For Jesus is here also answering a question that runs through the entire gospel of John: the question of the location of God's presence, of the new place of worship. This worship is no longer limited to a spatial center; in the light of the revelation of Christ the idea of a spatial "holy place" has become outmoded (cf. chap. 4). The community founded on faith is now the only legitimate locus for worship. In fact, faith makes even the individual person "the dwelling of God in the Spirit." To put it in figurative terms, in Jesus heaven has descended to earth, and the communion with God that begins through faith is endless as far as its own internal dynamism is concerned. What John has experienced in his meditative relationship with Jesus and has testified to in his gospel is the amazing miracle of God's coming to humanity. For John the heart of Christianity is to be found in the fact that in Jesus the mystery of God has disclosed itself to the extent of God's entering into a man and, through him, into humanity so as to be and remain present there throughout the entire future.

With this presence the practice of Jesus is unconditionally connected. If persons limit themselves to dogmatic assertions about the truth and do not connect them with the practice of Jesus, their assertions lack credibility. Even the community of Jesus is subject to the abiding danger of being satisfied with "cheap grace" (D. Bonhoeffer) and with propagating, zealously and even fanatically, an abstract, cold, dogmatic faith. If it does so, then even for it the promise is thrown into doubt.

Verse 24 may be a warning against the possibility: "He who does not love me does not keep my words." This is a warning against false security. Behind the word of Jesus stands the entire authority of God, since the word of Jesus is also the word of God, the Father. This authority makes the word of Jesus obligatory. But because it is linked with the practice of Jesus, it cannot be manipulated. For, whatever one may expect to accomplish by manipulation, one thing is certain: every form of manipulation is a renunciation of freedom and love! It excludes freedom and love in dealing with others and is a conscious or unconscious effort to outmaneuver them. The word of Jesus, on the other hand, lays claim simultaneously to all who appeal to it, and this creates the space of freedom and love in which it can take full effect.

Under its opening rubric of love for Jesus, the text raises the question of the relation between faith and Jesus, and seeks to answer it from various standpoints. Christian faith has a vital interest in this question because on the answer depends the solution to the problem of Christian identity. That is to say, how does Christian faith retain its sameness and identity through the vicissitudes of time and history? The history of Christianity shows us that Christianity and Christian faith could be understood in widely differing ways through the course of the centuries.

The question is an especially urgent one today. In its origin and nature Christianity, linked as it is with the Old Testamental and Jewish experience of faith, is a historical religion, as contrasted with nature religions or folk religions. This means, to begin with, that Christianity is very conscious of its historical origin. The statement in the Acts of the Apostles, "All this did not take place in a corner somewhere" (26:26), is correct in a broader and deeper historical sense. Apart perhaps from Islam, there is no other religion about whose historical circumstances, origins, and formative forces we have such precise and extensive knowledge (limited though it is in some ways) as we do about Christianity. From the viewpoint of historical criticism, Christianity came on the scene at an advanced stage of history; it came "in the fullness of time."

Historical, too, are the characteristic means by which Christianity gave expression to its unique nature and which it had to use if it was to perdure. The members of the early Christian communities were not recruited by the natural growth of the society in which they found themselves; that is, there was no Church of the people or all-inclusive Church, with infant baptism as the norm, in early Christianity. The mandate was to gain willing adherents, to recruit through mission. It was necessary to build gradually a tradition of faith and to establish a continuity based above all on a common doctrine and on the external cohesion of the communities. In this form, the problem of discovering a historical identity was present from the beginning.

This is also the situation reflected in the New Testament writings and especially in the four canonical gospels. It is clear in these documents that from the very beginning Christian faith was confronted with the difficulty that "Christian identity" did not consist in a pregiven set of fully formulated dogmatic propositions and that "Christian," therefore, did not refer to a fixed, clearly defined phenomenon, but was always a responsibility which each generation had to tackle anew. Jesus did not propose a basic set of systematically formulated new doctrines. Neither did he found a "church" as a ready-made institution that was fully equipped with functions, offices, and operating instructions and which would be fully capable of functioning after his departure. Rather, Jesus preached the message that God's reign was imminent. He expected that it would come in a very short time, although he gave no definite date and may perhaps have reckoned on a certain interval before the event. His entire life and activity proclaimed certainty that the end was near; he had no long-term plans.

After his violent death on the cross the community of Jesus saw itself thrown back and forced to begin all over. The Easter faith brought the surprising realization that this "new beginning" after the death of Jesus was to be understood as a creative new beginning. For the disciples, Easter was the divine commission to proclaim to the world that Jesus of Nazareth, who had been crucified, was "Lord and Messiah" (cf. Acts 2:29-36). Yet even at this point no one thought of a future history that would be of long duration. Rather, everyone expected the proximate parousia, or return of Christ and coming of the new, divine world.

After Easter, then, people had to become accustomed to the idea that there would be a historical period of long duration. In all probability, it was chiefly the death of the first generation of prominent disciples and apostles of Jesus that brought the problem fully home to them. The future would not simply fall like ripe fruit into the lap of the early Church; it would have to be conquered. In the process, the paramount importance of the person of Jesus, the historical Jesus, and of the tradition(s) of the early community(ies) about Jesus, became evident in an entirely new way to the early Church. This was especially true in 70 A.D. (destruction of Jerusalem by Titus) and the years following, when the links with the Jewish community of believers and the old Jewish-Christian tradition began to grow ever weaker. People evidently began to feel that the problem of a long-lasting future history was not to be solved simply by the expectation of a proximate parousia and by the fervor which the Spirit engendered. It now became necessary to turn back to the historical source of Christianity, and that source was the person of Jesus.

The most important evidence of this turning back to the person of Jesus is our four canonical gospels. As seen in the perspective of a history of origins, these books are the supporting pillars on which the weight of Christianity mainly rests. They, first and foremost, assure the connection of Christianity with its historical origin. At the same time, however, they are a bridge to the future! This they are because they present Jesus and the tradition about him in the framework of the proclamation of Christ. It is the "exalted Christ," and therefore the identity of the earthly Jesus with the heavenly Son of God, the identity of the crucified one with the Risen One, of Christ "yesterday, today, and forever," that is proclaimed in the gospels. The evangelists had no historical concern in the sense that they wanted to know or tell others what really happened. The focus of their concern was rather the proclamation of Christ now present. In the process, however, and to accomplish their purpose, they turned to the available tradition about Jesus. In their eyes, the truth and binding force of their own preaching depended on the binding force of Jesus' preaching. The evangelists consciously held on to two realities that were in tension: the historical tradition about Jesus and the preaching that made this tradition a present reality for the community.

In following both of these directions—the quest for the earthly Jesus of the past and the making present of that past in the kerygma—the evangelists have probably disclosed the basic structure of Christian proclamation and in the proces have given us an important indication about how to answer the question of Christian identity. This question can never be answered without inquiring into the beginnings and especially the person and cause of Jesus. This fact finds expression in the canonization of Jesus and the New Testament writings. Theology and preaching alike are bound by this early Christian norm ("canon"). It is impossible for the Christian or Church history to begin anew at point zero.

On the other hand, these same New Testament writings bid anyone who is looking backward simply from historical curiosity, to turn and look forward. Here the other term of the relation—the inter-pretation that renders the past present—has its say. In the last analysis, the important thing is the meaningfulness of speaking *today* of God's revelation in Jesus. Since the intellectual movement of Christian faith and theology follows the rhythm of this twofold struc-ture with both its poles, it too is inevitably historical in character. Seen in this light, Christian identity is not a fixed, self-enclosed, static concept, but is rather an identity in movement and needs to be achieved ever anew; it is identity in process. The gospel of John is a typical example of such an achievement of identity.

The attainment of Christian identity requires in the first place an imitation of the practice of Jesus, the keeping of his commandments. This has already been set down in 13:35 as a distinguishing mark of the disciples of Jesus. It is not enough to carry love for Jesus in one's heart or to profess it in words. On the other hand, amid all the talk we hear on every side today about practice, we must not forget that the practice of Jesus is much less eyecatching and sen-sational than many other forms of practice. For it is largely con-cerned with something that is simply human and obvious: giving help where help is needed. The only motive that can sustain this kind of practice, however, is a love that is concrete, related to the real world and adapted to it.

In the determination of Christian identity the question of the Holy Spirit must play a very prominant role. The important thing here is to understand the nature and action of the Spirit according to the Johannine text. The "Supporter, the Spirit of truth," appears in 14:16-17 as the successor or representative of Jesus in relation to the community. He is not a nondescript aura; his meaning and function must be understood by relation to Jesus. The person and message of Jesus, then, play the decisive part in determining, as far as content goes, the Spirit with whom we are dealing.

Also to be taken into account is the statement that the Spirit-Supporter will remain *forever* with the community. He is promised to the community for the entire future; there is a continuity of the Christian faith and Christian community that is effected, in the last analysis, by the Spirit. Important, too, is the fact that no particular individuals are given special prominence as possessors of the Spirit. The entire community receives the Spirit; he is given to the Church as a whole so that all may share in him. The various offices and charisms are therefore to be understood (as they are in 1 Cor. 12, for example) as the various gifts and services of this one Spirit. The presence of the Spirit also distinguishes the community from the world. It is the Spirit himself, then, that assures the Christian identity of the community as seen from within. For the Spirit is power that works in the word of Jesus and therefore in the preaching of the community in order to bring all to faith, hope, and love.

Second Statement about the "Supporter"
(14:25–26)

Exegesis

The first paraclete-saying (14:16-17) asserted that the Father would "give" the Spirit-supporter at Jesus' request. By his presence in the community the spirit of truth makes the community a reality over against the unbelieving world. He forms the community to be, as it were, the place for the abiding presence of Jesus' revelation in the world.

The second paraclete-saying develops this same thought. It contrasts two periods in the history of salvation, the time of Jesus and the post-resurrectional time of the Church. At the same time, however, the two periods are also linked and related by the activity of the Spirit. The sentence, "I have told you this while I was still with you" (v. 25), refers to the activity of the earthly Jesus. This John understands to be par excellence the "time of revelation," the presence of the light amid the darkness (cf. 12:35-36, 44-50), and to which the text looks back as to a completed whole. It is evident here, once again, how much John's thinking is dominated by his own location in the history of the Church and of theology. The time of Jesus is finished, and a new period in the history of salvation has begun. This new period is characterized by the presence of the Spirit-supporter who is here explicitly called the "Holy Spirit." God the Father will send this Spirit, and will do it "in my name."

The concept "send" has a wealth of meaning in John; it expresses, first and foremost, the divine commission and authentication of Jesus as Son and revealer of God.[55] Since the supporter is sent by God just as Jesus is, we have another parallelism: the Spirit takes Jesus' place. Just as Jesus, as revealer, is the representative of God the Father, so the Spirit is the representative of Jesus. To say that the Spirit is sent in the name of Jesus is to say that by reason of his function as heavenly intercessor Jesus plays an active part in the sending. Father and Son collaborate, each in his own manner, in the sending of the Spirit. Two functions of the Spirit are next given special mention. "Teaching" and "reminding," are both related to Jesus' words, "everything that I have told you." The Spirit-supporter will not add any materially new revelations to the revelation of Jesus, but will make the revelation of Jesus present and will disclose its meaning.

The Spirit is active in the community as a teacher (cf. also 6:45). This is frequently understood to mean that in the community the Holy Spirit himself teaches all believers interiorly in their hearts. This idea probably goes back to the well-known passage in Jeremiah 31:31-34, which speaks of the new covenant and says, "I place my law in their interior and write it in their hearts. I will be their God, and they shall be my people. Then they shall no longer need to instruct one another: 'Know the Lord!' for all of them, great and small, shall know me. It is the Lord who speaks. Yes, I pardon their guilt, and their sin I remember no more." When the Spirit is called teacher of the community, the intention is to emphasize the authority of Jesus as the abiding teacher of the community (cf. the similar idea in Matt. 23:2-12). The teaching authority of the Spirit is simply the enduring teaching authority of Jesus himself.

If we ask how this teaching of the Spirit is accomplished, we must surely not think solely of the Spirit giving Christians interior enlightenment, but must also take into account those learning and teaching procedures that were customary in the Christian community from the outset. Teaching played a very important role in the earliest communities. The most significant model was the teaching activity connected with the Jewish synagogue, together with the teaching activity, especially philosophical, in the ancient world generally. The early Christian communities probably looked very much like associations for teaching and learning, with instruction of adults being primary. As a matter of fact, the author of the gospel of John was in all likelihood one of the teachers, persons often possessed of prophetic gifts.

A special characteristic of this particular school is that for the Christian communities the teaching of Jesus or of the Gospel (for Paul) was the unquestioned norm. In the communities Christ is at the center as the teacher whose authority surpasses that of all other teachers. In comparison with him all Christians are disciples, learners. In this respect there was certainly a universal equality in the early days. In John this primitive state of affairs is still clearly visible: in his eyes an appeal to the paraclete as teacher is identical with the commitment of the community to the exclusive teaching authority of Jesus. It is not yet possible to appeal to the Spirit alongside Jesus or in addition to Jesus.[56]

The second function attributed to the Spirit-helper is reminding. The verb is an active one: to call something to someone's remembrance, to call to mind and thus make present. The object of the reminding is given in specific terms: "Everything that I have told you." The community is to be reminded of the words of Jesus. The concept of reminding plays an important role in John.[57] The reminding, as done by the paraclete, is not simply a calling the past to mind but a making the past present, together with a specific interpretation of it. In other words, reminding is not simply a literal repetition of what Jesus once said, but a living process in which the history of Jesus is applied to the present and explored anew. As understood in the gospel of John, the theology taught by the Spirit helps by its very nature to a "remembering" of Jesus in the sense of a constructive appropriation and extension of the revelation of Jesus. The reminding is thus a creative reminding. The best example of this is the gospel of John itself, for this gospel apprehends the message of Jesus with the help of new concepts and presents its circle of hearers and readers with an independent interpretation of Jesus. This interpretation is linked to the tradition of the primitive Church about Jesus, but goes far beyond it and creates its own portrait of Jesus.

It is not easy to grasp the unique blend of *commitment* and *freedom* that marks the relationship of the postapostolic Church to its origin, Jesus of Nazareth. If we return once again to the question of Christian identity and reflect on it in this new context, we may say that the identity consists in a harmonious balance of these two factors. Throughout history, it must be added, the balance is constantly threatened by an excessive emphasis on the one or the other factor, and must therefore be sought and found ever anew.

If the *commitment* is unilaterally emphasized and the element of creative freedom in reinterpreting the Christian reality is neglected or even regarded as heretical, the result is sterile or even reactionary traditionalism that not only loses all contact with its own age but crushes the vital impulses of faith itself. Without the freedom to rethink the tradition regarding Jesus and indeed the whole of Christian tradition, faith does not attain its full vitality. It cannot become the individual's own conviction for which he or she can render a personal account. On the other hand, if *freedom* is unilaterally emphasized, then there is great danger of losing touch with tradition and thus with history, of not doing justice to what is central in Christian faith, and of seeing enthusiastic freedom degenerate into an uncritical acceptance of the latest novelty or bog down in the vacuum of its own ideas. Admittedly, in the course of history the danger of reactionary traditionalism has been by far the greater of the two, and the need is usually to encourage believers to exercise freedom in their personal Christian thinking.

It is probable, however, that we must radically rethink both of these concepts, commitment and freedom, in their relation one to the other. When viewed in greater depth, they form a unity, as two sides of one and the same thing. For commitment to Jesus is not only the acceptance of a pregiven doctrine, it is always the acceptance of Jesus' practice as well, and this practice sets everyone who enters into it on the road to greater freedom and independence. The teaching of Jesus contains a liberating power no catechetical formulas can. If we accept the contemporary definition of learning as "altering, through external influences, the dispositions (capacities, attitudes) according to which one acts,"[58] then the message of Jesus looks to this kind of learning. From Jesus people can and must learn genuine freedom.

Since the learning process here is of a very comprehensive kind, it can hardly be directed by means of specific rules and regulations. There are too many imponderable, elusive, open factors that must depend on the Spirit and his action, and these play an important part in getting the process started. In this context Christian doctrine regains its *maieutic function* (maieutic means "relating to midwifery"; according to Socrates, teaching is essentially the art of bringing knowledge to birth). For the aim of the learning process is to bring the student into a personal relationship with the cause of Jesus. Since for John, as we have seen, the teaching authority of Jesus is unconditionally normative for the community, no Christian teacher can think of claiming the place of Jesus. Even the teaching office of the Church itself has no other role but to give selfless service to the authority of Jesus and to make that authority visible. The function of the Church's teaching authority is, in the last analysis, not authoritarian but *deictic*, that is, it points to Jesus.

This subordination emerges most clearly when we reflect that, as far as the Gospel and cause of Jesus are concerned, every teacher is and remains a student of Jesus. The reference to the Spirit as sole teacher of the community points to this relationship clearly. St. Augustine (354-430) is still aware of it, for in his theory of the Holy Spirit as the "interior teacher" he is always conscious that even his own episcopal teaching authority is insufficient by itself to lead to vital mature faith.[39] When taken seriously, the appeal to the Holy Spirit as the true teacher of the entire Church does away with the two-class model of a *teaching* and a *hearing* Church (this is the language used at one time; in practice people often think in these terms still). Within the community, teaching and learning are mutually related concepts that together constitute the learning process in its entirety. That is, teaching includes learning, and learning is intended to fit the learner to teach by liberating him or her and giving faith a Christian independence. In a Christian community all are both teachers and hearers.

The remembering of Jesus serves this same purpose. The point, then, is not the cultivation of a pious remembering of Jesus, although the human capacity of remembering should not be undervalued. In fact, the entire biblical history contained in the Old and New Testaments can be viewed as a remembering, while the instruction, "Do this in remembrance of me," is to be found in an important passage, the account of the institution of the Lord's Supper. But the remembering here consists primarily in making the past history of Jesus a present reality. Under the guidance of the Spirit the remembering of Jesus becomes a creative process and therefore always a critical one as well. The important thing, here again, is the intellectual stimuli and the changes which are set in motion by the remembrance of Jesus and which in the last analysis have as their purpose the salvation or renewal of humanity. In this sense, the remembrance of Jesus is disturbing and dangerous.

"Peace" as the Farewell Gift of Jesus: Conclusion of the First Farewell Discourse (14:27–31)

Exegesis

The section 14:27-31 forms the concluding part of the first farewell discourse which, as the final words, "Rise, let us go hence" (v. 31b), make clear, was originally an independent unit. At this point, in all probability, the account of the short journey to Mt. Olivet began.[60] Verses 27-31 probably belong together as a literary unit; an internal material-thematic structure is discernible in them. Verse 27 contains Jesus' wish for peace; in verses 28-29 there is another explicit reflection on the departure situation of Jesus; verses 30-31 prepare for the journey to Mt. Olivet and thus for the account of the passion.

According to verse 27 Jesus leaves his disciples "peace" as a farewell gift. The very situation in which the gift is given already tells us that peace is to be understood in a full and especially meaningful sense, as the gift and promise which contains everything that Jesus offers to faith.

In biblical language the concept of peace (Hebrew: *shalom*; Greek: *eirēnē*) has such a broad and comprehensive content that it cannot be reduced to any single unified formula.[61] The basic meaning of the Hebrew word *shalom* is " 'well-being,' with a strong emphasis on the material side" (von Rad). The term describes a positive state that not only excludes the presence of war and personal enemies—this is a precondition for *shalom*—but includes prosperity, joy, success in life, auspicious circumstances, and salvation in the religious sense of the word. People in Israel and the Near East still use *Shalom!* as a greeting.

In a blessing addressed to the king we read, "May the mountains yield peace [*shalom;* some translate, "salvation," "prosperity"] to the people, and the hills justice. May he [the king] defend the rights of the oppressed among the people, deliver the children of the poor, crush the oppressor. May he live as long as the sun and the moon shall give light, from generation to generation. May he drop like rain on the meadow, like rain showers that sprinkle the earth. In his days may justice flower and the fullness of peace [*shalom*] until the moon shines no more!" (Ps. 72:2-7). And in the well-known poem of Isaiah 11:1-11 on the Messiah, peace is a cosmic state and comprises outward security, prosperity, fruitfulness, and universal well-being; it is a great reconciliation of human society and nature. There is no doubt that the messianic age, the coming time of salvation, is to be a time of all-encompassing peace. This is precisely the meaning of the angelic message at the birth of the messianic child in Luke's gospel: "Glory to God in the highest, and peace on earth to men whom he favors" (Luke 2:14).

The coming of the Messiah inaugurates the true eschatological age of peace. Peace, therefore, is understood to be more than simply an interior reality, peace of heart, although this aspect continues to be important; thus Paul says, "May the peace of God which transcends all understanding fills your hearts and minds in Christ Jesus" (Phil. 4:7). The concept of peace is broad enough to include everything from the everyday greeting *Shalom!* "All good wishes!" to the peace and salvation of all people and the entire world. In the background is the idea that peace at every level is ultimately a gift from God.

In the New Testament, which here again continues and develops Old Testament thought, peace is connected with the Christian message of salvation, the Gospel. It is noteworthy, however, that Jesus himself uses the term peace only rarely. In fact, we even find him saying, "Think not that I have come to bring peace to the earth! I have come to bring not peace but a sword" (Matt. 10:34; Luke 12:51), although the words are possibly directed against superficial and false talk about peace (cf. Jer. 6:14: "And they heal the wounds of my people easily, saying, 'Peace! Peace!' But where is the peace?"). We must therefore avoid interpreting the concept of peace in a superficial and insipid way.

On the other hand, the disciples on their mission are to give the greeting of peace to those they meet (Matt. 10:13). The more the primitive Church became conscious that messianic salvation had entered the world with Jesus of Nazareth, the more it was convinced that because it believed, it had already been given eschatological peace (cf. Rom. 5:1-3). In the Letter to the Ephesians we find this statement, "For he himself [Jesus Christ] is our peace" (2:14), which already brings us quite close to the Johannine conception of peace.

From a purely formal standpoint the words Jesus speaks here in John are modeled on the customary everyday greeting of peace, but in content they go far beyond such a greeting. What Jesus means is peace as a gift of the last times, a call to salvation and life. "Peace I leave with you" is meant here in a definitive sense; that is, it refers to the eschatological blessing pure and simple, which Jesus, as it were, bequeaths to his community as a legacy. There is nothing more he can give his disciples; but then, no one who understands what is included in peace will want anything more.

When Jesus adds, "*My* peace I give you," the point once again is to emphasize that peace acquires its special character and its content from Jesus himself. Here again the gift is not to be separated from the giver, the person of Jesus. Consequently, peace is above all the gift of the risen Christ (cf. 20:19, 21, 26, where it is also made clear that the forgiveness of sins is part of peace). In 14:27 it is likewise the exalted Christ who is speaking. In the last analysis, what we have in peace is the presence of a new world that is given with the presence of Jesus himself in the community.

This peace of Jesus is contrasted with peace "as the world gives it." We are confronted once again with the distance separating Jesus and his disciples from the world. The world too has its peace, it too has its way of making peace and preserving it, by force of arms if need be. In its own domain the world too faces the endless task of being concerned about peace and standing up for it. But this peace is radically different from the peace of Jesus; it belongs to another realm. And yet through Jesus the peace that is not *of* this world is nonetheless present *in* this world.

The locus of this peace of Jesus is first and foremost the Christian community insofar as it is the place of Christ's presence: that is, insofar as it lets its life be shaped by the word of Jesus. In the process the community experiences the fact that it is a contradiction to the world, which confronts it with hostility. To that extent the peace of the community is never unchallenged. The exhortation not to be troubled or afraid is always necessary because the peace which Jesus promises does not lead to any experience of great success in dealing with the world. Neither faith nor the community of believers lives in a strife-free zone; rather, both are exposed to conflict with the world, and this not despite the fact that they believe but precisely because of it. It is genuinely possible, nonetheless, for Jesus'promise of peace to continue and prove efficacious even amid this constant exposure to conflict, amid all temptations and threats.

The reference to the departure situation (vv. 27-28) makes us aware once again that the situation portrayed in the farewell discourses is a literary fiction. But, from a theological viewpoint, it expresses a basic fact of Christian life—Jesus goes away, but comes back. To the extent that the disciples really love Jesus and are linked to him through faith, they should rejoice over his departure, because he is going to the Father; and there is a further reason: "because the Father is greater than I."

This theme runs through the farewell discourses and must be made clear to both the disciples and to the readers and hearers of the text. The departure of Jesus was not simply a passing from the stage of world history, but his going back to God. Moreover his return to the disciples has already begun at Easter and continues in his ceaseless coming to his community. That can be put in more general terms. For the post-Easter community Jesus has two locations: he is present in the community through the Spirit-Paraclete and through his own word, but he is at the same time with the Father, with God. Neither location excludes the other; in fact both belong together, and it must even be said that the passing of Jesus to the Father is the condition for his abiding presence in the community.

The reason given, "because the Father is greater than I," fits the whole tendency of Johannine teaching on Christ. On the one hand, this teaching emphasizes the close solidarity of Jesus with God; on the other, it holds fast to an order in rank or a subordination of Jesus as Son to God the Father.[62]

In this passage the subordination of Jesus to God is emphasized; it is the purpose of Jesus' revelation to glorify God and make him known as Father. Joy that Jesus is going to the Father is eschatological joy, since the way to God has now been opened once and for all (14:1-6), so "mankind now has its abode with God" (J. S. Bach). Verse 28 thus specifies once again, in conclusion, the "place" of the community. This place is determined by its relation to Jesus, who as the risen Christ is with the Father, but who at the same time is constantly coming anew to the community and working in it through the Spirit-Paraclete. The statement, "and I have told you this now, before it happens, so that when it happens you may believe" (v. 29), is addressed to the present-day community and its situation. The community is exhorted to faith; it must not see anything anomalous about its present situation. If it has been reflecting on its relation to Jesus, it has long since prepared itself for this situation.

Verses 30-31 end the first farewell discourse and by their content lead into the story of the passion. The time for talk is now gone for good. Like the other New Testament writers, John sees in the passion of Jesus not simply the obvious historical event but, in the background, a conflict of immense significance for the history of salvation, between Jesus, the Son and revealer of God, and Satan, the "ruler of this world." The description of Satan as "ruler of this world" is characteristically Johannine (12:31; 14:30; 16:11).[63] In the passion of Jesus Satan was stripped of his power as ruler of this world, and the world acquired a new ruler in the person of Jesus Christ. John conceives of the redemptive event as a cosmic change of rulers. As the turning point of the ages, this change has placed the world in a new situation that derives its character from the divine salvific will. In the cross and resurrection of Christ God's love-inspired will has finally had its way.

It is against this conceptual background that the text must be interpreted. According to verse 30 the hour of the crucifixion represents Satan's definitive assault on Jesus. But Satan finds in Jesus nothing which he can legitimately claim as belonging to the sphere he controls, that is, death, sin, lying, hatred, and so forth. There are no points of contact between Jesus and Satan, to say nothing of any essential relatedness. Consequently, every claim of Satan comes to naught where Jesus is concerned. In this struggle, it is clear in advance that Jesus will be the victor. Verse 31a tells us why the power of evil is helpless against Jesus: "The world must recognize that I love the Father and do as the Father has commanded me." It is the total commitment of Jesus to God his Father, his perfect love, that radically and in principle separates him from evil. "My food is to do the will of him who sent me and to complete his work" (4:34). Thus the circle is completed. By traveling the way to the cross in obedience to the divine will Jesus now becomes in a definitive way the revealer of divine love. That is how John interprets the death of Jesus. That is also precisely what the world must come to understand about Jesus.

Accordingly, with the exhortation, "Rise, let us go hence!" this farewell discourse ends.

Meditation

"Peace" is a catchword that is popular all over the world today. It captures, first of all, the desire to limit and, as far as possible, avoid wars and their devastating consequences. A glance at the political history of our day will show us, of course, how difficult a task this is and how little progress has been made in this area despite the bitter experience of protracted world wars. Yet the significance of the idea of peace and even of a universal peace for the world[64] is not to be measured by palpable successes. The fact that this idea of a universal peace exists and that people feel it to be a political and moral summons which should direct their political activity is in itself already something quite important, and at the same time shows the goal on which the hopes of millions are focused.

But is not this world peace, which is today regarded as the only sensible and reasonable goal of world politics, the opposite of the eschatological peace of which Jesus speaks? Is it not precisely a "peace as the world gives it," a peace on which apparently no reliance can be placed? What is there in common between these two conceptions of peace: eschatological, divine, and heavenly peace, and a universal political peace?

There is a Christian tradition which in fact makes a sharp distinction between the two; in this tradition are to be found great names such as Augustine and Martin Luther. According to it, the peace Jesus promised is primarily a spiritual, interior reality that is promised to humanity but reaches its full unfolding only in the next world or at the end of time. Thus in his commentary on this passage Augustine writes:

> He leaves us peace as he is about to depart; he will give us his peace when he comes again at the end. He leaves us peace in this world; he will give us his peace in the world to come. He leaves us his peace, and if we remain in him, we will overcome the enemy; he will give us his peace when we shall reign without any enemy . . . . Therefore we have a certain peace, because we find delight in the law according to the interior man, but it is not peace in its fullness, because we have another law in our members that resists the law of our mind.[65]

Those who appeal to this tradition are mostly of the persuasion that this religious peace of the heart (which is usually understood in an individualistic way) should not be connected at all with political conceptions of peace and the efforts to implement them. Religion has to do with the salvation of the soul, and any political or social conclusions drawn from it they regard as an adulteration.

On the other hand, this view is precisely why the objection is raised against Christianity that it has done so little in its two thousand year history to limit or do away with wars and other social conflicts. Western Christians have been unable to prevent the great conflicts; in fact, they have even undertaken expeditions of colonial conquest, and instead of the peace of the gospel have brought slavery and oppression. This justified criticism has caused Christians during the last thirty years to reflect more carefully on the political significance of the biblical conception of peace. In his encyclical *Pacem in terris* Pope John XXIII presented a plan of work for political peace that caught the attention even of the non-Catholic world and was received with great enthusiasm in some quarters. The Second Vatican

Council devoted a whole chapter of its Pastoral Constitution on the Church in the Modern World[66] to the problem of peace: "As it points out the authentic and most noble meaning of peace, this Council fervently desires to summon Christians to cooperate with all men in making secure among themselves a peace based on justice and love, and in setting up agencies of peace."

The argument for this understanding of peace is as follows. It is true enough that eschatological peace is not identical with political peace; the two are not coextensive. We must be very much aware of the distinction between them. We must also acknowledge that the messianic realm of peace, the full reign of God, cannot be had in this world (this is the so-called "eschatological proviso"). Eschatological peace in its full extent can only be understood as a divine reality. On the other hand, faith in the reconciliation achieved in Christ can and must be so efficacious that Christians who believe in it will do their best to establish peace in this world. The peace of Christ that is to reign in hearts urges us to strive for the establishment of peace at every level of human coexistence and in the socio-political realm, and to dedicate ourselves to this task. Relevant here is the realization that wars are made by people and are not inevitable natural catastrophes. We can search out their causes, and it is even possible, at least in principle, to avoid wars.

Christians convinced of the peace of God should be especially open to such a quest. Here, surely, we have one of the most important tasks facing political thought and action that are based on a sense of Christian responsibility. The concrete difficulties connected with it should not, of course, be underestimated or thought nugatory. But since humanity in our day must learn peace in a thoroughly new way if it is not to destroy itself, Christian dedication to peace in the world is inherently meaningful. It makes just as much sense, of course, to reckon on the task being a long-term one indeed. But precisely because of the difficulties involved, faith in the eschatological peace already given in Jesus Christ takes on a new significance. That is to say, the believer can lend powerful support to a long-term effort, and can help all face up to disillusionments and inspire them with courage to go on when failures make it seem senseless to continue. The believer will not be confounded and discouraged by failure but can help others to a critical and yet confident realism. In so doing, justice in our day to Jesus' legacy of eschatological peace can be done. For in our day Christianity or, more accurately, Christians, cannot permit themselves the luxury of cultivating a secret little garden of the soul, leaving humankind outside to struggle with its most difficult problems.

In this way the socio-political involvement of Christians will become a witness to the presence of Jesus in the community. Commitment to peace and a fitting life for humanity, to social and political justice and freedom, as well as to the fight against hunger, distress, and oppression of every kind, acquires in these circumstances a special value as witness. On the contrary, a Christian community that allies itself with the ruling powers in order to assure its own domination has no power to bear witness, no matter how much it talks of God and Christ. The way that Jesus bids his community of disciples travel is the way of free, responsible discipleship.

THE SECOND FAREWELL DISCOURSE
(15:1–16:33)

Although the second farewell discourse deals with themes similar to those of the first, it is possible to see a shift of emphasis. The first discourse had focused chiefly on the question of the community's new relationship to Jesus; in so doing, it reflected the theologically important distinction between the pre-Easter and the post-Easter community. In the second farewell discourse, on the other hand, the community as such comes to the fore in an essentially greater degree, and *ecclesiological themes* become explicit. We learn, above all, what is the Christian community in John's eyes, what are the determinants of its existence, what its situation is in the world, and what are the foundations of its hope.

The True Vine (15:1–10)

Exegesis

The second farewell address begins immediately with an "I am" discourse which makes use of a symbol: "I am the true vine."[67] This discourse deals with the relationship of the disciples to Jesus in terms of the foundation and life of their community.

Basic to an understanding of the text is the question of what the image of the vine means. From what tradition did John derive it, and what did he wish to express with its help?[68] R. Borig especially has studied the numerous Old Testament passages in which the vine is a symbol of the Israelite people.[69] He has shown above all that the link between the vineyard/vine and the production of fruit (a link typical as well of our present parabolic discourse) is firmly rooted in the Old Testament tradition. From this and other observations[70] he has drawn the conclusion that "the use of the image in John 15:1ff. can clearly be traced back to the Old Testament, except insofar as it has been inflected by John's own special use of it."[71]

This assertion need not preclude an openness on John's part to other traditions as well. In fact, we should probably regard the Parable of the Wicked Vine-Dressers (Mark 12:1-12) as a mediating link between the Old Testamental and Jewish vineyard/vine image and the Johannine parabolic image of the true vine. It is true, of course, that in the synoptic parable Jesus is not expressly identified with the vineyard. It is clear enough, however, that in the Markan version the parable has a christological point: The son and heir to the vineyard is slain by the vine-dressers, but he is honored by God. The saying, "I am the true vine," must therefore be regarded as being first of all a christological revelatory statement.

The adjective "true" is not intended primarily as part of a contrast in which the true vine would be distinguished from others that make a similar but unjustified claim. It is meant rather as a characterization of Jesus who, as revealer of God, is himself the truth.[72] Being the Son of God, Jesus describes himself as "the vine in the sense in which only the Son can be a vine."[73] This radical superiority then includes also, of course, the aspect of contrast. The quality expressed in the image of the vine is denied to all others that make a similar claim. In other words, "the origin of the Johannine imagery allows us to infer that in the Johannine image of the vine Jesus is taking the place hitherto belonging to the people of Israel."[74] This interpretation, according to which the Jewish image of the vine as a symbol of Israel is now transferred to Jesus and that Jesus therefore replaces the old Israel, also fits best with Johannine theology. For, according to John, the coming of Jesus has brought an end to the Israelite-Jewish temple worship and to the worshipping community that was associated with the temple (cf. 2:13-22; 4:21-26; 8:31-59).

In this view of the history of salvation the Christian community does not automatically become the new Israel and replace the old Israel. Rather it is directly *Jesus himself*, as Son of God and revealer, who takes Israel's place. He is the center of the new worshiping community. Thus the image of the vine represents a *christological concentration* which is a presupposition of the *ecclesiological ex-*

pansion of which the text will also speak. At the same time, John succeeds in keeping the history of salvation grounded in *God*: the Father, or God, is the vine-grower in this parabolic discourse, just as in the Old Testament image of the vineyard he is usually the owner and master.

The text is concerned with the new (eschatological) community of salvation, the Church, which Jesus, the true vine, establishes.[75] We should, of course, avoid giving a strained interpretation of the parabolic discourse or misunderstanding it by treating it as though it were a synoptic parable. Parabolic discourse and realistic train of thought are frequently very closely intertwined in John, and we must therefore take the text at its face value.

The introduction of "the branches" (v. 2) follows rather suddenly. The fact that the text can speak of them without any transition shows that in the idea of the true vine that of the branches is present from the very beginning.[76] It is in keeping with Old Testamental and Jewish thinking that as soon as there is a question concerning the vine, branches "bearing fruit" should also be mentioned.[77] In fact, of course, the concern of the vine-grower is that his vineyard bear fruit as richly as possible. As far as John's image is concerned, the concept of bearing fruit is left completely open; even the context does not give any specific indication of what is meant. The reference is to the total yield of a life lived in communion with Jesus, and not simply or primarily to the fruits of mission (the idea of mission does not come up in the discourse on the vine). The Old Testament frequently speaks of Israel, Jahweh's vineyard, as not having produced the expected fruit (e.g., Isa. 5:2, 4). It is to this situation that bearing fruit is contrasted here. In other words, the point is the bearing of fruit as such, and how this is effected.

In the continuing image of the vinegrower, two activities are specifically mentioned: cutting away unfruitful branches, and trimming (cleansing or purifying) the good branches so that they may produce even more fruit. The image, which is only briefly interrupted by "every branch in me" (v. 2), points in passing to the divine judgment which faith must take into account. But the allusion to it is probably meant chiefly to underscore the fact that in the community of Jesus more than in any other what matters is to bear fruit. If the community and the individual disciple fail to bear fruit because

108

they no longer live, through faith and love, by the power that is given in communion with Jesus, then they must expect to be cut away. Otherwise they will only be trimmed and cleansed.

Verse 3 says that the disciples are already clean, and this through the word of Jesus. "The purity is to be understood in terms of the vine imagery; it is the preparation for bearing fruit. There is no reference here to moral or cultic purity."[78] The encounter with the word of Jesus that forces a person to the decision of faith has led to faith and thus contributed to the cleansing which makes it possible to bear fruit. Here again, a gift, the word of Jesus, stands at the very beginning; bearing fruit, consequently, is not to be understood as a human achievement.

Nevertheless, the gift does give rise to a challenge: "Remain in me, and I in you" (v. 4). The word "remain" (Greek: *menein*), which keeps occurring throughout the rest of the passage, signifies in John the definitive and permanent character of the relationship with Jesus that faith grounds, a relationship of mutual reliability and fidelity between Jesus and his disciples. The formula, "remain in me . . . remain in you," which specifies the relationship as one of personal reciprocity, is especially characteristic of John. The relationship accounts for the believer's remaining in Jesus, while this remaining in Jesus is the basis, in turn, for bearing fruit. Verse 4 shows how radical a meaning must be given to this reciprocal remaining: Unless the branch is connected to the vine it cannot possibly bear fruit; it can do nothing, absolutely nothing, by itself, by its own strength and power. The disciples are just as incapable of bearing fruit if they do not remain united to Jesus.

The climax of the entire discourse now follows: "I am the vine, you are the branches" (v. 5a). It has been pointed out that the Johannine Jesus does not speak of himself as the vinestock or trunk, as distinct from the shoots, but as the vine, which already includes all the branches.[79] We would misinterpret the image, were we to identify the vine with Jesus alone. We are dealing rather with something that is already a totality. Jesus establishes it but it already includes the branches, so that even here the reference to the community is clear. In any event, Jesus has, of course, an inalienable priority, and one from which there is no derogating: "For apart from me you can do nothing" (v. 5c). Only union with Jesus carries the promise of abundant fruit; separation from him means utter unfruitfulness.

The contrast between bearing fruit and being unfruitful points to definitive salvation or damnation, just as remaining in Jesus refers to a definitive state. This is clear from the example given in verse 6 of the extreme negative possibility: Anyone who does not remain in Jesus but attempts to live and act apart from him will be cast out (cf. Matt. 5:13; 21:39), just as the branches that have been cut off and have withered are piled up and burned. John is here unmistakably taking the traditional language of judgment and integrating it into his vision. Separation from Jesus, that is, unbelief, already carries judgment with it.

If we look back over the parabolic discourse up to this point (vv. 1-6), the following basic lines of thought emerge. The discourse is answering the question of the ground of the community. Jesus himself is the true vine who has replaced the old Israel and who (we may add) by his obedience to the Father forms the new basis for all the fruitbearing of believers. If one allows the word to be decisive and if one thus believes, one is already cleansed and participates in the fruitfulness of the vine. Bearing fruit and remaining in Jesus are coextensive ideas. There is no bearing fruit without remaining in him, and there is no perduring communion with Jesus that can be permanently fruitless. Only separation from Jesus causes unfruitfulness. In order to express the relation of the community to Jesus, John uses the formula "You in me—I in you,"[80] which pulls together all the various aspects we have mentioned.

With its reference to prayer verse 7 introduces a new thought. The remaining is now specified as a remaining of Jesus' word in believers. Faith is connected with the word of Jesus and includes obedience to the word, or the *following of Jesus*. To this assent to the word of Jesus a promise is now attached: that prayer will be heard without reservation. In this context of faith, assent to the word of Jesus, and fruitfulness, prayer is not a practice of magic but rather a training in the spirit and practice of Jesus; prayer thus understood is certain of being answered. Prayer too is thus connected with fruitfulness and is to be regarded as the form of meditation that is ordered to this fruitfulness.

The train of thought is rounded off in verse 8 by the reference to the glorification of the Father. As the Father is glorified by the Son and by the latter's destiny (cf. 13:31-32), so too he is glorified by the fruitfulness of the disciples. In the last analysis, bearing fruit, and therefore the entire Christian life in union with Jesus, is for the greater glory of God and consequently for the true life of all.

Verses 9-10 may be regarded as a further variation within the vine discourse, as a "more profound interpretation of the parabolic discourse,"[81] or even as an introduction to the following section (vv. 9-17).[82] In any case, the verses form a bridge between 15:1-8 and 15:11-17 by establishing a thematic link and thus showing the internal unity of 15:1-17. In contrast to the parabolic discourse with its thoroughly allusive and open-ended mode of expression, a more objective kind of language now comes to the fore. It concretizes what has been said in the parabolic discourse and interprets it in terms of practical love. Jesus has loved the disciples just as radically as the Father has loved the Son (v. 9). The past tense (aorist) indicates not that this love is a thing of the past but that it is a permanently operative reality. According to 17:24 the Father loved Jesus "before the creation of the world" and therefore from eternity; there can be no time in which the Father did not love the Son. It is this eternal, abiding, and imperishable love that Jesus promises to his disciples as well. It is a part and expression of eschatological salvation. To this extent love is also the objective reality with which the entire parabolic discourse on the true vine is concerned.

For this reason the summons here to "remain in me" can be changed to read, "Remain in my love." Bearing fruit, consequently, is nothing but the activity and rule of love. Here the idea of immanence ("you in me—I in you")[83] is given a practical, dispassionate interpretation and protected against the misunderstandings to which a mystical enthusiasm can lead. For, as verse 10 says, to remain in the love of Jesus means simply to "keep his commandments," that is, to do the works of love. Jesus himself is the exemplar: "As I have kept my Father's commandments and remain in his love." But in what way has Jesus kept the Father's commandments? Simply by following the way to the cross, and therefore as indicated by the meaning of the washing of feet. Once again, the exemplary practice of Jesus becomes the model for the practice of the disciples. The latter remain in his love when they take their bearings from Jesus and set their course by his example.

Meditation

Of all the concepts in theology probably none has fallen into such discredit today and is associated with so many difficulties, misunderstandings, or emotional antipathies, as the concept of the Church. This is all the more surprising since an enormous amount of theological work has been devoted to the theme of "Church" in this very century. The best minds have shared in the work, and the Dogmatic Constitution on the Church of the Second Vatican Council represents to some extent the fruit of it. The discontent is directed chiefly at the Church as institution, the official Church. Our concern here is not with the question of the many causes that have led to this change of mood. We want only to use the fact as the occasion for inquiring into the Johannine understanding of the Church or, better, the community. It may be that a look at the Johannine conception of it will help us see contemporary defects and shortcomings more clearly and to judge them more accurately.

To do this, we must take the following facts into account. At the time when the gospel of John was written there was no fully organized, inclusive Church. A centralized ecclesiastical government with the pope and the Roman Curia at its head was still far in the future. None of the New Testament writers could even have imagined such a development (the legitimacy and necessity of which does not concern us here). "Church" meant first of all each local community, each local group of Christians with its regular assemblies, as depicted most clearly in the First Letter to the Corinthians (cf. 1 Cor. 14).

In his famous letter to Emperor Trajan Gaius, Plinius "the Younger," who was Roman governor in Pontus-Bithynia in about A. D. 110/112 and found Christianity rather widespread there,[84] gives us an interesting glimpse of life in a Christian community as seen by an outsider. He writes:

They [former Christians delated to the governor] affirmed

the whole of their guilt, or their error, was, that they were in the habit of meeting on a certain fixed day before it was light, when they sang in alternate verses a hymn to Christ, as to a god, and bound themselves by a solemn oath, not to any wicked deeds, but never to commit any fraud, theft or adultery, never to falsify their word, nor to deny a trust when they should be called upon to deliver it up; after which it was their custom to separate, and then reassemble to partake of food—but food of an ordinary and innocent kind. Even this practice, however, they had abandoned after the publication of my edict, by which, according to your orders, I had forbidden political associations.[85]

In sociological terms, this description reflects the behavior of a fringe group within official society, a group that defines itself by opposition to its social world but also, by way of compensation, develops a strong internal cohesiveness. The composition and internal structure of these early Christian communities differed greatly from group to group. There was, as the Johannine writings (gospel, letters) clearly attest, no unified conception of offices. To be sure, the local communities seem very soon to have established lively contacts and engaged in exchanges with one another. There were many interconnections that strengthened the sense of solidarity. Otherwise, however, the communities were independent, so that it is impossible, from a historical viewpoint, to say that a universal and uniform ecclesiastical organization with a central organization, such as in fact gradually developed in Western Roman Catholicism, was the only form of Church government that could possibly have emerged. As far as the New Testament evidence goes, other forms were conceivable.

A further point: In the present state of biblical research it is no longer possible to defend the traditional view that the historical Jesus instituted the Church at a certain point in time and provided it with a kind of deed of foundation in which all the essential constitutional elements of an ecclesial structure were already set down.[86] The formation of a community occurs only after Good Friday and Easter. The decisive thing about this process, of course, is that it took place under the egis of an *appeal to Jesus and his preaching* or *in the name of Jesus*. Both the letters of Paul and the gospels

113

bear witness in their various ways to the highly significant fact that Jesus of Nazareth, who had been crucified and had risen, was regarded by all the Christian communities as the *normative authority;* this fact finds expression chiefly in the titles of Messiah/Christ, Son of man, Son of God, Lord, and so on. The community is conscious of being linked by the Spirit to Jesus Christ, and it is thoroughly convinced that in the last analysis it is the risen and exalted Lord himself who rules the community, so that, in comparison, all human leaders occupy a very secondary position.

If we combine both aspects—the social situation of the community as a fringe group in an indifferent or hostile social milieu, and the faith-inspired conviction, set down in the gospel, regarding the presence and permanently binding authority of Jesus Christ in the community—we will better understand the background of the revelatory discourse on the true vine. This discourse is addressed originally to a small group, a limited local community, and cannot automatically be applied to a Church organized on all-inclusive lines. Moreover, the discourse maintains with the utmost firmness that the community or Church can be understood only in relation to Jesus Christ himself and that it is never to be thought of apart from this basic theological and salvation-historical principle. In the language of the image, this is to say that between the "vine" and the "branches" there is the very closest and most vital connection. The immanence formula, "you in me—I in you," brings out very clearly the intimate and personal character of this communion. In this vision of things, ecclesiastical authorities or community leaders exercise no absolute control. Instead, the community is seen as a place in which the primary focus is on the authority of Jesus and his cause.

In such a context the statements about "bearing fruit" likewise acquire a further meaning. The community and its members are promised fruitfulness, which includes success, only to the extent that they have the courage to make the cause of Jesus their own and to stand up for it in the face of the world. Just as Jesus is the salvation-historical ground and permanently binding authority for his community, so also labor for the Gospel and its proclamation in the world and society is the permanent task of the Church. Part of the process of carrying out this task is the critical differentiation and, if need be, elimination of the power, prosperity, and official

114

influence which the Church has accumulated over the centuries for all sorts of historico-cultural reasons, but which are not an inherent part of the Gospel.

Self-critical reflection on the Gospel, in order to hear its promises and demands with new ears in our own day and consequently to attain to genuine fruitfulness, is permanently necessary if the cause of Jesus is to be effective. In the measure that the Church desists from this most important task and focuses its concern on securing its traditions and position of power, it becomes a branch that does not bear fruit and must therefore be cut off and burned. Abiding communion with Jesus, then, is in fact the presupposition of all authentic Christianity and all Christian activity. As the text has made clear, this communion may not be understood as a guarantee of salvation, since it depends on the word of Jesus and the works of love. Both of these—the word of Jesus and love—are the most important criteria that must govern the ecclesiastical realm and ecclesial activity, and all Christians must contribute to making this ideal a reality.

The Friends of Jesus (15:11–17)

Exegesis

This loosely linked series of statements gives a further interpretation of the theme, which has been introduced in the discourse on the true vine, of the communion of the disciples with Jesus. Verses 11-17 describe the community as the circle of Jesus' friends.

First, verse 11 speaks of the "joy" which Jesus wants to communicate to his disciples through his word. Like peace in 14:27-28, joy is to be understood as an eschatological gift[87] in which believers are to share. And just as in the earlier text the peace was emphatically described as "my peace," so here we read, "that *my* joy may be in you and your joy may be full." Thus joy is to be regarded as a gift of Jesus that is proper to the last times. Consequently, in 20:20, joy is inspired by the encounter with the risen Lord, the Jesus who is abidingly present. This joy, then, bears the mark of Easter. Eschatological existence means a new attitude and outlook, while joy in its perfect form—endless and unlimited—characterizes the emotional state and enthusiasm of the person who through the gospel now grasps the full meaning of life and salvation.

According to Acts 2:46 joy and jubilation were also an essential trait of the community assemblies; to this fact the early Christian hymns and songs bear eloquent witness. Thus, in a song from the *Odes of Solomon*, which is the oldest known collection of early Christian songs and is close to the gospel of John in time and content, we read the following:

> My joy is the Lord, and it is to him that I run.
> This way of mine is beautiful,
> for it helps me to reach the Lord.
> In his generosity he makes himself known to me without jealousy,
> for in his friendliness he makes himself small.
> He became as I am, so that I might lay hold of him.
> Nor did I shrink back when I gazed on him,
> for he is my mercy.(7,2-5)

Verse 12 gives the commandment of love[88] in its Johannine form of "love one another." New here is that in verse 13 the *nature* of this love is defined as it were or, more accurately, clarified by an example: "Greater love than this no one has: to lay down his life for his friends." Here we find once again the typical Johannine formula: to lay down, or give, one's soul or life.[89] The essence of love is to commit oneself to the other, and the giving of one's life for one's friends is certainly the highest conceivable form of such love. There is no greater love because no one can do more.

John is thinking, first and foremost, of the example of Jesus himself. Jesus is the good shepherd who gives his life for his sheep (10:11, 15) and does so, as is explicitly stated there, with complete freedom: "For this reason the Father loves me, because I give my life and take it back again. No one can snatch it from me, but I give it of my own accord. I have power to give it and power to take it back again. This is the commandment I have received from my Father" (10:17-18). As applied to Jesus, the expression "to give his life *for* the sheep" or "*for* his friends" contains John's interpretation of the death of Jesus as an expiatory death for the sake of others, as their representative. According to John this death is the highest

116

form of love-inspired commitment to the salvation of the world: "Having loved his disciples who were in the world, he loved them to the end" (13:1). Indeed it was not simply a case of Jesus giving himself for his friends because they deserved it and he had no other choice; rather, the death of Jesus has foundational significance for the community. It is *because* he dies for his disciples that they become his friends.

In 10:17-18 the emphasis is on the fact that Jesus as Son and revealer of God has full power over his own life; it cannot be taken from him against his will. Thus the absolute freedom and voluntariness of Jesus' death are once again made plain; in every respect Jesus is and remains master of himself and his destiny. Since, then, the self-giving of Jesus even to the point of dying is the result not of an external or internal failure, but of a definitive freedom, the real superiority and genuineness of Jesus' love for his friends becomes clear. In surrendering his life Jesus realizes in a radical way a *being for others*. Consequently, in Jesus freedom and service, freedom and radical commitment to friends, are inseparable; it is precisely this union that constitutes the essence of *agapē* ("love"). It is clear, once again, how fundamental a role the example of the washing of the feet, at the beginning of the farewell discourses, is meant to play. It also follows that if the disciples are Jesus' friends, their love will consist in the same kind of dedication (v.14). Only if the disciples fulfill the commandment of Jesus will they be his friends.

Now the disciples learn that they are in fact the friends of Jesus and are thus drawn into full communion with him (v.15). "Servant/slave" (Greek: *doulos*) is a term used in Israel not only, as elsewhere in the ancient world, to describe those belonging to the slave-class, but also as an expression of one's subordination to God. To be a "servant of God" is, in Old Testament thinking, perhaps the most exalted thing that can be said about a human being. Of Moses we read in Exodus 33:11: "But the Lord spoke with Moses face to face, as a man speaks with his friend," but that is an extraordinary exception (cf. Deut. 34:10 where the same statement is made but the term "friend" is omitted; the only other person of whom it is predicated is Abraham in Isa. 41:8). The distance between God and his creatures makes the concept of "friendship" inapplicable.

From this point of view, then, there is a *revolution in values* when, according to John, Jesus calls the disciples his friends ("calling" here means making them his friends). The faithful attain to this new condition of friends of Jesus by participating in his communion with God. Through Jesus the disciples—all without exception (there is no question here of a distinction between clerics and laity)—have become sharers in God's revelation. Jesus has made known to them "everything" that he has "heard from the Father." Moreover, as Son of God, he is himself the entire content of revelation, and the disciples have acknowledged this fact. The climax of the revelation is Jesus' surrender of his life for his disciples as the perfect proof of his love. Because the disciples have let this love of Jesus lay hold of them, they have been transformed from slaves to become friends of Jesus.

Verse 16 expresses the same idea with the help of the concept of *election*. It is not the disciples who have chosen Jesus as their leader and hero, but just the opposite: with a power and authority that are inherently his Jesus has chosen the disciples for himself (cf. the account of the calling of the disciples in 1:35-51). Like the synoptic writers John maintains the irreversibility of the relationship between Jesus and the disciples. In his relationship with them Jesus is not simply the most fully human person anyone can imagine, but also the Lord, the one through whom God carries out his liberating and elective action in regard to humans. With this election by Jesus goes a commission, a determinate task, the reference to which is a flashback to the discourse on the true vine with its talk of bearing fruit. This fruit is to remain: to make the meaning explicit we might add for eternal life, for the "remaining" is another name for the state the individual attains when the self is given to the works of love. It is also part of communion with God or the friendship of Jesus that prayer in the name of Jesus (cf. on 14:12-14) should be assured of an unreserved response. As friends of Jesus the disciples have been drawn into Jesus' sphere of life, so that as far as God is concerned they too have all things at their disposal. The new circle of friends that Jesus has inaugurated thus becomes a place of new freedom and ease in dealing with God.

It is in this context that the idea of election also acquires its real meaning. What is meant is not an arbitrary act on God's part whereby he determines, for example, that some be chosen while others are excluded or damned. Such a double predestination to salvation or damnation is unknown in the gospel of John. The term election brings out rather the unqualified priority of Jesus' freedom and love in relation to believers. The acknowledgment of this priority is, of course, a necessary presupposition. Finally, the circle of ideas is completed by a reference to the commandment of love (v.17).

In connection with this section Bultmann emphasizes that faith and love "are, in fact, a unity." "The fact that the Word assures faith of the love of God manifest in Jesus, and that this love is only received when it becomes the means whereby a man is himself freed to love, means that the Word is only properly heard when the believer loves *in that he is a believer*."[90] This description gets to the heart of what John is saying, for he is in fact talking of the unity of faith and love. Only to the two of these together is the friendship of Jesus promised, and the prospect of remaining held out.

Meditation

Joy, enthusiasm, and jubilation are at the very heart of religious experience in the biblical tradition. The encounter with the God who saves and liberates gives rise to joy: "And the angel said to them, 'Fear not, for see, I bring you news of great joy that is meant for all the people. For today, in the city of David, is born to you a savior who is Christ the Lord' " (Luke 2:10-11). So runs the joyous message of the angel to the shepherds regarding Christ's birth. Where salvation is proclaimed and experienced, joy reigns. The presence of the salvation that was manifested with Christ was, and continues to be, the meaning of the Christian feastdays during the Church year. A feastday is marked by festive joy and high spirits.

It must be admitted, however, that nowadays Christians and the Churches no longer take the lead when it comes to spreading joy, and this is surely a bad sign. To be sure, one cannot produce true joy on command; it is to be compared rather to an unrestrained irruption against which there is simply no defense, an irruption that seizes and overwhelms a person. Or, if you look at it over the long

119

term and as an everyday reality, it can be likened to a friendly, benevolent atmosphere. Does the absence of this joy in today's Church have its source perhaps in a discordant relation to the Gospel? According to the New Testament, joy is the effect of practiced love, or a fruit of the Spirit, and is connected with the happiness which the reign of God brings. It communicates itself to people by freeing them and waking to life their capacity for love. Legalism, with its lists of prohibitions, gives rise instead to anxiety. Practices of repression beget a servile spirit and foster inhibitions that enslave. We should not object that what is meant is primarily a spiritual, interior joy! For even eschatological, spiritual joy lays hold of and liberates the entire person so that life can be lived in a new and creative way.

The liberation of the human person for joy is very important, and religion can bring it about if it allows itself to be permeated by the spirit of Jesus' Gospel. In this area religion would probably have no competition from other supposed providers of joy, because it is able in fact to offer an evangel, a *message of joy* that brings fulfillment to the whole person and the whole of life. Admittedly, while joyous human beings have creative ideas and manage to accomplish all sorts of things, they are also not so easy to control and dominate. Possibly this is why there has been so little chance for a revolution of joy.

Where joy reigns, friendships are easily formed. The Church and the Christian community as the circle of the friends of Jesus!—you need only write these words and you immediately feel the vast distance between this *Johannine* conception and the now prevailing forms of Church life. In our day it is perhaps small groups or circles of friends that come closest to embodying the New Testament ideals of what "Church" should be. We ought to find food for thought in the fact that this Johannine conception of the friends of Jesus has never been successful in the history of the Church and that nonetheless there have at all times been groups which have endeavored to make this ideal a reality: the medieval Fratcelli, the Bohemian Brethren, the pietist brotherhoods, and many nineteenth-century communities, for example. Such groups have each in their turn embodied the realization that if Christianity is to be a reality in the world, it needs to take shape in a concrete congregation of limited size, in a form of community which in its internal structure still resembles the rather free association characteristic of an extended family. Such a community would not have the inflexible juridical structures that seem in the long run to be unavoidable in an inclusive Church. Love and friendship cannot be practiced over a long period without a certain degree of intimacy.

In any event, the clerical interpretation of 15:15, "I no longer call you servants . . . ," represents a gross misunderstanding of the text. The verse is sung at the ceremony of ordination to the priesthood and is thus taken to mean that only the ordained priest is a friend of Jesus, while the laity are still only servants of Jesus. According to John, all believers are friends of Jesus.

As we saw, the text understands love, in the light of Jesus' example, to mean "giving one's life for one's friends," that is, commitment to others. Even this formula can be abused, of course. The history of the most recent world war, in which a hero's death for his country was often lauded in the words of 15:13, may serve as a cautionary example. Yet what the formula is really saying remains important, as its interpretation in the First Letter of John shows: "We have known what love is from the fact that he gave his life for us; consequently we too are obliged to give our life for the brethren. Now if anyone possesses this world's goods and sees his brother in need but closes his heart to him, how can the love of God remain in him? Little children, let us love not solely with words and tongue, but with deeds and in truth" (12 John 3:16-18).

Here we have the oldest social interpretation of *agapē* as a commitment to others. It is important for us to realize that primitive Christianity had already derived this social interpretation from the Gospel, and this in a community of which our first impression is that it inclines to a spiritualizing interpretation of things. But it is precisely the concrete, practical social interpretation of agape that seems to distinguish the group of Johannine communities from gnostic spiritualism. The new factor in our own day is that the distinction between those who possess this world's goods and the brothers in need is on a world scale. Consequently, help must reach beyond the concrete community; if need be, we must face up to the necessity of structural changes in society. If there is to be a long-term, effective, and, in the best sense, helpful commitment to the underdeveloped peoples, then Christians too must familiarize themselves with socio-critical analysis and the idea of structural social changes. If the Church is to be ready for these and related large-scale tasks, it will have to liberate itself more than it has done from its traditional bourgeois ideas. These ideas are handicaps which did not yet burden the Johannine communities of ca. A. D. 100. At that period the communities were marginal groups that lacked social and political recognition, and this fact must have been a help in their radical commitment to one another.

The Community of Jesus' Disciples and the Hatred of the World (15:18–16:4a)

Exegesis

The passage 15:18–16:4a speaks in detail of the precarious position of the community in the world. "World" here means, concretely, the pagan and, to some extent, the Jewish society of antiquity, toward the end of the first century and the beginning of the second. The specific character of the situation is given in the fact that the community is viewd with disfavor by the society around it or is even directly persecuted. In either case there is a vast gulf separating the community from the world in which it is forced to live. John's task as a pastor is to supply the motivation that will enable the community to persevere and will even make such perseverance meaningful.

The text may best be approached by dividing it into three sections. a) 15:18-25 deals with the theological principles governing the situation: As the community of Jesus the disciples must also share the lot of Jesus. Resistance to revelation did not cease when Jesus was crucified, but is now directed at the believing community which clings fast to the witness of revelation and holds a brief for it in the face of the world. b) 15:26-27 introduces another Paraclete saying that likewise relates to the situation of the community: In its real-life circumstances the community is called on to bear witness to Christ, but it is given power specifically for this purpose. c) 16:1-4a takes an overt stand on the urgent problem of the exclusion of Christians from the Jewish community.

THE COMMUNITY OF DISCIPLES
AND THE HATRED OF THE WORLD (15:18–25)

The opening words, "If the world hates you, then realize . . . " (v. 18), are evidently an answer to a pressing question. The question arises from the fact which the text describes as the "hatred of the world." "World" (Greek: *kosmos*), here and in the following verses, means the world of persons who show hostility to the revealer of God and to his community. This enmity reached its symbolic climax in the passion and crucifixion of Jesus. Even after Easter, however, the communities found that they would meet not only with non-acceptance from the world around them but with persecution as well.

From the beginning of Christianity persecution and its attendant phenomena—suspicion, misunderstanding, ridicule, and so forth—were elements in the characteristic image people formed of this new religion. These were also the great trials the disciples of Jesus had to face, conscious as they were of having committed no crime. Paul is already able to report such persecution (cf. 1 Thess. 2:14-16; 2 Cor. 11:23-33). According to the synoptic gospels, too, the disciples of Jesus are to expect rejection, hatred, and persecution.[91] More than any other passage, the missionary discourse in Matthew (10:5-11:1) offers a series of parallels to this passage in John.

The idea of a parallelism between the lot of the community and the lot of the revealer thus has a broad basis in the widely divergent New Testament traditions.[92] In addition, society's rejection of Christians was a hard reality with which the community had to come to grips every day. Moreover, ever since the Neronian persecution of Christians in A. D. 64, the threatening possibility was always there that the representatives of the Roman state would once again turn against the Christians.[93] Finally, it is highly likely that the gospel of John was composed in the period immediately after the Decian persecution (A. D. 95) and that the martyrdom of Bishop Ignatius of Antioch occured soon thereafter (cf. A. D. 107/110). Thus there were quite enough real reasons for the theme of the persecuted community.

The exhortation to the community begins with a lapidary reminder: the summons "then realize" or "recognize" challenges the hearers to reflect on their basic situation and to think of him to whom they have united themselves through faith. The disciples are meeting hatred from the world; they probably did not anticipate this when they first accepted the faith. The fact that faith meets with hatred instead of love can be confusing to believers, especially since Christian teaching obliges them to love. Then, too, there is the danger that is present from the beginning that in the face of threatening persecutions and difficulties Christians may capitulate and fall away. That is why in the present passage the first thing John does is give his hearers a forcible reminder of Jesus. When the disciples meet with hatred from the world, they are meeting only what Jesus himself experienced: "They have hated me before you."

Verse 19 provides a theological reason for this hatred: the disciples do not belong to the world any more. The Johannine idiom "be of the world" or "not be of the world"[94] is a *description of origin*; it indicates a specific whence. The underlying idea is that the origin of persons leaves its stamp on their nature, their character, and, finally, on their ways of acting as well. Two possibilities are contrasted here: "to be from above" or "from God," and "to be from below" or "from the world." Being from God applies first of all to the revealer, and then to all who belong to him. Being from the world, on the other hand, describes the factual situation of all who have not yet found their way to faith; then, and above all, it describes in a specifically negative way the situation of those who have taken a conscious position against the revealer and his message.

The disciples are "not of the world"; they have passed "from death to life" (5:24) and in so doing have put off the characteristic ways of the world. They are no longer the possession (Greek: *to idion*) of the world, but are the possession (Greek: *hoi idioi*) of Jesus. By his election of them Jesus has made them his own. Because they no longer belong to the world, the world no longer bestows its love on them and shows itself unconcerned about them. Because they belong to Jesus, the disciples now experience the strain of the radical opposition between God and the world. Paul says that they are "crucified with Jesus." This is to say that although they are no longer of the world but have been born of God and are children of God (1:12-13), they must yet continue to live in the world, without ever again being understood by the world or feeling fully at home in it.

The disciple can no longer identify with the world, and the world takes this attitude in bad form: "Therefore the world hates you."

According to verse 20 Jesus had predicted this situation. This is primarily a reference back to an earlier passage (13:16) which says, "The slave is not above his master." Perhaps the reminder of this particular passage has a further significance, inasmuch as the saying resembles one that occurs in Matthew and, in fact, in a similar context: "A disciple is not greater than his teacher, nor is a servant greater than his master; a disciple must be satisfied when he fares as his teacher did, and a servant when he fares as his master did. If they call the master of the house Beelzebub (devil), how much more will they do the same to the members of his household" (Matt. 10:24-25; cf. Luke 6:40). This suggests that in the tradition of the Johannine community there was a saying of the Lord which was similar to this one of Matthew and to which appeal was made: "We cannot be better off than our Master was!" Evidently Matthew understands the saying in the same way as John. It is inevitable that the disciples should share the lot of Jesus, for ill as well as for good.

In verse 21 the hostile attitude of the world is explained more fully. The world is hostile because of Jesus and because it does not know God. In the last analysis, the world cannot help acting as it does, because it does not know the Father. This ignorance of God on the part of the world and its representatives is not, however, the kind of ignorance that can be eliminated by additional information. Rather, according to the biblical conception of knowledge, what is lacking is the acknowledgment and acceptance of God and his revealer. According to the Bible, there can be no neutral, objective attitude to God; knowing or not knowing God always implies an attitude toward him. Ignorance of God as such is sinful; it is nothing but unbelief as verse 22 emphasizes.[95] Once Jesus has come as revealer of God and has brought the eschatological revelation, the world cannot be excused. Its unbelief is sinful, and this precisely because "it turns itself against Jesus, who has shown himself to be the Revealer by his words and his actions."[96]

Jesus was the first to experience the world's hatred. The hostility directed against him was, in John's view, at the same time a hostility against God (on this cf. 8:31-59), since in the person and work of Jesus it was God who was encountering humanity (v. 23). Verse 24 is to be understood as parallel to verse 22, since the words and works of Jesus form a unity in John. But the words, "works such as no one else has done," are intended to remind the reader of the miraculous signs as well. The miracles are to be understood as revelatory signs. Here again the meaning is that despite the actions of the revealer in the world his message was not accepted. Despite the fact that the world has seen, it persists in its hatred and therefore in its sin.

Nor did such a situation arise by chance. Verse 25 says that the world's behavior is the fulfillment of a text from the law, that is, from the Old Testament: "They have hated me without cause" (Isa. 35:19; 69:4). The citation from Scripture is not meant as a strict proof. Rather, the persuasion that the lot of Jesus was the fulfillment of Scripture is an expression of the idea that in his life and death the divine plan of salvation was being carried out. In our present context this means that the utterly undeserved and rationally unintelligible hatred of the world of Jesus has a place in God's plan and derives its meaning from this. It plays a role in effecting the salvation of the world.

The Paraclete and the Disciples as Witnesses to Jesus (15:26–27)

John now introduces a further saying about the Paraclete or Spirit-supporter, and attributes to him another function of which nothing has hitherto been said, namely the function of "bearing witness" to Jesus. Also to be noted here is the unity of Father and Son: Jesus "sends" the supporter from the Father, and the supporter "proceeds" from the Father. That the text has to do primarily with witnessing is clear from the parallel statement that the community too will bear witness to Jesus. The testimony of the Spirit-supporter and that of the community run parallel, as it were.

The concept of witness plays an important part in the gospel of John.[97] The truth of revelation can, in the last analysis, only be attested. The kind of response this truth calls for is not, as in the process of knowing that is proper to the natural sciences, observation that is as objective as possible or the construction of an experiment that can be repeated at will. The response is rather an acceptance of the knowledge along with a commitment to it, and a personal, existential sense of shock and wonder. Jesus is by his entire existence the witness par excellence to God and therefore to the truth (cf. 18:37). But the disciples too must become witnesses for Jesus, since faith is not susceptible of demonstration but is always communicated through living witness.

These verses also contain a historical reference, which is to be seen in the words, "because you have been with me from the beginning." The witnesses of Jesus in the primitive Church were primarily those disciples who had been with him from his first public appearance (cf. the introduction to the gospel of Luke, 1:1-4, or Acts 1:21-22: "Therefore one of those must join us as a witness of his resurrection who accompanied us during the entire period when the Lord Jesus went in and out among us, beginning with the baptism of John and down to the day when he was taken up from us"). The faith-inspired witness of the disciples of Jesus is also a witness to history.

There is another aspect: It is precisely in the face of the world which hates and persecutes the community, that the latter is constantly summoned to bear witness, even authoritative public witness. The concept of witness or martyr became a peculiarly Christian concept.[98] In bearing this kind of witness before a hostile world the community needs the help of the Spirit.

In this promise of the Spirit's help John once again is in the broad stream of primitive Christian tradition. Thus we read in Mark 13:9, 11, "Take heed for yourselves. For they will hand you over to tribunals, they will chastise you in the synagogues, they will hale you before governors and kings, for my sake, to bear witness before them . . . . When they lead you off and hand you over, do not worry beforehand about what you will say. Say what is given to you at that moment. For it is not you who speak but the Holy Spirit." Even in 15:26-27 we may well think primarily of *public* witness to Christ in the face of the unbelieving world. In this testimony, the Spirit will be acting with the disciple, and as with Jesus' own testimony to God, so here the result will be that people take sides and are divided.

127

In this passage we can see a concrete historical cause that led to the formation of the Johannine community, and represents one of the most difficult problems offered by primitive Christianity. The cause was the rejection of the Christian message by the Jewish faith-community. From a historical point of view, the separation of Christianity from Judaism in the early Church is an extremely complicated matter that has not been studied in sufficient detail.

The separation did not take place all at once. In the beginning there was a period of relative friendliness. Tensions and conflicts began at a rather early date, however, as can be seen from the example of Paul who, before his conversion in ca. A.D. 35, was a resolute persecutor of the Christian community. As a missionary to the pagans he himself came into conflict with the synagogues and was scourgd on five occasions (2 Cor. 11:24-26).

After the Romans had destroyed Jerusalem and the temple in A.D. 70 relations became even more strained. It is generally accepted today that Rabbi Gamaliel II, who after the fall of Jerusalem became head of the recently established rabbinic academy at Jabneh (or Jamnia) in succession to Rabbi Johanon ben Zakkai, the Founding headmaster, was the one who caused the definitive exclusion of Christians as heretics (*minim*) from the Jewish believing community. The introduction of the twelfth blessing against the heretics into the prayer of the Eighteen Blessings is attributed to him.[99] The twelfth blessing reads as follows, "May the hopes of the persecutors be crushed in the bud! May the kingdom of arrogance (the Roman empire) be uprooted swiftly in our day! May the Nazareans and other apostates vanish in an instant! May they be erased from the Book of the Living and not be enrolled with the devout! Praised be you, Lord, who crushes the insolent."[100]

The expression "expel from the synagogue" (v. 2; cf. 9:22: "For the Jews had already decided that anyone who confessed him [Jesus] to be Messiah should be expelled") does not here have the meaning of impose a major or minor excommunication from the synagogue. Excommunication was a corrective punishment, and must be distinguished from the complete expulsion imposed on heretics and apostates. "Since apostates and heretical groups had emerged from the synagogue itself, they were regarded as its most dangerous enemies. They were not met with excommunication but were simply expelled from the synagogue according to a discipline that could not but make even the simplest Jew aware that there could no longer be communion of any kind between the synagogue and such groups. Every form of personal and business dealings with them was prohibited."[101]

John evidently presupposes a situation of complete separation, at least within his own limited geographical environment (for we may not without examination generalize this supposition). It is possible that the Johannine community(ies) also had to face persecution from Jews (cf. Rev. 2:8-11), since the statement that "anyone who kills you will think he is doing a service that is pleasing to God" (v. 2b) can hardly apply to pagan persecutors, who would not think in these terms. If the statement is not just a rhetorical flourish, we must regard it as referring to Jewish persecutors; such people, as the example of Saul/Paul shows, could very well be religiously movitated.

Against this background of contemporary fact 16:1-4a becomes fully intelligible. It is also clear that what we have here is not an authentic saying of Jesus but an interpretation of the writer's own situation in the light of Christ. By any accounting, exclusion from the Jewish community and persecutions (whether from pagans or Jews can be left undecided here) add up to a hard trial. Verse 1, which tells us that the passage is a prediction, would have the disciples learn to gauge the situation correctly. For this, remembrance of Jesus is the best help. For, if it looks back to him, the community will realize that it will itself not be preserved from conflicts and that in this respect too it must follow in the steps of the master. The community must expect the same misunderstandings, the same rejections, that Jesus met. But it must not on this account allow itself to be shaken and turned aside from its course.

Meditation

In a passage such as 15:18–16:4a, which evokes the idea of persecuted community or Church of the martyrs, we can see most clearly how necessary it is to understand the text first of all in terms of the historical situation and not to generalize too hastily. In John's time the community was only a little flock. It had only recently been separated from the bonds of the Jewish community of faith, probably unwillingly rather than with enthusiasm. On the other hand, it had as yet no support from the society in which it now had to live. It was anything but firmly established. It had no history on which it could meditate and from which it could draw confidence.

Given these circumstances, John was undoubtedly right in referring the community first and foremost to the word and example of Jesus and in trying to make clear to the community that it and its way of life were no longer of the world but that its existence as a chosen band of disciples was now grounded in God. The dignity and world-transcending self-awareness of the community were based precisely on the fact that as the disciples of Jesus they were not just any group of people but God's community in the world. In this light we can also understand why John should explain the "hatred of the world" for the disciples as hatred "on account of Jesus" and as having its deeper cause in ignorance of God. And we understand why he says that hatred of Jesus is in the last analysis hatred of God. As we said, the situation of the author and his readers makes these statements intelligible.

We for our part must ask whether in all this we are to see only a higher theological wisdom, or whether the statements do not also carry peculiar dangers with them, especially when we understand them in a purely dogmatic and unhistorical way, as though they described the timeless essence of every historical situation in which the Church finds itself. In other words, in our day we cannot avoid comparing these statements, which were written over nineteen hundred years ago at the beginning of Church history and which at that time had an innocent, uncompromised meaning, with what has been made of them throughout the centuries.

To begin with, the Church's situation has changed dramatically in comparison with the beginnings! John's characterization of the community applies at most to the pre-Constantinian period, approximately until the Edict of Milan in 313: it applies even then only with certain limitations. After 313 conditions were completely different. It is astonishing to see how quickly a Church that was hitherto insecure, although by no means always and everywhere persecuted, came to terms with its new establishment state.[102] It was not long before the Church began to use against outsiders and deviants, heretics and Jews the same repressive methods it had had to suffer during the first three centuries. So quickly were the experiences of the early period forgotten or suppressed!

> We authorize (*iubemus*) the followers of this law (*lege*) to assume the title of Catholic Christians; but as for the others, since, in our judgment, they are foolish madmen, we decree that they shall be branded with the ignominious name of heretics, and shall not presume to give to their conventicles the name of churches. They will suffer in the first place the chastisement of the divine condemnation, and in the second the punishment which our authority, in accordance with the will of Heaven, shall decide to inflict.[103]

Thus reads the edict with which in 380 Emperor Theodosius the Great (379–95) made the Catholic Christianity of the inclusive Church the official religion of the state.

And when we read, "The hour is coming when anyone who kills you will think he is performing a service pleasing to God" or, as the text might be translated, "is celebrating a solemn liturgy," who can fail to think of the victims of the Inquisition? During the period of the Inquisition Christians were convinced that by burning individuals who remained faithful to their convictions or, as in Spain, by burning countless Jews, they were celebrating a liturgy and saving the souls of the afflicted. The official title for these cruel proceedings was *Auto da fè* or, in Latin, *Actus fidei*, that is, an "act of faith" and therefore "a solemn confession of God" that was accompanied by high masses, processions, and public pageantry.

Countless other examples could be adduced. They would only reinforce the conviction that the Christian Church may no longer appeal unreflectingly and in good conscience to such texts as we are reading here in John. In the interim the Church has absorbed so much of the world and worldly behavior, especially the behavior of the powerful, that it and its practice can no longer provide the basis for an unbiased answer to the question of whether someone or something is of the world or not of the world.

Some time or other, we ought to entertain (simply as a possibility) and think through to its logical conclusion the thought that a statement such as "but now they have seen, and yet they have hated me and my Father" (15:24) may apply even to the Church. Certainly, in the course of its history, and in the highest ranks of its members, even the Church has at times acted in ignorance of God. As long as we do not honestly admit the distorted relationship to the Gospel and the cause of Jesus which has cropped up often enough in the history of the Church, there can be no productive encounter with the New Testament and therefore no constructive change. The appeal to the Scriptures has frequently been only a legitimation of a pregiven practice and doctrine; even then, all that has been sought is a confirmation, without any honest acknowledgment of the human and historical reality behind the texts. Today, however, and in the time ahead, only a critical confrontation can be of any help. This does not mean criticism solely in the theoretical and scientific sense. It likewise means a Christian self-criticism and a criticism of the Church in which we draw upon the history of the Church for a critical reconsideration of the past.

If this sort of critical stance were taken, it would surely also be a Spirit-inspired credible witness before the world. We do, of course, celebrate the great founding personages and the martyrs. But the impression is often given that such a celebration of the fathers is intended simply to render them innocuous: Thank God, they belong to the past! The real martyrs of the present time are troublesome people whom others avoid if they cannot muzzle them.

The Church's relationship with Judaism has been and still is an especially sad story. In the preceding exegesis I was concerned to show that the beginnings of the alienation between Jews and Christians are extremely difficult to assess and that if we follow the data given in our sources, we must admit that in these beginnings there was fault on the Jewish side too. Even Jewish scholars recognize this. The persecuted community of the early period was very much a minority. Moreover, the mistake must not be made of reading back into the very earliest period later relations that were undoubtedly conditioned by the shift in power and predominance.[104] In that early period Christians could still think of themselves as a "third race" between pagans and Jews; in practice this meant that they fell between the two stools.

132

All this, however, does not justify the behavior Christians adopted toward Jews once the former had achieved success in society. Even in the fourth century we learn of numerous synagogues being destroyed. M. Simon sees in this active hostility a specifically Christian form of the anti-Semitism current in the ancient world. In the pre-Christian pagan period hardly any measures were taken against synagogues; in the Christian period such measures suddenly become more frequent. The anti-Semitism is no longer directed simply against Jews as a distinctive people but against the Jewish religion. The fact that such highly placed and cultured individuals as Bishop Ambrose of Milan (388) and Patriarch Cyril of Alexandria (414) could approve anti-Jewish activities remains a blot on the Church's record.[105]

We are not interested here in pursuing the later tragic history of Western Christian anti-Semitism. The point we wish to make is simply that it would be incorrect to view the problems of the initial period in the misleading mirror of later Christian practice. The exclusion of Christians from the Jewish community that is depicted in John 16:1-4a was a single historical event, although it had momentous historical consequences. In this respect, the New Testament texts call for careful reflection and discriminating judgment.

The Activity of the Spirit-Supporter (16:4b–15)

Exegesis

16:4b-15 forms a coherent textual unit, and its meaning can best be understood if we start with the assumption that it contains the Paraclete-sayings of the second farewell discourse, sayings that were originally independent units. Only then does it make sense to have the discourse start with the theme of Jesus' departure, as though nothing had yet been said of this. In addition, the two aspects or facets of the Spirit-supporter's activity are clarified: his activity with regard to outsiders in the form of "judgment on the world," and his activity with regard to the community in the form of "leading into the truth." The two facets are interrelated as two aspects of a single activity. For the action of the Spirit-supporter does not take place in a hidden free-floating manner but in and through the community which in its faith and its proclamation holds fast and bears witness to the saving event. At the same time, the two facets of the action of the Spirit-supporter are to be understood as aspects of the existence of the Christian community itself, for in them the interior face and the external face of the latter are manifested.

As in the previous pericope (15:18–16:4a), so here again the passage can be subdivided into three sections: (a) Verses 4b-7 are concerned with the departure situation and emphasize the necessity of Jesus' going away; (b) verses 8-11 deal with the judgment of the Spirit on the world; (c) verses 12-15 specify the action of the Spirit within the community

THE DEPARTURE OF JESUS (16:4b–7)

This section renews the reader's awareness of the situation in which the farewell discourses are spoken: Jesus is about to leave his disciples. We are also reminded of the character of the farewell discourses as historical fiction, for here again the evangelist intends to raise a question that is important from a theological viewpoint. The reader is once more made aware of the difference between the time of Jesus and the time of the Church. During the time when Jesus was with the disciples, such questions did not have to be asked.

Verse 4b evidently looks back to the prediction of persecutions. "But now"—and the "now" is not only temporal but refers to the entire new situation—Jesus is going to the Father, and his departure raises new problems. The text once again is to be read at two different and contrasting levels of meaning, one being simple and obvious, the other theological. On the level of the obvious, the text is speaking of the departure of Jesus which has his death for its premise. He is leaving the disciples alone behind him, a little band lost in the vast world. The disciples react with shock and do not even ask Jesus where he is going. Instead they are overwhelmed with sadness. The sadness meant here is of a radical kind, since it is a characteristic of being in the world; it is intensified by the eschatological distress of persecution and trial. The theme of sadness will be expressly developed in 16:16-25.

The question is, then, how can the disciples successfully endure their situation without the presence of the revealer? The question brings out, once again, a basic problem of faith as it finds itself situated in the world and in history. The answer is correspondingly basic in its theological importance. this emerges when Jesus replies, first of all, that "in all truth it is good for you that I should go," since the departure of Jesus is the prerequisite for the coming of the Spirit-supporter. If we ask why Jesus had not given the Spirit to the disciples earlier and whether perhaps he had been unable to do so, the meaning of the statements emerges with greater clarity.

The real issue is not the time of the Spirit's coming but a matter of basic fact: It is only the Spirit who makes the entire event of revelation intelligible. He is the new understanding of reality that faith makes accessible. The historical as such is not yet revelation. Insofar as there was always need of faith in dealing even with the historical Jesus, it was already necessary to move beyond the obvious historical level (cf. 6:61-65). This need becomes fully clear, however, only after the death and departure of Jesus. Now the community must deal solely with the word of Jesus, the kerygma. But it is not on this account at a disadvantage compared with the first generation; rather, it has now become fully clear that the decisive step in any encounter with Jesus is the step from non belief (or unbelief) to faith. Jesus must therefore go away so that the Spirit-supporter can come, but the Spirit's action is wholly related to the activity of Jesus. Consequently, we must speak of Jesus returning to the community in the person of the Spirit. The historical presence of Jesus has now been replaced by his presence in the Spirit.

THE JUDGMENT ON THE WORLD (16:8–11)

If we are to understand these rather difficult statements we must begin with the fact that the Spirit is to make present through the community the entire revelation of Christ together with the re-demptive work of Jesus in his cross and resurrection.[106] The whole of John's gospel is the consistent example of a Spirit-effected, pneu-matic interpretation of the history of Jesus, understood as a reve-lation of God. The concise statements made here presuppose the entire gospel (chaps. 1-12); they tell us how the fourth evangelist viewed the history of Jesus. The Spirit will bear witness that through Jesus truth and life are already present for the believer. But he will also bear witness that in the cross of Jesus the judgment on the world has already taken place. The two testimonies are connected with one another. For this reason the Spirit's activity can here be described as an act of *convicting*.

The term convict belongs to the world of the court and the law and means to prove, demonstrate, indict, pass sentence. The con-victing which the Spirit does comes down in practice to a con-demning. The Spirit will execute God's judgment on the unbelieving world. In the background is the image of a legal proceedings.

According to John the revelation Christ brings is at the same time a "judgment on the world"; in its encounter with the revealer the world is confronted with the final decision regarding salvation or damnation. The final judgment does not take place only at the end; it is already taking place now, for the reason that (according to John) the eschatological verdict has already been issued in the cross and resurrection of Jesus. That is why John can say, " 'Now is the judg-ment on this world; now the ruler of this world is being cast out. But I, when I am lifted up from the earth, will draw all men to myself.' He said this to indicate what kind of death he was to die" (12:31-33). This passage states clearly that the final judgment takes place in the lifting up of Jesus on the cross. The cross is already the turning point of the ages. According to John, the judgment has already taken place in God's eyes and therefore in the eyes of faith as well. The Spirit, and in union with him, the preaching of the community have as their function to make this judgment and its result known to the world.

It is against this same background that we must understand that the Spirit-supporter will make known sin, justice, and judgment. The need here is not only to indicate the new meaning of these concepts but also to show how the world is already and will permanently be affected negatively by the saving event, even though it does not realize it. Faith will always call the world as such into question, and the world in turn will render faith precarious.

"What sin is: that they do not believe in me" (v. 9). Sin consists in unbelief. "Sin is not therefore any single ghastly act, even if that action be the crucifixion of Jesus; sin is not moral failure as such, but unbelief and the bearing that springs from it, i.e. the conduct determined by unbelief and taken as a whole. From now on that is 'sin.' "[107] This is also to say that according to John belief/unbelief is not a mere intellectual response on our part but an existential response in which the issue is our basic attitude to our own lives and to the world, but also to God and revelation, and that these *all-important* attitudes inflect our overall behavior in one or another direction.

The sin of the world is this: that in rejecting Jesus it closes itself to the Creator's love which comes to meet it in revelation. Since, however, the sin of the world, among other things, was removed on the cross (in 1:29 we read, "Behold the Lamb of God who takes away the sin of the world"), there is no longer any adequate reason, any pretext, for the world to persist in its attitude of rejection. If it continues to do so, then its unbelief reveals its radical alienation from God, and this estrangement is precisely the sin in which it remains forever.

"What justice is: that I am going to the Father and you will see me no longer" (v. 10). Justice here is the eschatological victory of Jesus over the destructive forces of the world. His departure is simply his way to the Father, and this way leads through the cross; therefore his departure also signifies the conquest of evil. It is at the same time the way of Jesus' exaltation and glorification, whereby he receives his divine rights. Admittedly, that which to faith is Jesus' way to the Father and to his glorification is for the world simply the final disappearance and absence of Jesus: he will be seen no more. According to 16:20 the world will rejoice because it believes that it is rid of Jesus. It is right, of course. It is finally rid of this Jesus— but in its blindness it fails to see that the worst thing possible has befallen it: this absence of Jesus signifies judgment and damnation.

The final judgment no longer takes the form of a mighty drama in which heaven and earth are shaken; it is simply the complete absence of Jesus in which the world is left to its own doings, without the love that liberates. That is the price it must pay to be rid of the disturbing presence of Jesus.

"What judgment is: that the ruler of this world is already judged" (v. 11). The action of the paraclete will bear witness to the world that the turning point of the ages has already come. In Jesus, judgment has already been passed on the world and its ruler.

In this sense, then, the Spirit-supporter, together with the community as witnesses to Christ, declares to the world what sin, justice, and judgment are. John evidently thinks that the life of the community and its testimony of faith are a permanent challenge to a world locked in unbelief. The confrontation between revelation and the world will continue to take place as long as the world contains a believing community. We can ask here, with Bultmann, whether something of this is not to be discerned in the world itself, and we can reflect on his answer: "This word and the claim it lays on man is heard in the world, and after hearing it, the world can never be the same again. There is no longer any such thing as an unprejudiced Judaism or an impartial Gentile world within the circumference of the word of proclamation." [108]

We may not, however, ignore the other side of the coin: This section says that the community is also in a position now to be able to raise critical questions to the world. In the background of our text was the anxiety of the community at its own isolation amid the world because Jesus had gone and because the hatred of the world was poured out on it. But, rendered bold by his convinced faith, John turns the tables and says it is not the disciples who have reason to be anxious, but the world that is convicted of sin. The world is in a state of injustice, especially when it resists the message of Christ. It is clear that the community cannot face up to the world by its own power or in its own right, but only in the power of its faith, its confession, and its union with Jesus. What it proclaims is not its own victory but the victory of Jesus and therefore the victory of God. But in so doing, it challenges the world, and such indeed is its duty.

138

The Spirit Teaches the Community (16:12-15)

The testimony of the Spirit to the world is matched by his action in the internal life of the community. This action or teaching consists primarily in disclosing ever anew the meaning of Christ's revelation. The present section of John's gospel is frequently invoked in order to paint in strong colors the lack of understanding and courage on the part of the disciples before Easter and, on the other hand, the great change that took place on Pentecost. But in this case, once again, the time difference expressed in verse 12 points to a more substantial difference. The text refers once again to the two levels already mentioned, that is, to a problem that constantly remains acute for faith. In very simple terms, the problem is this: It is always the Spirit, and he alone, who leads to an understanding of revelation, that is, of Jesus' message. Apart from the Spirit there is only a collection of "much" that we cannot endure or handle; the Spirit, however, "leads" the individual and the community "to the entire truth" (v. 13).

The formula "the entire truth" deserves our attention. The usual translations "all truth" or "every truth" do not capture the sense of statement and have led to many erroneous interpretations. The truth which Christ reveals is to be understood as being antecedently an all-embracing intelligible unity. There is a question here, therefore, not of a plurality of dogmas that the Spirit will continue to bring to light in the course of history, but of a revelation that is given from the beginning as one, simple, and definitive. For John revelation is not a doctrinal structure, that is, a gigantic complex of revealed propositions, but the person of Jesus. Consequently, to lead persons to the entire truth is nothing else than to lead them to an ever new and better or deeper understanding of Jesus. This leading to the entire truth marks the freely adopted vital movement of faith and of the believing community in its living, Spirit-inspired and Spirit-filled relation to Jesus of Nazareth. Whenever the community labors seriously and zealously for the cause of Jesus, this leading to the entire truth takes place.

As verses 14-15 explain, this process does not entail a new revelation to be set alongside that of Christ. Rather, the action of the Spirit is related to the already given revelation of Christ. The proclamation by the Spirit and the community cannot be detached from this basis, for it supplies the fundamental substance of tradition. John gives a further reason for this tradition: The historical revealed truth which Jesus brought and the truth of God together form an indivisible unity. In the Spirit's testimony to Christ the experience and communication of divine truth take place.

At the same time, however, the revelation also concerns the future. The message of Jesus cannot be superseded because it discloses the eschatological, eternal future. This also means that in the last analysis no age and therefore no Church or magisterium can exhaust the message of Jesus or explicate it fully or embody it totally in concrete forms and practices. The Gospel of Jesus Christ continues, therefore, to have a future because it has not yet been fully assimilated and translated into reality and action. It is first and foremost the prophetic office in the Church that gives expression to the still unexhausted futurity of the message of Jesus. Verse 13c refers expressly to this: The Spirit will make known the future. With these words John grants a permanent place in the Church to Christian prophecy (with which he was probably quite familiar). Just as the Jahwist faith was the basis on which Old Testament prophecy related to present and future, so too the revelation of Christ enables New Testament prophecy to analyze and interpret present and future in a critical but at the same time helpful way.

The Spirit-supporter's action leads the community to the entire truth in numerous ways which have in common a remembrance of and reflection on Jesus and his cause: theological teaching and exploration of the message of Jesus for the community; meditation; the critical and unsettling word of prophecy. A final point worth noting is that here again the activity of the Spirit extends to the entire community and by no means solely to a privileged group of official representatives of Jesus. The discovery of Christian truth in regard to the cause of Jesus is a process in which the entire community and all its members are engaged.

Meditation

The question of how the Christian community would handle the problem of the absence of Jesus and of eschatology (delay of the parousia) is not one of merely historical interest. It also defines Christian self-understanding down to our own day. In the early days of the community, immediately after Easter, things were in all probability relatively simple as yet, since at that time great enthusiasm was evidently still the dominant mood. In addition, a large number of the early disciples of Jesus were still alive. But with the passing of these disciples and the original apostles the early communities must have started asking, "How will we proceed now? Who will lead the communities? Who will be responsible for preaching? Who will answer the new questions that arise, and by what authority will it be done?" These and similar problems led gradually to the development of the idea of tradition and succession in apostolic office (or apostolic succession). The gospel of John precedes this development and goes its own way. It has Jesus himself answer these questions. The author uses the authority of Jesus in order to help the community carry on.

We are readily inclined to regard such a procedure as a form of plagiarism or at least as somehow irregular. But to do so is to mistake the intention of John's gospel. The appeal to Jesus means first of all that the author has no desire to speak in his own name and that in his view the authority of Jesus is binding permanently and in principle. The same kind of problem arises for us in the other gospels as well, when we find community productions (sayings, etc., produced by the community) being handed on as genuine sayings of Jesus. In fact, the very collection of Jesus' sayings in the early communities and the redaction of these in the shapes of books of good news by the evangelists are the most striking indication of how intensely the communities felt bound by the authority of Jesus.

The obligation was not simply a survival from the historical past; rather, the authority of Jesus was understood as an *abidingly present authority*. That is the point of the ending of Matthew's gospel: " . . . and teach them to observe all that I have commanded you. For, behold, I am with you always, to the end of the world" (28:20). The origin of the written gospels is thus directly connected with the effort to show the authority of Jesus as a present authority that is permanently binding. As the ending of Matthew shows, this authority is to be binding through all ages "to the end of the world." Throughout the entire future, the gospels will enable the Church

141

to align itself over and over again with the authority of Jesus. It is a question of basic importance, of course, to what extent in the course of history the Church has complied with this intention.

John shows that he has reflected explicitly on this point when he contrasts the time "when I was still with you" and the time of Jesus' absence. The sadness that fills the hearts of the disciples at the farewell not only describes the psychological state of the pain of parting. It also identifies a perduring problem: Whenever the community does not derive its essential self-understanding or its action from its relation to Jesus and his message, but seeks motivation instead from the historical or purely social circumstances of one or other present situation, then it will probably experience this sadness once again in the form of resignation, pessimism, crippling inability to act, and so on. To this extent the sadness corresponds approximately to faintheartedness in Matthew; it is the sign of a temptation regarding faith. In the last analysis, then, Christian faith derives its motivation and certainty only from deeper penetration into its own cause or concretely from deeper penetration of the word that has been handed down, and this in the form of a Spirit-effected meditative remembrance of Jesus, a reflection on his Gospel.

This is not to say that social circumstances are a matter of indifference. In large measure they show in fact the steadily declining influence of Christianity and the Christian proclamation as well as of the Church in contemporary society. But this decline of the Church's influence on society is not a univocally clear phenomenon to which people in the Church can respond in a purely negative way, as they often prefer to do. Rather, the Church must ask to what extent it has contributed to this development, for example, by preaching an outmoded morality that is not sanctioned by the message of Jesus; in other words, to what extent it is responsible for the declining social influence which history attests. Were the Church to ask this question, it would become clear that critical reflection on the cause of Jesus is one of the most important tasks incumbent on it.

There is doubtless also a danger of a wrong kind of adaptation, an effort to avoid conflicts as much as possible and to cozy up to the world, not only in the form of the moral worldliness that is often censured, but in the form, much more dangerous in the long run, of accommodation to the political powers, the rulers of the day. Here the question of criteria arises once again. What kind of adaptation can be regarded as legitimate and even necessary, and what kind is dangerous? In any attempt to answer this question the gospels have something important to tell us. We should not expect, of course, a quick and direct answer to such problems, a neat formula for handling them. What we may expect are guidelines we can follow. Thus, any adaptation can be readily accepted which fits in with the cause of Jesus or which at least meets with no important objection from this quarter .

Yet even this generalization is probably still too much of a formula. Individuals and Christian groups must work out their own answers; in the process of doing so they must pay attention to all the various viewpoints, among them those expressed in the New Testament (though not these alone), and give them all a say in the formation of a judgment. The final decision will admittedly have to be made on their own responsibility. The Church, and especially the ecclesiastical authorities, will have to represent, first and foremost, the living voice of the Gospel, for that is their authentic and most important task. But the Church cannot relieve anyone of personal responsibility.

The statement in John, "It is good for you that I go away, for otherwise the supporter cannot come," expresses the most important positive factor in coming to grips with our own situation. The Spirit takes the place of Jesus. In very simple terms, the disciples can no longer put questions directly to Jesus; it is no longer possible to go back and ask whether we have properly understood Jesus or even the apostles. But the community can rely on the Spirit of Jesus; it can and must learn, in reliance on the word of Jesus as preserved by tradition, to understand Jesus anew "by the power of the Spirit," and to think and act in accordance with his Spirit.

But what does this mean? After all, the Spirit of Jesus is certainly a very invisible reality that cannot be apprehended: "The gentle breath of the wind blows where it will; you hear its rustling but do not know whence it comes and whither it goes; so it is with everyone who is born of the gentle breath of the Spirit" (3:8).[109] The Spirit is intangible, free, not at our disposal (all of which is not simply to be equated with immaterial). He certainly does speak in the word of Jesus and in the community's proclamation of Jesus. To this extent R. Bultmann is correct in saying that the Spirit is "the power of the proclamation of the word in the community."[110] At the same time, however, if incomprehensible (to our mind) describes the being and action of the Spirit, then it follows that the individual believer and the community as a whole have their real roots in something that is unconditionally not at our disposal. Consequently, there is an open space here, as it were, a pneumatic realm that as such can be filled only by the lordship of Christ, that is, by the rule of the Spirit, and that, because of its pneumatic character, is and always will be a sacrosanct area beyond the reach of every human authority, including ecclesiastical offices and those who fill them.

The Spirit guarantees the eschatological openness which is part of the community's very being, and thereby guarantees as well a space of freedom for people against which every worldly power must prove ineffective. The presence of the Spirit of Jesus also assures the freedom of the community and its responsibility for itself. The community does not see its commitment to the person and word of Jesus as submission to authoritarian rule, but on the contrary as the unconditionally reliable and steadfast basis of its freedom. R. Bultmann has correctly pointed out the paradox that the living word spoken by the community is also the word of the Spirit who acts in the community.[111]

This is not to say that the community can dispose of Jesus' word as it chooses, so that any and every utterance of the community or Church authorities would automatically be the word of the Spirit. No, such utterances are and will be the word of the Spirit only to the extent that they remained related to the word of Jesus. The kerygma and the tradition about Jesus continue to be the norms for material content, so that the Spirit, especially in John's view, can never become a vague fluid thing or the source of what is willful and arbitrary.

As thus linked to Jesus himself by the Spirit, the community carries on Jesus' work in the world and in confrontation with the world. Just as Jesus by his word brought the world to that crisis which was both decision and separation, so the community will bring on the same crisis by its witness to Christ, inasmuch as it forces the hearer to the decision of faith. It is clear that the community cannot cause this crisis in its own right. It is not commissioned to pass judgment on the world; that is the business of Jesus alone. If the Spirit and the community together continue the work of Jesus, they do so (according to John) on the basis of a decision already taken, and one that has been established as definitive by the word and work of Jesus and especially by his cross. The Church's proclamation has nothing to add to the eschatological decision God has made in Jesus for the salvation of the world. That is why John says here that the Spirit will convict, that is, make known what has already taken place in the saving event.

If John understands sin to be unbelief, that is, if he simply identifies unbelief and sin, it follows that he is taking sin not in a moral sense (a violation of a divine commandment concerning morality) but in a deeper existential sense. No longer is there question primarily of active human behavior but of a basic decision which affects the very being of humanity, the innermost existence. John sees unbelief and faith as the decisive alternatives between which people must choose. In the background for him here is also the fact that in Palestine, among his own countrypeople, Jesus failed in his preaching and inevitably ended on the cross, even though in the community's view he was utterly innocent. Jesus, therefore, as revealer of God, confronts the human person in the ultimate questions of life, although Jesus, in the last analysis looks for a positive choice that will lead the person to faith and thus to salvation and life. According to John Jesus wants all to be saved, not to be judged or lost.

How is this theological principle to be understood today? The idea that people's ultimate decisions regarding themselves and the meaning of their lives is a decision between faith and unbelief is often no longer understood, or else it is dismissed as a Christian or ecclesiastical exaggeration, especially when the faith in question is primarily a dogmatic faith. The language of Church dogma and of traditional preaching has at many points become so alien to the people of today that it simply misses its mark; in other words, it is no longer capable of posing the decisive question in a meaningful fashion. A kind of short-cut mentality on the part of the Church in the past has also frequently led to the question of truth being asked in a rather superficial way. Finally, the question has often enough been accompanied by claims to power on the part of the various confessions. In consequence, the kind of outlook that prepares the way for the question of faith is frequently so hindered that the question can no longer be raised in its valid form.

At the same time, it can hardly be denied that human beings still have the thoughts, dispositions, reflections, and so on that are traditionally regarded as expressing the human question regarding salvation or meaning. The existential question of the meaning of life seems to be inseparable from human existence as such. The question, then, is evidently a primordial anthropological datum. But the question of meaning brings with it the possibility of decision; people obviously do not experience meaning as something self-evident (otherwise there could not be the contrary experience of the loss of meaning), but as something that must be found in history, and this means, above all, found in connection with the exercise of free choice.

This basic anthropological structure finds extremely varied expressions in the historical religions. The Christian name for the question of meaning is the *question of faith*, with faith representing the highest form of the discovery of meaning. In Christian tradition, the discovery of meaning is linked with the revelation of Jesus. In fact, the concept of revelation means precisely that in the encounter with Jesus and his word the highest, that is, the divine meaning of reality is disclosed. In this context we should not reach too quickly for traditional formulations, but rather learn to be attentive to the *human structure of meaning as such*. If we did, it would probably become much clearer that in faith we have to do with something basic in people, namely with the ability to believe in the sense of a radical trusting in the positive meaning of life and the world, despite any experiential evidence to the contrary. When Jesus confronts a person with the decision of faith, he, the revealer of divine love, is appealing to that person at the level of ultimate, positive, vital possibilities. The word of Jesus, when heard and properly understood, touches all at the level of these ultimate possibilities of the self. It also precipitates people into a radical life-crisis, but one that is to be sweated out as a sickness not unto death but unto life.[112]

According to John, the Church must be able in its proclamation

146

to articulate the question of faith as the question of human meaning, and, on the basis of faith, to carry on the critical discussion between revelation and the world. The Church must derive the motivation for this confrontation from what is central to itself, namely its union with Jesus. In John's time the community was conscious of the role it had as critic of the world and society in the light of prevailing conditions. Here is how an anonymous Christian of the second century expressed the community's relationship to the world:

> To put it briefly, what the soul is in the body, Christians are in the world. As the soul is diffused throughout all the members of the body, so Christians are scattered through all the cities of the world. The soul indeed dwells in the body but it does not take its origin from the body; in like manner, Christians live in the world but they are not of the world . . . . The soul is enclosed in the body, yet it is the soul that holds the body together; so too Christians are detained in the world as though they were in custody, yet it is they who hold the world together . . . . God has assigned them this post, and they have no right to desert it. (*Letter to Diognetus*, ch. 6)

The Christian message was addressed to all the world; encounter and critical confrontation with the world was always sought.

It is the very nature of the Gospel and Christian faith that they may not be restricted to a private religious realm but must leave their mark on people's thinking and action in relation to the world. But what if this kind of critical encounter and confrontation no longer occurs? What if the world's opposition to Christianity is no longer voiced, if at bottom people expect nothing further from the Church and simply find it uninteresting? This kind of indifference is essentially worse for the Church than any open rejection. In such circumstances we should not begin intoning a great lamentation but rather reflect on the words of Jesus: "If the salt becomes saltless, how will you season it?" (Mark 9:50). If there is no longer any critical confrontation with the world, then the first thing to do is to ask the Church whether in its life and activity it has not become saltless, insipid and tasteless, so that no one is interested in it any longer.

In the past, people liked to use the statements in 16:12-15 to render intelligible or give a biblical legitimation for the Church's formulated dogmas and developed doctrines. Such an application of the passage was not entirely unjustified, but it needs to be explained more carefully. The Johannine text, "I still have much to say to you, but you cannot bear it now" (v. 12), gives rise to many misunderstandings. It sounds as though before Easter and Pentecost Jesus had held back a series of statements or propositions, each with its specific content, because he thought the disciples' ability to grasp them was insufficiently developed. Later on, the Holy Spirit supposedly brought these previously withheld propositions, together with a new ability to grasp them, and communicated them to the Church in the form of dogmas. But this is not what the text is saying.

The word "much" (Greek: *polla*, which is plural) is doubtless to be interpreted as a global or all-inclusive term. It does not point to a multiplicity of particular statements and dogmas but is a vague and imprecise way of pointing to the problem of understanding as such. In the immediate historical present (the gospel of John is saying) the disciples have understood the revelation of Jesus only in a fragmentary and rudimentary way, and not in its comprehensive fullness. This second kind of understanding is possible only with the help of the Spirit. The context explicitly tells us, moreover, that the Spirit will not be bringing us materially new truths after Easter; rather he will cause Jesus and his message—and no other—to be esteemed and honored.

It is also clear that the entire truth cannot refer to a system of doctrinal propositions, a collection of articles of faith. For John, Jesus himself is the revelation and the truth in an unqualified sense. It is characteristic of the gospel of John that the concept of truth finds expression only as a noun in the singular number; there is no plurality of truths of faith. This one and singular truth, moreover, is given to us as an all-inclusive totality in Jesus Christ. As the Prologue says, "of his fullness we have all received, favor upon favor; for the law was given through Moses, but grace and truth have come to pass through Jesus Christ" (1:17). The fullness of truth comes in Jesus Christ. As such it needs no supplements.

If we reflect further on John's words, we see that the question of dogmas and dogmatic development arises at a different level. There can be no development of the full eschatological truth that came to us in Jesus of Nazareth. But, as verse 13 says, this does not

148

mean that the believer is not constantly in need of being "led to the entire truth."

I would like here to make note of an interesting point. The Greek text says, "he will lead you into the entire truth" (*hodēgēsei hymas eis tēn alētheian pasan*). The Latin translation (the Vulgate), however, has, "he will teach you all truth" (*docebit vos omnem veritatem*), and this version was interpreted in the Latin-Roman tradition as referring to a teaching office. But there is a considerable difference between "leading you to the entire truth" and "teaching you all truth"!

Although the entire truth as such has already been given in Jesus Christ, in the history of faith itself there is an ever new understanding of this truth, and therefore the necessity of constantly disclosing and interpreting it. Dogmas have their place precisely at this level of disclosure and interpretation. They can never replace the revelation Christ brought or even compete with it. As speech-utterances they take the form of propositions, but these are able in every case to grasp and express only a limited aspect of the fullness of truth. The fullness of truth is far more than all the dogmas can express, and for this reason the latter are always relative and can be superseded. In the course of history dogmas can also become obsolete and require alteration or a new formulation.

In all this we should not overlook a danger that has in fact arisen in the course of Church history: the danger that in official Church preaching dogmas may often become much more important than the revelation of Christ in its biblical form, despite the fact that they must constantly be referred back to this revelation. According to John, a person can be a believing Christian and yet have only a few central formulas. All that is required is confession of the revealer, Jesus Christ, who embodies in himself not a part of the truth (with others embodying other parts of it) but the entire truth of Christianity. All that is required is faith and love. The important thing is the truth in its totality and fullness, not the individual propositions of faith in their multiplicity.

On the other hand, provided we keep our eyes on this fullness of truth, the many and varied propositions of faith can be understood and allowed to stand; but salvation does not depend on them. Salvation is a total, unified, and single reality, and when the Gospel

149

is reduced to its simple, basic structure, the believer too attains to that personal unity, that identity, mediated by faith, which is meant in the concept of salvation. One may therefore defend the possibility, in the finite and historical world of human beings, of a plurality of propositions and interpretations of the Christian faith, or the legitimacy of a plurality of interpretations of the Christian reality, provided these are all seen in their relation to the original totality and fullness and acquire their meaning solely from it.

There is one further aspect of the text that may be mentioned. The Spirit will foretell the future; he establishes a *charism of prophecy* in the community of Jesus. Primitive Christianity experienced a revival of prophecy; there were prophets and prophetesses in the early Christian communities.[113] Prophets are Spirit-filled men and women who have the word at their disposal. It is assumed that in the early days individuals with the charism of prophecy were among the most important leaders of the communities, until their place was taken over more and more by institutional officials, the presbyters and the bishop. It was probably a chief task of the New Testament prophets to explain to others the message of Jesus and the tradition about him, and to interpret these in relation to new situations. In all likelihood, we should not draw any great distinction between the prophets and the teachers.

The classical example of such a prophetic reinterpretation of the message of Jesus is the gospel of John. But what did "John," the author of this gospel, do? He did not simply collect and put order into the old traditions available to him, but had the courage to proclaim the message of Jesus in a wholly new language, in wholly new concepts and words that were familiar to his hearers, so that they could understand and appropriate the message. In so doing he made the message of Jesus indigenous especially to the Hellenistic world. Educated Greeks, like Justin, Clement of Alexandria, and Origen, who might have found Christianity unacceptable, were especially captivated by the teaching of this gospel.

John thus accomplished for his age a work that every period calls for anew. He is a model not simply because as an inspired author he authoritatively preached the message of Christ, but also and above all because of the way he did it, namely, with unparalleled spiritual freedom and mastery. Prophecy evidently liberates the

Christian message from the fetters and incrustations of a paralyzing traditionalism. Its primary function is to relate the Christian message to the present age with its experiences and problems and to interpret it for the people of every today. If the message is to remain alive or to become alive again, the Church of every age and especially of today needs authoritative, Spirit-filled prophecy.

Quite clearly, prophecy is not simply to be identified with theology, although we may admit that all vital theology contains a prophetic element. Generally speaking, however, the prophetic spirit is not tied in with any office (recall, for example, writers like Kierkegaard or Reinhold Schneider). Rather, the prophet is a free spirit who is exposed to the often painful experiences of his or her own age and world. Authentic prophecy is marked above all by something that is often suspect today, a relation to the *kairos*, a response to the *spirit of the times*, to the unique challenge of the present hour. The prophetic spirit dares to confront the spirit of the times with the Gospel, whether to criticize the former or to help it. For, unless the seed of the word is scattered in the field of the times, it cannot produce any fruit. Consequently, the prophet is energized both by the Gospel, the living word of God, and by the expectations, trends, and views of the age. This often puts the prophet in the difficult position of being correctly understood neither by the devout nor by the rest of society. We must therefore take into account that the prophet, like the Old Testament prophets before, comes forward under the banner of radical criticism; for it is part of the task to bring to light the contradiction between the message and the wretched reality of Church and world.

The Promise of Jesus' Return (16:16–22)

Exegesis

The reinterpretation of the early Christian expectation of the parousia has already occurred several times as a theme;[114] it occurs again in these verses. The text makes it clear how urgently the problem of the delay of the parousia must have been felt in the Church toward the end of the first century. "Christians of this period regarded this chaos (i.e., the chaotic condition of the transitional stage from the Primitive-Apostolic to the Early Catholic form of Christianity) as a perilous crisis, in which both the legacy of faith, handed down from the beginning, and the Church itself were threatened with ruin."[115]

This formulation of the facts may be somewhat exaggerated, but there can be no doubt that the transition did bring on a real crisis. The important thing, here again, is that John endeavors to solve the problem of the imminent expectation of the parousia on the basis of his christology. His response is entirely determined by the idea that the salvation to be given in the last times has already become a reality; in other words, by the idea that salvation is now present and that this *eschatological present* also includes the *eschatological future*. This theological starting point finds expression in John in the kerygma of the cross and resurrection or the "exaltation and glorification of Christ."[116] It enabled him to retain the idea of the return of Christ and give it a new meaning. We will properly understand 16:16-22 only if we take it seriously as a Johannine interpretation and renounce any attempt to attribute it to the earthly Jesus. There can be an attribution of it to Jesus only in an objective and theological sense, namely, that faith in the exalted and glorified Christ also made it possible to understand the return of Christ in a new way.

The passage begins with an enigmatic statement of Jesus in verse 16: "Yet a little while, then you will see me no more; and again a little while, then you will see me again." What is the "little while"? John likes this kind of enigmatic expression that is frequently susceptible of two meanings. It enables him to make his readers face up to certain problems which he regards as important. As in the present instance, the possibility of a double meaning is linked to the stylistic device of misunderstanding. John's aim is to lead his readers to a new and deeper grasp of something with which they are already familiar: in this case, the return of Christ.

The return of Jesus had traditionally been thought of in terms of seeing him again, of a hope of seeing the exalted, heavenly Jesus Christ who would come with divine power and glory. In 1 Thessalonians 4:13-18 Paul had given a vivid dramatic form to this conception (cf. also Phil. 4:20-21). It is put less dramatically but in a really similar way in the First Letter of John: "Dear brethren, we are now children of God, but what we shall be has not yet been revealed. We know that we shall be like him when he manifests himself, for we shall see him as he is" (3:2). It is possible that this verse represents a complement to, if not a correction of, the view represented in the gospel of John.

John, then, was familiar with this tradition. Consequently it is easy for us to reconstruct the process of reinterpretation through which he went. The expression yet a little while uses the language of imminent expectation (cf. Rev. 22:20: "He who testifies to these things says: 'Yes, I am coming soon.' Amen. Come, Lord Jesus!") and gives it a completely new interpretation. It is now only a short while before Jesus goes away for good, by way of his passion and death, and it is only another short while before he is seen again, a term which in the evangelist's mind refers first of all to Easter and its apparitions. In not directly mentioning these two events but— it seems clear—deliberately leaving them out of consideration, the evangelist is being true to a basic principle. For him, as for the entire New Testament, the *question of the when* remains completely open.

The misunderstanding on the part of the disciples (vv. 17-18) underscores once again the problem to which John wishes to respond. It is noteworthy that not only do the disciples misunderstand the seeing again and discuss it among themselves—"They do not turn to him (Jesus) directly; it is as if he had already left them"[117]— but they also debate the meaning of "I am going to the Father." In other words, the subject here is the whole complex of ideas associated with the departure of Jesus and its meaning for the community of disciples. At the same time, the evangelist here indicates to us that these two aspects—the seeing again and the going to the Father—are objectively connected. This makes it clear that he links the seeing again with Easter.

The answer of Jesus (vv. 19-22) clarifies the meaning of his statement, which initially had been completely obscure. The reproach to the disciples for their failure to understand (v. 19) is a stylistic convention. Verse 20 refers to the imminent situation of Jesus' death and to the absence of Jesus which his death would cause. The death of Jesus also affects the situation of the disciples, since the latter is

153

characterized precisely by his absence from them. The community is left in the world without any visible support from Jesus, and is subjected to temptation, to sadness and lament, to distress and bewilderment (cf. 16:4b-6). John sees the disciples at Jesus' death and the community now as being in the same situation. It is a situation which the community must always take into account and with which it must come to grips ever anew.

Especially will the community encounter the striking phenomenon of the unbelieving world's joy: "But the world will rejoice" because it believes it has overcome and finally rid itself of the disturbing revealer of God. The world feels superior to faith; from its lofty position it smiles pityingly at faith and equates it more or less with stupidity or a lack of enlightenment. Believers must take this into account and try to prepare for it.

In the last analysis, however, the important thing is that the believer is not left to face this attack alone. Instead, there is the promise that could not have been anticipated: "Your sorrow will be changed to joy" (cf. 20:20: "Then the disciples rejoiced when they saw the Lord"). Temptation, distress, and sadness are certainly a real part of the believer's existence in the world, and these must always be taken into account. But within this very situation the believer has the promise that sorrow will be changed to joy.

The comparison between the situation of the disciples (v. 21) and that of a woman in labor who feels sorrow or, more accurately, pain before the birth of the child, but after the birth rejoices over the newborn child, is drawn from a universal human experience. In this case, however, it may have a special meaning. For John, the cross and resurrection of Christ are the saving action of the Messiah and therefore represent the turning point of the ages. Judaism, moreover, speaks of the messianic birthpangs when referring to the time of distress just before the end. According to a saying of Rabbi Issac (A.D. 300),

> in the year in which the King, the Messiah, will manifest himself, all the kings of the earth's peoples will rise up (for battle) against one another. . . . And all the nations of the world are perplexed and bewildered; they fall on their faces, and *labor pains as of a woman giving birth come upon them.* The Israelites, too, become perplexed and bewil-

154

dered, and say, "Where shall we go? Where shall we come?" Then God will say to them, "My children, fear not. All that I have done I have done solely for your sake. Why are you afraid? Fear not: the time of your redemption is here."[118] In this rabbinic passage the Israelites are addressed and consoled in the same way as the disciples in John. It may be, then, that John is taking over the idea of the messianic birthpangs, but at the same time giving it a christological interpretation: The time of sorrow and perplexity is now related to the passion and cross of Jesus, while the eschatological joy begins on Easter. So too the present time is a time of sorrow for the disciples (v. 22); their experience of the world is interpreted by reference to the passion of Christ.

But then comes the promise: "But I will see you again, and your hearts will rejoice, and your joy no one will take from you." The thing that immediately strikes us here is that Jesus himself is the one who sees again, whereas in verse 16 it was the disciples who do the seeing. The problem connected with the imminent expectation and with seeing Jesus once again is one that in John's view cannot be answered in terms of the disciples but only in terms of Jesus. Time and hour are here entirely in Jesus' power, as they are not in the synoptic gospels. Jesus comes when he wishes; he lets himself be seen when he wishes; he determines the time and manner of his presence, his appearing. When it comes to the parousia, the community once again has no power over Jesus. The fact that John links parousia and Easter changes nothing basic in this state of affairs, for it is precisely the manifestation of the risen Lord that is subject to the sovereign freedom and divine initiative of Jesus. Nonetheless the community is promised that it will see Jesus again.

Jesus will not abandon his disciples; he will see them again. This seeing again is accompanied by their experience of perfect joy which no power in the world can terminate. For the heart to rejoice means that the entire person experiences a joy springing from the innermost ground of being. And the fact that this joy cannot be taken away shows that it is unending, eternal, eschatological joy. In it all perplexity and temptation and confusion are a thing of the past. The text is here telling us what the return of Jesus will mean for the community. According to John this experience of the return of Jesus has been available since Easter. In his comprehensive vision Easter,

Pentecost, and the parousia form an interlocking unity; they are various moments or aspects of the appearing and return of Jesus to his disciples.

According to R. Bultmann the evangelist "has used the primitive Christian ideas and hopes to describe the stages through which the life of the believer has to pass, and on which it can also come to grief." [119] This is not an incorrect interpretation, but it does have to be modified a bit. John first had to face a problem that was agitating him and his community, the problem of the delay of the parousia. He thought the problem through with his christology as his starting point. In his view the cross and resurrection represent the turning point of the ages, and consequently even the messianic birthpangs receive a new interpretation. The disciples are already living in the time of eschatological distress, and the latter becomes a structural element of faith in the world. But in their faith in the risen Lord, in the kerygma, in their hope and joy they also experience the liberating, redeeming return of Jesus; as an ever new coming of the exalted Lord to the community, this return shapes the community's present existence.

Meditation

The problem addressed in the concepts of imminent expectation and delay of the parousia received hardly any attention in the Catholic theology of an earlier day. It was modern exegesis that taught us to see the problem and reflect on it seriously.[120] The chief hindrance at that earlier time was the dogmatic interpretation of Jesus' knowledge as being a participation in the divine omniscience itself. Given this dogmatic postulate, it was a course impossible to permit a development in the consciousness of the earthly Jesus or to claim that Jesus fell into any error. It was felt that if he were mistaken on even a single occasion, the credibility of the entire New Testament revelation of God would collapse. Even in the present century renowned theologians, K. Rahner among them, have struggled to give a speculative response to the problem with the aid of extremely complicated interpretations of the knowledge of Jesus.

Among the exegetes, meanwhile, it has been taken as a starting point, on the basis of certain texts, that Jesus expected and preached the proximate coming of God's reign. Now that the saying attributed to Jesus in Mark 9:1, "Amen, I tell you, some of those standing here will not die before they have seen the kingdom of God coming in all its power," has been accepted by many contemporary exegetes as an authentic saying of Jesus, the conclusion is also widely accepted that the earthly Jesus was in error about the imminent coming of the kingdom of God. That is what the modern reader at least will conclude.

The same thing holds for the post-Easter community. As Paul clearly did (cf. 1 Thess. 4:13-18; 1 Cor. 15), it expected the proximate return of Christ, the parousia of Jesus as the heavenly Son of man. Thus the community too was in error here. A critical confrontation with the problem of the delay of the parousia is already perceptible in the New Testament writings. In a sense, the evangelists Matthew, Luke, and John all thought of their gospels as being also (not *only*, of course!) a response to this question. The fixing in writing of the tradition about Jesus is already a sign that people had begun to turn from a short term to a long term expectation. This means that they recognized their mistake in expecting a proximate coming, and did what people usually do when they have made a mistake: they correct it openly or tacitly. That is precisely what the evangelists did. It follows that while they fully acknowledged the divine authority of Jesus they did not interpret it with the dogmatic inflexibility that would characterize later ages. The error of Jesus in no way detracted from his divine authority. This also means that this error on the part of Jesus and the primitive community was not regarded as a problem or an objection in principle against the message of Christ.

In this context, it was a help that neither in the message of Jesus nor in the post-Easter kerygma of the community was the imminent expectation given a specific date. No date was established that the community would have been obliged to accept. This fact prevented additional difficulties. It is typical, moreover, that the problem of the imminent expectation later on led to insoluble difficulties chiefly when an effort was made to turn christology into a theological system free of all contradictions. In reality, the imminent expectation is a sign that the eschatological future is radically open and not at our disposal. It is also a sign of the truly historical character of the Christian proclamation.

A further point is that the community was increasingly conscious of its dependence on *the fact that Jesus had already come.* This gave it firm ground to stand on and kept it from being any longer focused exclusively on the future. Or, to put it differently, as the expectation of Christ's return indicates, even the future reign of God showed the features of the Son of man, Jesus of Nazareth. Attention was now given mainly to the coming of *Christ*, and we have seen that John understands this coming as a coming through the Spirit, in the word, in the liturgy of the community, and so on. It is this coming that gives vitality to the community.

There is another point of view we may mention. Since Nietzsche people have talked of the death of God or said that we live in an age in which God is absent. For a while a death of God theology was even proclaimed; it seems now to have subsided somewhat, although there has been no careful evaluation of its basic concern. It is worth noting, in this connection, that there has never been any mention of the problem of the absence of Jesus as articulated by John, although the problem is a very important one for the community and for faith generally. The absence of God and the absence of Jesus are situated on the same line, while over against them is the experience of a presence of Jesus that is also the signal for a new presence of God. If it is true that the proclamation of the Gospel in its complete fullness can communicate the experience of the presence of Jesus, then this is something that should be regarded as of the greatest importance.

The appearing or return of Jesus is never a speculative demonstration of faith; it is not to be confused with a vision. When it occurs, it always comes on doves' wings, as it were. It remains hidden in the form of the word, the Spirit, the sacraments, the loving commitment of human beings to one another. Consequently, temptation and bewilderment are part of the experience of faith, since faith is the vital movement of a historical person. Consequently, too, the promises still hold: "Your sorrow will be changed to joy" and "your joy no one will take from you." We have a whole series of testimonies, for example, from the resistance movement against Nazism, during which people faced with extreme affliction and distress attested, just before their executions, how filled they were with the joy of the Lord.

One of the finest meditations on 16:16-22 was written by the poet Annette von Droste-Hülshoff for the "Third Sunday after Easter" in her cycle *The Church Year*. In it she describes the modern experience of God's absence and the experience of his gracious return.[121] The final two stanzas of the poem read as follows:

> On the mountain height
> stood a prophet and sought you as I do:
> a mighty wind shattered the branches of the giant spruce,
> a fire ate through the tree-tops;
> but the stranger in the wilderness stood there unshaken.
> Then there blew
> a soft breeze of grace, and trembling, overwhelmed,
> the prophet sank to his knees
> and wept aloud and found you.
> Your gentle breeze
> told me what was hidden in the wind
> and what was not unriddled by the lightning flash.
> Therefore will I presevere. Ah, the wood of my coffin
>   is already growing,
> the rain is falling on the spot where I shall sleep!
> Then, like smoke,
> shall the cloudy plans of empty wisdom disappear,
> then I too shall see,
> and my joy no one shall take from me.

The Clarity of the Day of the Lord
(16:23–28)

This passage has four parts which describe the eschatological condition of believers, once Christ comes back: (a) verse 23a: all questioning will end; (b) verses 23b-24: assurance that prayer in the name of Jesus will be heard; (c) verses 25-27: the clarity of life as a believer; (d) verse 28: a concluding doctrinal statement as "the background against which the discourses and conversations are to be seen."[122]

Verse 23a. This verse says: "on that day," that is, the day of Jesus' return, all the disciples' questioning will cease. "That day" is an apocalyptic idiom (cf. the *Dies irae, dies illa*—"That day, the day of wrath"—in the old sequence for requiem Masses). The phrase originates in the Old Testament and signifies originally the day of Yahweh and later the day of final judgment.[123] The New Testament tradition connects the idea of the last judgment with the expectation of Christ's coming, although the hope of the final resurrection and the consummation of the world by Christ's coming in glory pushes the thought of God's chastisement into the background. The New Testament stress was not always to be maintained later on, and increasing emphasis came to be placed on the final judgment as compared with the hope of the definitive coming of God's reign and thus of salvation for the entire world. In the early Christian view, then, that day is the day of our Lord Jesus Christ.[124]

John is familiar with the traditional expression, but for him that day is the day of the return of Christ that begins with Easter and Pentecost. He has thus *demythologized* traditional eschatology, although admittedly he sees, more or less distinctly, only some of the consequences of this move, consequences which in their root are already present in Jesus' message of the imminence of God's reign and in Paul as well. Because of the new post-Easter way in which Jesus is present in the Spirit and in the community, that day is already present for believers. When the evangelist, in keeping with the literary fiction he has adopted, speaks in the future tense, "You will have no more questions to ask me," he is referring in fact to what is already true for believers now.

What is he talking about? The statement (v. 23a) is linked to the final words of verse 22: "And your joy no one will take from you." In verse 22 the subject was the eschatological joy which is promised to believers and has already been given. Because of this joy, which is the essence of eschatological happiness, all questioning is at an end; it is as it were swallowed up in joy. "That, however, is *the eschatological situation:* to have no more questions! In faith, existence has received its unequivocal explanation, because it is no longer explained in terms of the world, and is therefore no longer a puzzle."[125]

Until now the disciples always had questions to ask of Jesus (cf.

14:5, 8, 22; 16:17-18); there were questions and misunderstandings. This indicates that in John the questions and misunderstandings are meant to point to an essential frontier, the frontier that distinguishes and separates the world, the cosmos, and therefore worldly thinking and acting, from the revealer of God and his words. In this sense, questioning is the mark of a person whose orientation is worldly; it is a sign that he is being tossed to and fro in his quest of his true happiness. When the questioning stops, it is a sign that the person has entered the realm of divine perfect truth and perfect joy.

What realm is this? It is the dimension of divine love, of which Jesus came as witness, revealer, and mediator. This love has been manifested in Jesus and especially in his death. With his death the turning point of the ages has come; since then the eschaton has been present in the world. The return of Jesus is constantly taking place whenever people open themselves in faith to the word of Jesus and let that word determine their lives. Then they should also have the experience that in the presence of faith a certain kind of questioning ceases. The well-known words of Augustine make this same point: "You yourself incite him to find delight in praising you, for you made us for yourself, and our heart is restless until it finds its rest in you (*inquietum est cor nostrum, donec requiescat in te*)" (*Confessions* I, 1, 1).

Verses 23b-24. Once again the subject is prayer in the name of Jesus (cf. 14:13-14 and the commentary on these verses). Here, too, assurance is given that such prayer will be heard. If the disciples ask the Father for anything "in the name of Jesus," he will certainly give it to them. With the words "until now you have not asked for anything in my name," the prayer of the disciples and therefore in principle all Christian prayer is integrated into the new eschatological situation. As the subsequent final prayer of Jesus (chap. 17) will confirm, Christian prayer participates as it were in Jesus' own relationship to God and therefore in the acknowledgment of Jesus by the Father. In saying this we are not referring primarily to the psychological or even the real effects of prayer but to *the very structure of the Christian relation to God as this finds expression in prayer*. According to John the permanent role of Jesus as revealer and mediator finds expression even in prayer.

The statements in John on prayer look to a dimension of prayer in which the emphasis is no longer on special particular things, objects, or wishes and in which petition cannot therefore be in any way interpreted as a magical conjuration of the divinity but rather becomes a participation in the divine conversation that goes on between Jesus, the Son of God, and his Father. It is a dimension, therefore, in which a completely disinterested speaking to God becomes as such the meaning and content of all prayer. Then communion with God is itself the content of prayer, or, to put it another way, prayer becomes the action in which human communion with God becomes definitively real. When this happens, the question of what effect prayer has is utterly out of place. For here again what we really have is perfect joy, eschatological happiness. The disciples who ask in this situation will receive; it is not at all important what concretely they receive. The important thing is the fact of being heard; the important thing is God's answer, "I am here," which the person praying experiences in the form of joy.

Verses 25-27. The thing that the day of eschatological joy, that is, the day of Jesus' return, brings and already discloses to the disciples is the full clarity of existence in the light of faith and, with this clarity, the immediate relationship of the disciples to God.

What is meant by the clarity in question is suggested by the contrast between a speaking in enigmatic images (Greek: *paroimia*)[126] and a speaking openly, directly, and without concealment (Greek: *parrhēsia*).[127] Until now Jesus has spoken to the disciples in images. The Greek word *paroimia* originally means a rhetorical figure, namely the striking proverb that sheds light by means of a concrete example. "It states an experienced truth of popular wisdom in short and pointed form."[128] The parabolic discourses of John's gospel, on the contrary, are obscure and difficult for the hearers to understand. They even give rise to misunderstandings, some of which we have already met. Thus in 10:6 the introduction to the parabolic discourse on the good shepherd or the door is described as this kind of parabolic discourse that conceals its meaning: "Jesus spoke this figured discourse (*paroimia*) to them, but they did not understand what he was trying to tell them."

Now in 16:25 everything that Jesus had said during his earthly life is described as having been obscure and enigmatic. The evangelist is evidently referring to the revelatory discourses of Jesus in general and is therefore offering a comprehensive evaluation of the historical Jesus as he saw him. This overall evaluation has yielded a principle for the literary and technical construction of John's gospel. His book, after all, is largely a collection of parabolic discourses which are deciphered by means of misunderstandings and Jesus' replies to them. According to John, moreover, it is only faith and the action of the Spirit that can produce a true understanding of these discourses. "It is the spirit that gives life; the flesh avails nothing; the words I have spoken to you are spirit and life" (6:63).

It has been pointed out, and rightly, that the obscure parabolic discourses of John are not out to be confused or compared with the synoptic parables. The synoptic parables have a different literary form and a very different didactic function. They usually refer to a concrete situation that is deliberately entered into and may be deliberately changed. The Johannine discourse, on the other hand, undoubtedly has a dualistic element that reminds us rather of Platonic thinking. Thus, for example, the terms bread, water, life, and shepherd admit of various interpretations; they can be used as symbolic words and therefore, in their context in John, can point to a bread of life, a living water, a true light, a good shepherd. The evangelist makes deliberate use of the ambiguity of individual words or whole sentences.

The misunderstandings reflect the realm of the world and unbelief. In the last analysis, the failure of the Jews to understand what Jesus is saying is not, according to John, a sign of defective intelligence but of unbelief or a lack of readiness to believe. The obscurity of the discourse is geared to a human existence that is unenlightened and is dominated by the world and its standards. Conversely, faith grasps the true meaning of the figures because, being eschatological existence, it is geared to the understanding of the eschatological truth that revelation brings.

In the hour of Jesus' glorification and return there will be no more parabolic discourses; they will be replaced by straightforward talk about the Father. The concept of *parrhēsia*, which means candidness, frankness, and "enthusiasm" (Luther's translation of the word), especially in connection with speech, has a number of aspects.[129]

Originally it designated the right of free speech at the civic gatherings in the cities of antiquity, a right which only the free native citizen possessed. The concept was a political one. In the Acts of the Apostles *parrhēsia* describes the frankness of the apostles as they fearlessly preached the message of Jesus Christ to a Jewish or pagan audience or to the authorities.[130]

In John, too, the term has in view, for the most part, the public character of Jesus' activity, but it also refers to the manner in which Jesus speaks before the world, that is, without reservation, candidly, openly, and, at times, in a way that gives scandal.[131] Consequently, when he is interrogated before Annas, the high priest, he can say, "I have spoken candidly and openly before the world. I have always taught in the synagogues and in the temple where all the Jews gather, and I have said nothing in secret. Why do you question me, then? Question those who heard what I said to them! They know what I said" (18:20-21). According to this claim Jesus had always spoken openly. A look through the gospel also tells us that in speaking to his Jewish audiences Jesus does not pass over in silence anything essential which he tells his disciples only later on or communicates to them as a kind of esoteric teaching.

As a result, the eschatological hour when Jesus speaks openly and candidly about the Father cannot bring anything materially new, for he has always spoken about the Father. This makes it quite clear that the point here is not the intellectual grasp of what Jesus says. Rather, it is precisely this that the disciples must realize, namely that the commitment of one's whole existence is required to understand these words.[132] Only the commitment of faith makes understanding possible.

But we must go a step further. John indicates a temporal succession between speaking in obscure images and plain speaking, with the hour or that day as the point of transition. The hour, here again, is the hour of the exaltation and glorification of Jesus that makes possible the new eschatological saving presence of Jesus. As a quick examination of the entire gospel shows, veiled and plain speaking are always interconnected, so that in fact no real temporal distinction can be made. This means that the real dividing line is something objective. The two types of speaking are in fact juxtaposed or coexistent. The discourses of Jesus become clear and plain only and

164

always in the crossover of faith; the clarity is not a fixed possession but must be derived ever anew from the obscure speech. Only at the return of Jesus is such clarity to be gained, and this over and over, but each time only for the moment, as it were. Consequently, the contrast between obscure speech and plain speech is something with which the faith that exists in the world must constantly come to grips.

The promised *parrhēsia*, the enthusiasm and frankness, also points to something further, namely the candid unreserved and matter-of-course dealing of the disciples with the Father. In the eschatological hour of that day the disciples will indeed continue to ask the Father in the name of Jesus, but they will no longer need the helpful intercession of Jesus himself! The reason given for this assertion is, "For the Father loves you because you have loved me and have believed that I have come from the Father" (v. 27). Here again we have the idea of divine love as the innermost core of the Johannine understanding of revelation. Because the disciples are united with Jesus through faith, they, just like Jesus, become the objects of God's love. And when Jesus says that they no longer need him as intercessor and mediator with the Father, he is telling them that faith, as a bond uniting them with the person of Jesus, by no means leaves them in the subordinate position of minors but rather places them in a position of equality with Jesus and gives them the same immediate relation to God that Jesus has.

John is here making his own an idea that finds varied expression in the New Testament. Jesus' manner of addressing God as "Father" (*Abba*) evidently helped the early Church to conceive its own religious condition as one of authentic emancipation, in contrast to Judaism and especially to paganism. Paul says, for example, "For you are all children of God through faith in Christ Jesus. For all of you who were baptized into Christ have put on Christ. No longer is there Jew or Greek, slave or free, male or female, for you are all one being in Christ Jesus" (Gal. 3:26-28). And again, "But that you are children (you know because) God has sent the Spirit of his Son into our hearts, and he cries out (within us), 'Abba, Father!' So through God you are no longer a slave but a son, and if a son, then also an heir" (Gal. 4:6-7; cf. also Rom. 8:15; Heb. 2:10). The Letter to the Ephesians also speaks of free access to God: "Through him

165

(the crucified and glorified Christ) both of us have access to the Father in one Spirit. Therefore you are no longer strangers and aliens, but fellow citizens of the saints who have the right of domicile in God's house" (Eph. 2:18-19).

In this last text the political aspect emerges clearly: Christians are citizens of the new eschatological city of God or members of God's household, with assured rights of domicile there. The message of Jesus about God as Father opened the way for a new experience of God that was characterized chiefly by a new relationship of trusting love to God. People now understood themselves to be the new family of God, the *familia Dei,* or the "household" (*oikos*) of God, where household had its ancient implications of a comprehensive communion of life. The clearest indication of this outlook is that the members of the Christian community addressed one another as brother or sister. The fraternal aspect of primitive Christianity is an eschatological phenomenon; it is unthinkable without the idea of the fatherhood of God.

This fraternal spirit is not a manifestation of fanatical zeal, but represents a self-understanding derived from the tradition regarding Jesus. In this context, Jesus himself was understood to be "the firstborn of many brothers" (Rom. 8:29). Mary Magdalene receives this commission from the risen Jesus, *"Go to my brothers* and tell them, 'I am ascending to my Father and your Father, to my God and your God' "* (John 20:17). This last text is all the more significant since John at the same time makes a distinction between Jesus and the disciples. When, therefore, as in this text, the disciples are called brothers of Jesus, it is a sign that, in the fourth gospel too, the relationship to God which has been established by Jesus includes a new fraternal bond between Jesus and his disciples, whatever be the distinctions required at this point. Jesus, the Son of God, belongs therefore among the many brothers and sons, sisters and daughters, or children of God.[133]

Verse 28. The final verse of this section sums up the Johannine theology of revelation in a concise sentence that sounds like a doctrinal statement; it resembles a kind of short formula of the faith. Jesus of Nazareth is the revealer of God; he appeared in the world for a short time in order to bring people the truth about God, and then, when his saving work had been completed, he returned to the Father. Using the language of myth, the formula includes the entire coming of Jesus: that is, according to the gospel of John, the incarnation of the revealer, the "becoming flesh of the divine Word" (1:14), and his earthly activity as well as his passion and resurrection (glorification), are all a totality, a single way. In verse 28 only the two ends of the chain are mentioned. The "coming from the Father" and the "return to the Father" give the divine background against which the activity of Jesus in the world is to be understood theologically.

As revelation this activity is a single comprehensive witness to the Father, and the Father is present by way of the testimony of Jesus. The fact that Jesus again leaves this world does not in any way rescind his revelation of God. As an eschatological saving event the activity of Jesus remains permanently valid.

By its permanent commitment to the word, work, and person of Jesus and, through him, to God the Father, the community attests that though it lives in the midst of the world and history, the ground of its existence is not to be found in this world but solely in the God whom Jesus has revealed.

Meditation

Is it possible to be a human being and have no more questions to ask? If we were to cease asking questions, would we not in fact have come to an end as human beings: either the end which is resignation, a state in which we no longer expect anything at all, and certainly not any answers, no matter from where they come, or else the end which is total fulfillment, in which utter clarity would solve the enigma of existence and answer all questions? In fact, it is of the very nature of human beings to be able to ask questions, and this in regard to everything that is. Question-and-answer is the pattern of all our dealings with reality.[134] We are not talking here, of course, about the countless individual questions we can ask but about the one radical question we do ask regarding ourselves: the question regarding the very meaning of our existence. From the theologian's point of view, this question already contains also our question regarding God. What we are talking of here is Augustine's "I became a question to myself" (*quaestio mihi factus sum*).

This questionableness of people is so radical that it cannot be escaped or dismissed at will or overhastily answered. The question is rather one that a person must live, in a literal sense. It can, of course, be suppressed for a while; it can be drowned by counterfeit certainty. But it breaks through again from time to time. Hardly anyone has formulated the questionableness of humanity with the pitiless clarity of Blaise Pascal (1623-1662):

> What a monster then man is! What a novelty, what a portent, what a chaos, what a contradiction, what a prodigy! Universal judge and helpless worm; trustee of truth, and sink of uncertainty and error; glory and off-scouring of the universe.

> Who will unravel this tangle? I cannot be a sceptic unless I smother nature; I cannot be a dogmatist without renouncing reason. Nature refutes the sceptics, and reason refutes the dogmatists. What will you do then, ye who seek to discover your true condition by the light of your natural reason? You cannot avoid one or other of these two sects, nor abide in either.

> Know then, proud man, your own paradox. Down, helpless reason! Silence, futile nature! Learn that man is infinitely beyond the reach of man, and hear from your Master what is your true condition, so far unknown to you. Hearken to God. [135]

It is faith in God and in his revealer, Jesus Christ, that will put an end to the radical question humans ask themselves, and give them peace. That is what the text is saying: "On that day you will have no more questions to ask of me."

This kind of assertion stirs suspicions that it is a vast oversimplification, an illusory consolation; that it cannot really help people and will even keep them from seeking real help. In Karl Marx's view, for example:

> *Religious* suffering is the *expression* of real suffering and at the same time the *protest* against real suffering. Religion is the sigh of the oppressed creature, the heart of a heartless

world, as it is the spirit of spiritless conditions. It is the opium of the people.

The abolition of religion as people's *illusory* happiness is the demand for their *real* happiness. The demand to abandon illusions about their conditions is a *demand to abandon a condition which requires illusions.* The criticism of religion is thus in *embryo* a *criticism of the vale of tears* whose halo is religion. [136]

According to Marx, religion is an "ideological superstructure" and therefore a form of "false consciousness"; it is an "illusory happiness," a "halo on the vale of tears." "And indeed religion is the self-consciousness and self-regard of man who has either not yet found or has already lost himself." [137] In response we may point out that Marxism has rightly brought to light and criticized pseudoreligious modes of behavior. People who are starving and living in unjust and asocial conditions ought not to be mollified by spurious religious consolations or put off with alms; their fellows must help them, even if this requires structural changes in society. But, when all such changes have been made, people's questioning about themselves and the meaning of their existence will begin again, for human needs include more than mundane needs.

We have also been forced to learn, since Marx's day, that the question of meaning does not arise solely or primarily in an abstract, purely theoretical, philosophical or theological form, but is embedded in a context created by human existence as a historical being. The question of meaning is directly connected with our situation as a member of society, but conversely the social situation has a depth-dimension. Many Christians and theologians see more clearly today than formerly that questions of faith and questions of life are inseparable, even if the connections cannot be reduced to a neat and simple formula.

If we are to urge John's statement in a credible fashion, we must endeavor to hear the various questions people ask about life, and this in all areas of human existence. Even the political dimension must not be excluded. Once these conditions have been met, we must listen to John's answer without trying to lessen its force in any way. His answer is that when we radically trust in the God of love,

we are liberated from our impatient, hopeless questioning; our restless, futile questions about ourselves cease, in the manner indicated
in Psalm 131:

> LORD, my heart is not proud,
> my eyes are not raised in arrogance.
> I do not busy myself with things
> too marvelous and lofty for me.
>
> I let my soul grow calm and quiet;
> like a child near its mother,
> my soul is quiet within me.
>
> Israel, hope in the LORD
> from now on and for ever.

Such tranquillity is due to the fact that faith has its own proper kind
of certainty because of the divine foundation on which faith rests.
The peculiarity of biblical faith is that *it is ultimate certainty based
on God himself.* This certainty may be accompanied by a feeling of
security, but it need not be. Just as the depths of the sea are calm
and still, so in the experience of God human questioning is
superseded. But—to anticipate an obvious misunderstanding—this
does not mean that ever new questions will not arise at countless
other levels, and precisely in connection with faith. Here we have
the other side of faith, and it too is considered in the gospel of John.
For faith must persevere in its situation as faith existing in the
world; it cannot withdraw from this situation; it may not become an
acosmic faith or pure interiority. Consequently, faith is unques-
tioning certainty on the basis of its divine ground, but it is at the
same time questionable and is in fact called into question because
it is faith existing in the world. To that extent, faith itself constantly
raises new questions.

Similarly, our experiences of life and the world raise new questions for faith, because these experiences are constantly changing.
Faith should not evade such questions. In the past, the refusal to
ask questions in matters of faith was even regarded as a virtue. For
a person to ask questions and manifest doubts was taken as a sign
of imperfect faith. This mentality has by no means disappeared even
today; in many circles within the Church we can frequently encounter an anxious fear with regard to questioning. But where this

happens, whatever be the reasons and motives, the emphasis is being put in the wrong place. There is a failure to distinguish the two sides of faith: its security in God, where questioning is unnecessary because this God is accepted and experienced as the truth and love that sustains all of reality; and its existence in the world, of which questioning, temptation, doubt, continued reflection, and continued seeking are a necessary part, as is the questioning of traditional forms, dogmas, rites, and so on.

It seems to be inherent in the situation of faith that it must frankly and honestly accept and come to grips with all the questions that arise with regard to it. What John says here can give us the courage to do so. Whenever faith endeavors to attain its full flowering as radical trust in the God and Father of our Lord Jesus Christ, it relies on the groundless ground of truth and love. In so doing, faith secures its lines of retreat, as it were, and is able to address itself unhesitatingly to the problems that crowd in upon it. This kind of ultimate certainty even encourages faith to ask its questions with confidence.

According to a profound Old Testament image praying is seeking the face of God:

> Hear, O LORD, my loud cry;
> be gracious to me and hear me!
> My heart ponders your words, "Seek my face!"
> Yes, LORD, I want to seek your face.
> Hide not your face from me;
> do not in anger turn your servant away!
> You became my help:
> do not reject me, do not abandon me,
> God, my savior!
> Even though father and mother abandon me,
> the LORD receives me. (Ps. 27:7-10)

What a person aims to do in prayer is to be situated in the presence of God or face to face with God. More so today perhaps than ever before, success in this effort requires practice, and especially recollection and quiet. If we are to pray we must set aside time for it. We must withdraw from the multifarious activities, demands, and distractions of daily life, turn our attention to ourselves, and muster the courage to be alone. In Pascal's opinion "man's unhappiness arises from one thing only, namely that he cannot abide quietly in one room."[138] We must learn to let the voice of our own soul be heard, and we should not run away from ourselves even if the voice tells us only of our own wretchedness. The important thing in praying is not the number of words we speak:

> And when you pray, be not like the hypocrites who like to stand and pray in the synagogues and on the street corners so that men may see them. In truth, I tell, they have already received their reward. As for you, when you pray, go into your room and close the door and pray there in secret to your Father, and your Father who sees what is hidden will reward you. But when you pray, do not speak a great deal, as the pagans do; they think that if they say a great deal they will be heard. Do not be like them, for your Father already knows what you need, even before you ask him for it. (Matt. 6:5-8)

Quiet prayer does not mean that we turn away from the world and the affairs of life. On the contrary, to pray is to bring the whole of life into the conversation with God and in God's presence. Goethe's short prayer in his *West-östlicher Divan* is a good example of this: "I go astray and am perplexed, / But you can set me straight. / Whether I act or write my verses, / Give me guidance for the way."

The Johannine statements on the contrast between veiled parabolic discourse and clear, plain speech might well be taken as an occasion for discussing the problem of religious language. The gospel of John, in fact, offers a good entry into the problem. It may be taken as true of religious language that it is always marked by the swing back and forth between obscurity and clarity. It prefers images with several meanings; it likes analogy and metaphor, nor may paradox be overlooked. We shall not inquire further here why this should be so. The important thing is for the reader to be stimulated by the images to reflection and meditation, and to follow their trail and see where they lead . . . .

There is another point to be emphasized in connection with the *parrhēsia*, the frankness and directness of the disciple of Jesus in dealing with God. John's view is that the revelation brought by Jesus confers on people an adult status in God's eyes and that this adulthood has a liberating emancipatory effect on our thinking and acting or on our entire existence. The statement that Jesus intends to speak of the Father frankly and openly, and no longer in images, corresponds to a verse of Scripture cited earlier, in 6:45: "It is written in the prophets, 'You will be taught by God' " (cf. Isa. 54:13: "All your sons will be disciples of the LORD, and profound peace will reign among them"). Reference should also be made to Jeremiah and the well-known passage on the new covenant:

> For this will be the covenant that I shall make with the house of Israel after these days—this is the word of the LORD. I will place my law within them and write it on their hearts. I will be their God, and they shall be my people. No one shall any longer teach the others, and they shall no longer say to one another, "Know the LORD!" but all of them, small and great, shall know me—this is the word of the LORD. For I will forgive their wrongdoing, and will remember their sin no more. (31:31-34)

The idea expressed in these texts is that in the last times, because of the utter clarity of the eschatological revelation of God, there will be no need of any teaching, written or oral, for all will receive true teaching directly from God. According to the passage in Jeremiah, this teaching will be communicated by God putting the law (the Torah) within each person, so there will no longer be need of any teaching from outside. According to John, it is the words of the revelation of Jesus that make us disciples of God. Or it is the Holy Spirit who communicates the divine teaching to us, for he is the interior teacher who not only addresses our understanding but also instructs our hearts. It may be worth our while to delve further into this conception. It seems to be based on the experience that instruction of one person by another, however necessary or indispensable, is nonetheless a kind of stopgap measure, because it also creates dependencies. The adult especially no longer likes to be instructed but feels that it is incongruous, especially if certain overtones creep into the relationship.

This view, which is also to be seen in Paul and Matthew, is that *due to the knowledge faith gives a radical equality exists among Christians* and that since the Spirit instructs all there is no need to divide the Church into a teaching Church and a learning Church. Only at a later time did the opinion become prevalent that the share in the possession of the Spirit must be differentiated, as it were, and a greater measure allotted to the teaching office of pope and bishops than to the rest of those making up the Church. It makes a vast difference, in fact, whether the entire Church, along with pope and bishops, regards itself as a community of people who are basically free and equal, and all equally disciples of God, or whether we are dealing from the outset with a two-class Church.

In the former view, the teaching office will be understood rather in terms of a division of labor, as providing a function and a service that are required even in the Church since the learners are a very large group. Besides, as far as revelation and the understanding of it are concerned, even the magisterium does not guarantee a superior truth. Teaching is in the service of the proclamation of the word, and its presupposition is that the Spirit of God and not, for example, the pope, is the real teacher of faith to the entire community and therefore at least to every Christian who is mature.

In the second of the two views, the teaching office would be regarded (and unfortunately it is still often so regarded) as an institution endowed with power and special privileges concerning the truth, an institution which seeks to keep the faithful in a structural position of subordination and immaturity that is supposedly based on God's will. Here the teaching office creates a dependence of the people of the Church on the official Church; no dialogue among partners is to be found in this view. It is taken for granted from the outset that the representatives of the official Church are more correct, not because they convincingly prove their position but simply because they represent the official Church.

St. Augustine (A.D. 354-430), a father of the Church, and bishop of Hippo, a community of about five thousand people, was still aware, as bishop and preacher, of this problem of Christian instruction. He asked how it is possible in fact for one person to teach another at all. And he took the very interesting position that in the last analysis no human being can teach another anything, *unless the truth itself*, that is, the learner's own insights and capabilities, instruct him. Even in matters of faith, only the divine Spirit can instruct us interiorly in our understanding and heart. External instruction, especially through the medium of the word, is an indispensable help, but should not be made an end in itself. When it

174

does become an end in itself, it fails its real purpose, which is to make the learner active so that maturity and independence may be attained. The ideal, then, is that the teacher should be rendered more or less superfluous; the goal of Christian instruction is the mature Christian with the full right to have his or her say in the community. This, of course, is directly contrary to the two-class Church which has turned a structure based on a division of labor and on historical development (namely the duality of official Church and people) into a datum of divine law with a metaphysical status.

To put the matter another way: even the representatives of the teaching office need to be taught: by God, by the Gospel, by all the members of the Church. In reality, there is no independent teaching office that can dispense with dialogue, except at the cost of almost complete ineffectiveness. In our world today this is becoming daily more evident. We see on every side that the unilateral interpretation of the teaching office as being represented solely by the official Church does not do justice to contemporary fact. This is so if for no other reason than that the traditional teaching of the Church has largely gotten sidetracked, to the profit of modern theology with its scientific methods for determining truth and of the entire development of the sciences generally and of society.

In order precisely to carry out their proper function as representatives of the magisterium, the members of the official Church need a continuing dialogue with the people. The people or laity, moreover, have long since ceased to be the simple flock of earlier times. They are the authentic, qualified *professionals in modernity* who in virtue of their competence and abilities may rightly expect to be taken seriously as equals even in the Church. The same holds for the equality of women in the Church. In this regard, too, the two-class Church is outdated as a model for thinking about the Church.

In the monastic Rule of St. Benedict, the father of western monasticism, there occurs the regulation that the abbot in chapter is to hear what all the monks have to say, "since the Lord often reveals to someone younger what is best" (*quia saepe juniori Domines revelat quod melius est*) (ch. 3). In his monastic constitutions Benedict made full room for the immediate relationship of each monk with God, and this relationship was given a chance to operate. It is fitting that we call to mind this ancient bit of monastic wisdom.

175

Conclusion of the
Second Farewell Discourse (16:29–33)

This passage, 16:29-33, brings the second farewell discourse to a close; it also includes a transition to the passion narrative (vv. 32-33). Whether it was the evangelist or a later editor who introduced these final two verses here, there is no denying that from a material viewpoint they fit in very well. This factual appropriateness makes the questions of literary criticism that have often been given pride of place seem quite secondary.

Exegesis

Verses 29-30 give the answer of the disciples to Jesus' words about the clarity and plainness of his discourse. The disciples say, "See, now you are speaking plainly and using figures no longer." The response is suggested by the context. Jesus' statement that the disciples will not put any more questions to him and, strictly speaking, will not even be able to ask questions because Jesus is going away for good, is beginning to be fulfilled in the disciples. The actual beginning of the eschatological day is thus indicated at the level of the text itself.

On the other hand, this beginning is also connected with the imminent passion and glorification of Jesus. For, as is made clear over and over, the real point of the farewell discourses was and is to bring the disciples, and with them all subsequent generations, to this threshold of the understanding of Jesus. Now the actual upshot of the endeavor is this: the understanding of Jesus, according to John, depends essentially on the saving event of his cross and resurrection, on his exaltation and glorification. Consequently, in the cross and resurrection the goal of the farewell discourses and indeed of the entire preceding revelation-in-words is reached. For the disciples this means that they have now begun to understand Jesus and have come to grips with his word.

Their understanding is also manifested straight off in their next words, which are a confession to Christ and may be regarded as the

176

response of the disciples to the christological-doctrinal statement in verse 28. The confession is in two parts: Verse 30a: "Now we know that you know everything and do not need anyone to put questions to you"; and verse 30b: "Therefore we believe that you came from God."

The meaning of verse 30a is that Jesus is in fact the revealer of God and participates in the omniscience of God, although of course the omniscience is not to be understood in a fairy-tale sense. The reference is rather to the knowledge which Jesus has of the Father and which he communicates to his disciples, as well as the special knowledge he has of humanity. In this regard verse 30a says nothing new but supplies a handy formulation of a datum long since brought out in the gospel.

Thus Jesus says to Nathanael, a young man coming to meet him for the first time, "Behold, a true Israelite, in whom there is no deceit." When Nathanael asks, "How do you know me?" Jesus answers, "Before Philip called you, I saw you as you sat under the fig tree." At this Nathanael can only say, "Rabbi, you are the Son of God, you are the king of Israel." Jesus replies, "Do you believe because I told you I saw you under the fig tree? You shall yet see greater things than that" (1:47-50).

In like manner, Jesus is aware of the questionable life the Samaritan woman has led (4:17-19): "You are correct in saying 'I have no husband.' For you have had five husbands, and the one you have now is not your real husband." To which the woman replies, "Sir, I see you are a prophet."

Or, in a generalization: "When he was in Jerusalem for the feast of Passover, many believed in his name, because they saw the signs he performed. But Jesus did not trust himself to them, *because he knew them all* and did not need any one to give testimony regarding man; *for he himself knew what was in man*" (2:23-25).

In their association with Jesus the disciples came to realize that he had knowledge of God and knowledge of the good and evil in people. Knowledge of God and knowledge of humanity go together. Revelation, in John's sense of the word, not only brings the intelligence of God; it also discloses at the same time the problematic situation of people, their sinfulness, their unbelief and hatred. In

John the idea of Jesus' omniscience is strictly related to these two points; the Johannine Jesus is no more of a soothsayer than is the synoptic Jesus.

In view of the knowledge Jesus has as revealer all the questions of the disciples become unnecessary. Perhaps we can derive clarification from the statement in the First Letter of John: "That is how we shall know that we belong to the truth, and shall be able to set our hearts at rest in his presence; I mean, when our heart accuses us, for God is greater than our heart and knows everything" (1 John 3:19-20). This passage is marked through and through by Jesus' experience of God. So clear is the revelation Jesus brings that it answers humanity's most radical questions about itself, and these certainly include its questions about injustice and guilt, about failures in dealing with neighbors, and about love; in other words, the questions which in the heart find utterance. Consequently, the statement that Jesus knows everything and has no need of anyone to ask questions has something consoling about it; it resembles Pascal's saying: "Take comfort. Thou wouldst not be seeking Me, hadst thou not found me."[139] The faith which understands that the salvation of humankind is already given in Jesus and his revelation, has grasped the essential point.

Verse 30b, "Therefore we believe that you came from God," is a confession of Jesus as revealer. If a person does not look for Jesus' origin at the purely human, historical, and worldly level but accepts him as coming from God, if Jesus is seen as first and foremost the witness to God, then such a person has attained to a correct faith in Jesus. As a matter of fact, it is only through faith that people can have the proper relationship to Jesus. This too is one of the many focuses of the farewell discourses. All other categories of a nonreligious nature may prove necessary and justified as one draws near to the person of Jesus, but the final word must be a confession of faith in him.

When John, in the present passage, juxtaposes the expressions "now we know . . . " and "therefore we believe . . . ," he is declaring the unity of faith and understanding. In John faith always includes the element of understanding, just as unbelief involves not understanding. Conversely, understanding, as it applies to revelation, is always connected with faith in the sense of a positive decision, a yea-saying. The fourth gospel knows nothing of a blind faith that would be utterly devoid of insight and incapable of understanding. The alternative to faith is not knowledge, though people often say this, even today, but unbelief. In its very origin faith includes the element of knowing, primarily in the form of understanding.

The reply of Jesus, "Do you now believe?" (v. 31), is interpreted in quite different ways: either as a confirmation that the disciples do believe, that is, that after so many questions and misunderstandings they have at least attained to faith; or else as a "great question mark"[140] which Jesus puts after their confession of faith. Or, "His response does not cast a radical doubt upon their faith, yet their faith must accept being questioned."[141] Jesus' question must be interpreted strictly in accordance with its context. Then the evangelist is seen to be referring once again to the departure situation and specifically to the event of the coming passion, as verse 32 makes clear. This is to say that here, once again, Jesus does not separate faith from its situation in the world, no more than elsewhere does faith here become clear vision. Faith can never become an absolutely sure possession; it always retains its element of risk. Moreover, faith is also reminded of its connection with the historical Jesus and his way, and this way is the way of the passion. The approaching passion of Jesus will be another test for the faith of the disciples, and this is true not only of the faith of the original disciples of Jesus but of faith generally. Faith must ever anew defend itself against the attacks of the world.

An explicit reference to the passion follows, and this in the context of the behavior and the lot of the disciples. The hour of Jesus' arrest and passion will be an hour of scattering for the disciples. Here the evangelist harks back once again to the traditions known to us from the synoptic writers: "Then Jesus said to them, 'You will all lose faith in me, for it is written, "I will strike the shepherd, and the sheep will be scattered." But after my resurrection I will go before you into Galilee' " (Mark 14:27-28; the citation is from Zech. 13:7). Mark's account evidently supposes a tradition according to which the disciples scattered immediately after the arrest of Jesus; that is, they fled and probably returned to Galilee. This was not something of which the disciples and the primitive community could be proud. At the same time, however, it was possible even in this situation to appeal to a passage of Scripture that could serve as a prophecy. According to Mark, the first apparitions of the risen Christ likewise took place in Galilee (cf. Mark 16:7, where the angel at the empty tomb says to the women, "Now go and tell his disciples and Peter, 'He is going before you into Galilee; there you will see him, as he told you' ").

John's version is, "You will be scattered, each to his own" (v. 32a). This may mean that John is deliberately leaving unspecified the whither of the scattering, since according to his account the Easter apparitions take place in Jerusalem and not in Galilee (20:11-18, 19-23, 24-29), although the Johannine tradition is also able to report apparitions in Galilee (chap. 21). For this reason he may have avoided a reference to Galilee and replaced it with a vague "to his own" (or, "to the special [place]"); this kind of vague allusion is frequent in John.

Another possibility is that the text is a reminiscence of Isaiah 53, the Song of the Suffering Servant, where we read, "All of us like sheep went astray, each of us intent upon his own way. But Yahweh allowed the guilt of us all to rest on him" (53:6). This second conjecture seems to me the more probable one. According to 18:8, when Jesus is arrested he explicitly stands up for his disciples so that nothing may happen to them.

Along with Peter's denial, the scattering of the disciples at Jesus' arrest is doubtless the strongest objection to the confession of faith which the disciples have uttered so confidently. That is why Jesus' question, "Do you now believe?" with its slight tone of doubt, is quite justified. Here again Jesus is in the position of superiority, as with his question he confirms the confidence of the disciples (they are right in saying that there is no need of asking Jesus questions) and at the same time circumspectly reproves it. The disciples will not (yet) follow Jesus in his passion, although later they will do so. In the first test of their faith they will fail and will leave Jesus isolated, humanly speaking. That is the sad upshot, as far as the relationship of the disciples to their master during the passion is concerned.

But John emphasizes another point as well: Even when abandoned by his followers Jesus is not alone, for the Father is with him. God has in no sense deserted Jesus. "The final part of the sentence, 'but

I am not alone . . . ,' sounds like a correction of the synoptic account of the crucifixion with its cry of abandonment by God."[142] It is quite possible that John did intend to correct Mark 15:34-35. In any case, it is certain that an abandonment by God does not fit into the Johannine account of the passion, as we shall see. Jesus is indeed abandoned by his friends, but he is not abandoned by his heavenly Father. For as verse 33 says in lapidary form, the passion of Jesus is *his victory over the world.*

Verse 33a picks up the catchword peace once again (on this, see John 14:23-32). The words of Jesus communicate peace to believers, or, more accurately, the peace of Jesus, which is to be had only in union with him. This peace is the eschatological salvation that is the lot of believers amid a world lacking in peace and salvation."The certainty of his faith does not rest on the believer himself, but on the Revealer in whom he believes. And precisely this uncertainty, which the believer meets with again and again, teaches him how to direct his gaze away from himself to the Revealer, so that it is indeed possible to speak of *felix culpa.*"[143] In the last analysis, it is Jesus' work of salvation that is the basis and definitive guarantee of peace.

Verse 33b, on the other hand, in a sentence that gets to the heart of things, describes the situation of faith in the world: "In the world you have distress; but take heart, I have overcome the world." This statement needs to be understood against the background of Jewish eschatology (apocalyptic). Distress refers to the time of final affliction before the end. "Before the devout may enter the broad plains of salvation, they must pass through the gloomy defile of suffering; before a new time can come, the old must be shaken to its foundation. The time immediately preceding the final act is the last and most dreadful period; it is the last evil time."[144] This is the same period that is elsewhere described as the time of messianic birth-pangs (cf. on 16:21).

In early Jewish apocalyptic this period of distress is painted in the darkest colors; the same is true of the New Testament Apocalypse (Revelation) of John, where it is described in terms of the four apocalyptic horsemen and the various plagues (cf. Rev. 6; 9:1-12; etc.; also Mark 13). In the gospel of John, however, the distress or affliction of the final period is not described in any specific way. It is simply contrary to the peace Jesus promises, and is therefore a time of unqualified non-peace and non-salvation. Moreover, it is inherently connected with the situation of being in the world. Distress becomes, as it were, a structural characteristic of the believers' situation in the world. Existence in the world and existence in faith can therefore never be made completely coextensive; rather, they are constantly in friction, constantly jostling one another, as it were. The world and its distress, on the one side, and faith and the peace of Jesus Christ, on the other, are engaged in basic and unavoidable conflict. According to verse 33 there is no identification of world and faith that would eliminate all questions, disputes, and conflicts, nor can there be any such in the world.

Martin Luther translated the verse thus: "In the world *you have dread.* But take heart, I have overcome the world." This brilliant translation emphasizes the subjective element in distress, namely, the sense of being cornered and the resultant fear a person experiences. Here, being in the world and dread are so fused that dread becomes the special mark of being in the world. In the last analysis, moreover, the dread is a dread of death and nothingness that as such is never to be shaken off, since the power of death is present in the midst of life. It is therefore the situation of all humanity as faced with death that is addressed in the words: "In the world you have dread (or: distress)." If Jesus can nonetheless say, "But take heart, I have overcome the world," he can say it only because he is *the risen Lord, the victor over death.* The victory of Jesus over the world is his victory over the power of death that reigns in the world.

Only if we understand the words of Jesus in this way do they have a serious meaning; only then are they not triumphalistic blustering; only if the power of death has been overcome has the cosmos with its dread and affliction been truly conquered. Faith already shares in this victory of Jesus, and this is why it truly and effectively makes people be of good cheer. For as the risen Lord Jesus is the giver of eschatological life. Faith in this way becomes the power that liberates people unto life in the midst of the world of death. From beginning to end the gospel of John proclaims this message of eschatological victory. This can be seen above all in the way the evangelist describes the passion of Jesus, namely as an account of his victory. It is therefore completely in keeping with the whole tendency of his presentation that the farewell discourse should end with this heartening assertion of victory.

Meditation

The text speaks of the eschatological victory of Jesus over the world: "In the world you have distress; but take heart, I have overcome the world." We seem to hear an echo of these words when we read in the First Letter of John, "For everything born of God overcomes the world; and this is the victory that overcomes the world: our faith. Who then is the victor if not the one who believes that Jesus is the Son of God?" (1 John 5:4-5).

The immediate addressees of these words were in fact members of a hard-pressed community which was rendered insecure by its lack of standing before the law and was also being persecuted by the pagan world around it. For this community affliction from the world had a very concrete meaning. For the most part, pagan society was unsympathetic and even hostile to the friends of Jesus.

When the community was bidden to focus its attention on the victory of Jesus, the strength and encouragement it derived therefrom (cf. also Rev. 19:11-16) were not meant primarily to render its existence in the world more secure but rather to enable it to persevere to the end. The conquest sayings in the Apocalypse of John give us a keen sense of the situation:

To the victor I will grant to eat of the tree of life that stands in Paradise. (2:7)

Be not afraid of what you must suffer. Behold, the devil will imprison some of you, so that you may be tested, and you will suffer affliction for ten days. Be faithful unto death, and I will give you the victor's crown of life. Let him who has ears hear what the Spirit is saying to the communities: The victor will not be harmed by the second death. (2:10-11)

The victor I will make a column in the temple of my God, and he shall never leave it, and I will write on him the name of my God and the name of the city of my God, the new Jerusalem that comes down from heaven from my God, and my own new name. Let him who has ears hear what the Spirit is saying to the communities. (3:12-13)[145]

The concepts "victory," "to conquer," "to become a victor," are meant in an intraworldly sense, as the Apocalypse of John especially makes clear. Victory is not a synonym for success in this world. On the contrary, the victory is understood as being entirely eschatological; it will become apparent only at the end when Christ returns and the new, heavenly Jerusalem is manifested. Until then, the community on earth is a community living amid all kinds of affliction and care, with these originating not only from outside the community but from within as well, in the ranks of the community itself; these latter afflictions are just as momentous as the former. Among the afflictions arising from within the community there are the slackening of first love, all sorts of erroneous teachings and wrong behavior, hypocritical Christianity and tepidity: "I know your works . . . . You are neither hot nor cold. Would that you were either hot or cold! But since you are lukewarm, neither hot nor cold, I will spit you out of my mouth" (Rev. 3:15-16; cf. 2:4, 14, 20; 3:1).

The reference to eschatological victory is therefore to be taken as a powerful encouragement to persevere through the earthly period of distress until the end. The reference to the victory of Christ that has already been achieved serves the same purpose. We should not forget even for a moment that according to John the victory of Christ is essentially connected with the cross. Here again, there is no question of an intraworldly victory; this becomes even clearer when we reflect that the essence of the victory is Christ's resurrection to eternal divine life.

Admittedly, the statement about the victory of faith over the world (especially in its second formulation in the First Letter of John, where it is said that "our faith" is the victory that overcomes the world) rings much too shrilly in our ears today for us to be able to make it our own without reservations and all sorts of doubts. A chief objection is the past history of the Church with its triumphalism, in which this victory over the world was frequently, and with great confidence, interpreted in terms of intraworldly success on the stage of world history, but had only a tinge of the Christian in it. Here are some examples:

The Church of the patristic period regarded the Constantinian turning point, which brought an end of persecution of Christians (Edict of Milan, A.D. 313) and the recognition of Christianity by the state, as a victory of Christ and the true faith. The dominant mood of the time may be gauged by the following passage from the *History of the Church* by Eusebius of Caesarea (A.D. 262-319):

> Thus all men living were free from oppression by the tyrants; and released from their former miseries, they all in their various ways acknowledged as the only true God the Defender of the godly. Above all for us who had fixed our hopes on the Christ of God there was unspeakable happiness, and a divine joy blossomed in all hearts as we saw that every place which a little while before had been reduced to dust by the tyrants' wickedness was now, as if from a prolonged and deadly stranglehold, coming back to life; and that cathedrals were again rising from their foundations high into the air, and far surpassing in magnificence those previously destroyed by the enemy.
>
> Emperors too, the most exalted, by a succession of ordinances in favour of the Christians, confirmed still further and more surely the blessings that God showered upon us; and a stream of personal letters from the emperor reached the bishops, accompanied by honours and gifts of money.[146]

The same triumphalistic mood permeates the following passage from a sermon which Pope Leo I the Great (pope in A.D. 440-461) preached for the feast of the Princes of the Apostles, Peter and Paul, in a year that cannot be precisely determined:

> Beloved, all our holy feasts are the common possession of the whole world, and the reverence due to the one same faith requires that a like urgency should mark all the commemorations of what was done for the salvation of mankind in its entirety. Today's feast, nonetheless, in addition to the veneration which it merits everywhere on earth, must be greeted with very special jubilation here in our city. For where the Princes of the Apostles ended their lives so glo-

riously, there too should joy on the day of their martyrdom be chiefly felt. These are the men, O Rome, who brought you the light of Christ's Gospel. You were once the teacher of error but you became the disciple of the truth. These men are your holy fathers and true shepherds, who, because they made you a member of the divine kingdom, founded you in a much better and happier sense than did those whose efforts laid the first foundations for your walls; for of these latter the one who gave you your name befouled you by murdering his brother. It is these two apostles who have exalted you to the glory that is now yours. For because of the sacred Chair of Blessed Peter you have become a holy nation, a chosen people, a priestly and royal city, and head of the world. By reason of this divine religion you were to rule far more widely than by any earthly domination. For although you grew great through many victories and extended your imperial rule over land and sea, yet the realm you mastered by the toil of war was smaller than that which Christian peace made subject to you.[147]

This text gives us a good idea of how the triumphalistic ideology of Christian Rome developed. The very language of the passage shows the concepts connected with the old imperial Roman ideology, especially political and symbolic concepts, being transferred to Christian events and facts. There are some fine differentiations we should not overlook. What is being celebrated is the martyrdom—the victory, in the original Christian sense of the term—of Peter and Paul, who are now called, in the grand style, the Princes of the Apostles (literally: "leading or principal apostles"—*praecipui apostoli*). These men, the text goes on to say, brought the light of the Gospel to Rome, and for this reason Leo regards them as second founders; founders, that is, of Christian Rome. They are the new holy fathers, that is, the new senators of Rome. The rhetorical verve of the passage is achieved by the use of an argument from the lesser to the greater (*a minori ad maius*): the political power of the old imperial Rome was very great, but the spiritual power and effectiveness of Christian Rome is far greater still. In all truth, religion has widened the sphere of Rome's power beyond anything the generals and politicians had been able to accomplish. Moreover (attention is expressly drawn to this point), religion has done this without the use of violence.

We may also recall the ideal of soldierly piety that was cultivated by the Christian Middle Ages with their faith in the sword; the crusades against the Albigensians and the Cathars; the forced conversion of the Saxons; the conduct of the Portuguese during the conquest of India and of the Spaniards during the conquest of Mexico and Peru. Since the last-named events are still too little known, I shall give in some detail an example from Pizarro's conquest of Peru.[148] Fray Celso Gargia describes as follows the climactic meeting between Francisco Pizarro and the Inca, Atahualpa, which occurred on Sunday, November 16, 1552.

Soon after sunrise a loud blast of trumpets called the Spaniards to arms. At roll-call Pizarro explained his plan to the troops. Then the account continues: "After these arrangements had been made, a Mass was read. The God of battles was invoked to extend his protecting hand over these soldiers who were ready to fight for the spread of the Christian realm. All joined fervently in the singing of *Exsurge, Domine, et iudica causam tuam* (Arise, O Lord, and conduct your proceedings). "In the late afternoon the Inca arrived with his army. When he hesitated and wanted to wait until the next day to appear for the negotiations with Pizarro, he was lured into a trap. Pizarro

> sent a message to the Inca with the request that he would enter the city today, since everything had been prepared for his entertainment. Atahualpa acceded to the request. He struck camp, and the column began to move forward again. Atahualpa had already told the Spanish commander that he would leave behind the larger part of his soldiery. . . . No news could have been more welcome to Pizarro. It seemed as though Atahualpa desired nothing more than to fall into the trap set for him. I venture to say that the hand of divine providence was directly at work here.

When the Inca reached the main square of Cajamarca with an escort of six thousand men, the square was completely empty, for the Spaniards had concealed themselves in ambush. Only a Dominican monk and priest named Vicente de Valverde, who was also Pizarro's confessor, was to be seen; he spoke the Quecha dialect. With crucifix and Bible in hand he immediately began to preach a sermon aimed at their conversion. After he had explained the Christian creed he continued,

> "The Savior left the Apostle Peter behind him on earth as his representative; Peter handed on his office to the pope, and the latter in turn to succeeding popes. The pope, who now has authority over the rulers of the world, has commissioned the Spanish emperor, mightiest of all princes, to make subjects of the natives of the Western hemisphere, and to convert them. Francisco Pizarro has now come to carry out the task given him. I now call upon you, Atahualpa, to abjure the false beliefs in which you are ensnared. In addition, you must acknowledge that from this day forward you owe tribute to the Spanish emperor."

> When the Dominican had finished speaking, Atahualpa stood there as if turned to stone. Then he said in a voice filled with hatred, "I will pay tribute to no one! I am the greatest prince on earth, I have no equal. How can the man you call pope give away lands that do not belong to him? I will not abjure my faith. Your God was slain by the very men he had created. My God"—as he said this he pointed to the sun—"lives in heaven and gazes down on his children." By now Pizarro was in the square. He saw Atahualpa snatch the Bible from the monk's hand and dash it to the ground. The time had come. A gun was fired and the Spaniards poured into the square. With the battle cry "Santiago!" on their lips footsoldiers and cavalry in closed ranks threw themselves upon the crowds of Indians.

Atahualpa was taken prisoner and later killed. With a sense of cruel irony we read of Father Valverde that "he sought to console Atahualpa and make it clear to him that all who resisted the warriors of Christ were doomed to destruction."[149]

Catholics usually do not like to be confronted with such incidents as these from the Western Christian past. For centuries the Jews were repressed from Christian consciousness; today it is the events connected with the conquest and christianization of Latin America of which people are in large measure simply unaware. After reading

188

an account like the foregoing one asks, "What kind of God was it that these Spanish conquerors believed in: this cruel God of battles who regards some of his creatures as enemies; who not only allows but requires forced conversions; who allows the mass murder of peoples and even, in Pizarro's day, the annihilation of countless Indian tribes?" Our Dominican in this account is not bothered by the slightest scruple when he allows the pope and the Spanish king to dispose of the newly discovered lands and calls for the Inca's submission. Does not the Inca emerge as the much bigger man when he says with perfect truth, "Your God was slain by the very men he had created. My God lives in heaven and gazes down on his children"—just like the God and Father of Jesus, who makes his sun to shine on good and evil alike?

But this is the decisive point: the God of battles is not in fact the God and Father of Jesus. He is rather the God of the ruling classes, an idol representing power, whose function is to legitimate the domination of some people over others and who annihilates his enemies, be they the enemies of the state or the enemies of the Church. We must get it clear in our own minds that this God of battles has repeatedly in the course of Western Christian history been passed off and regarded as the true God, the Christian God! Many Christians have never known any other God; they have not met the Father of our Lord Jesus Christ, the God of love, but only the God of those in power and the ruling classes.

Beyond a doubt, it is not this God to whom the statement about the victory of Christ refers. If we look back at the triumphalism of Western Christendom, we find that St. Paul's words are directed against Christians: "On your account the name of God is blasphemed among the pagans" (Rom 2:24). Modern atheism, too, is at bottom undoubtedly a product of that incredible history of victory of European imperialist faith in the sword which completely identified the conquest and annihilation of foreign peoples and cultures with the mission and expansion of Christianity. The story of Atahualpa is striking proof that we Christians have a large share in the responsibility for the present state of the world, especially with regard to the former colonies.

As can be seen, the idea of the victory of faith proves extremely dangerous when we seek to connect it in any way with intraworldly

189

political success, even if the latter be put in the long-range terms of world history. Martin Buber made a remark which is well worth pondering: "Success" is not one of God's names! The important thing for us today is to see that the world which is now making things difficult for faith is also the historical world which Christianity has helped shape and for which it shares the responsibility. Because of the historical freight it carries—which has of course not only a negative side but a positive one as well, which we obviously presuppose—the adjective "Christian" has become thoroughly ambiguous. Christianity has allied itself with the ruling powers; its representatives, including even popes, have in the course of history acquired bloodstained hands. This makes it difficult today to speak freely and naturally of the victory of faith. This kind of language is in fact true only when applied to Jesus, the pioneer of faith. He alone has won the victory—but as the victim of the religious and political powers that be.

THE FAREWELL PRAYER OR
HIGHPRIESTLY PRAYER OF JESUS (17:1–26)

Exegesis

In the version of the gospel of John that has come down to us, the farewell discourses are followed by a lengthy prayer which is also known as the "highpriestly prayer" of Jesus. The name goes back to David Chytraeus (1531–1600), a theologian who evidently saw in this prayer of Jesus an expression of his highpriestly office, possibly with reference to the passion, in which, according to traditional theological teaching, Jesus offered himself as a sacrificial victim. In this interpretation the prayer would be Jesus' prayer of consecration for his approaching death.

From an exegetical point of view the name "highpriestly prayer" is not without justification, since among other things Jesus here exercises on behalf of his disciples the function of intercessor with the Father (cf. 17:6-24) which the early Christian mind ascribed to the exalted Christ (cf. Rom. 8:34; 1 John 2:1-2; Heb.). If we take this intercessory role as our point of departure, we immediately have an important standpoint for studying the prayer. Here again John is transferring a function of the heavenly post-Easter Christ to the earthly Jesus, or, to put it the other way around, the earthly Jesus exercises a function that, properly speaking, belongs to the exalted Christ. This makes it clear once more how much the earthly Jesus and the exalted Christ are fused into a single reality in the Johannine approach. It follows from this that the prayer has been formulated by the evangelist. We are not dealing here with a prayer composed by Jesus himself as we are in the Our Father, the basic content of which very probably goes back to the historical Jesus (cf. Matt. 6:9-13; Luke 11:24).

On the other hand, a traditio-historical link can be seen with the

Johannine logion or "hymn of praise to the Father," which comes from the discourses source:

> In that hour Jesus answered and said,
> "I praise you, Father, Lord of heaven and earth,
> because you have hidden these things from the wise and clever
> but have revealed them to children.
> Yes, Father, such was your will.
> Everything has been handed over to me by my Father,
> and no one knows the Son but the Father,
> and no one knows the Father but the Son
> and anyone to whom the Son chooses to reveal him. (Matt. 11:25-27; cf. Luke 10:21-22).

There is no doubt that the Johannine farewell prayer and this prayer from the discourses source show similarities in language but far more similarity in the kind of thinking they embody. In particular, the second part of the Matthean prayer (Matt. 11:27; Luke 10:22), and the farewell prayer are in agreement in their conception of Jesus as the exclusive and absolute revealer of God as Father. It is clear, then, that John's special conception of the revelation brought by Jesus is located within a broader stream of early Christian tradition. In the farewell prayer of Jesus in John, as in the Matthean prayer, the salutation "Father" for God is central to the prayer (vv. 1, 5, 11, 21, 24, 25). The important thing for John is Jesus' relationship to God as manifested in his characterization of God as Father. It is into this relationship with God that believers are drawn. John has certainly captured here a principal concern of the message of Jesus and plumbed it more deeply in his own way.

A further point is that the farewell prayer of Jesus is, in a way, a summary of the entire gospel of John and of its theology of revelation. The significance of what is said in this prayer becomes clear only to those who are to some degree familiar with the gospel of John and especially with the farewell discourses; without this knowledge it is not possible to gauge the real depths of the prayer. E. Käsemann rightly observes, "Regardless of how the question of the original position of this chapter is answered, it is unmistakable that this chapter is a summary of the Johannine discourses and in this respect is a counterpart to the prologue."[150]

The prayer contains, then, the entire Johannine theology of revelation, with the difference that the content is no longer given in the form of teaching by the revealer, as it is in the various revelatory discourses, but in the form of a living embodiment of that revelation in prayer, in a kind of liturgy that is at once earthly and heavenly. In this prayer, the heavenly intercessor with the Father and the earthly community of his friends are brought together in a unity that is effected by the Spirit. The prayer makes it clear that in the last analysis revelation is a matter not of instruction in theory but of new life and a living communion with Jesus and with the God and Father of Jesus.

In this prayer, then, John shows us what he believes Christian community to be in its inmost nature and not simply in its external sociological embodiment. John does not develop an explicit doctrine of the Church (ecclesiology); for him the Church is not an independent theme. But insofar as he portrays the community of Jesus' disciples and identifies it with his own community (or the other way around), he clearly shows his own conception of the Church. This will emerge especially in connection with the recurring term *unity*.

The prayer falls into four parts: (a) 17:1-5 sums up the revelation of Jesus and its significance; (b) 17:6-19 is a prayer for the disciples who are remaining behind in the world; (c) 17:20-24 is a prayer for the community of the future; (d) 17:25-26 forms the conclusion of the whole prayer.[151]

In his commentary R. Bultmann places this farewell prayer after the account of the last supper (13:1-30) and before the farewell discourses.[152] In my view, however, there is no convincing ground for this procedure. Or, to put it more accurately, there are many good and convincing reasons for leaving the prayer where it now is. As a compendium of the Johannine theology of revelation it is in a much better position after the farewell discourses than before them. In this position it also serves as a bridge to the ensuing narrative of the passion. The prayer may originally have been an independent composition (although such a view is a hypothesis pure and simple), but in the final redaction of the gospel it has certainly ended up in its proper place. In this matter it seems clear, once again, that textual transpositions and the various procedures of literary criticism do not advance us very far in the understanding and interpretation of John's gospel. The decisive thing is the subject matter that finds expression in the text.

The Revelation of Jesus (17:1–5)

In a brief introduction, "After speaking these words Jesus raised his eyes to heaven and said . . ." (v. 1a), the evangelist signals the end of the farewell discourses and the beginning of the prayer. That Jesus is about to utter a prayer is clear from his taking the posture of prayer: he raises his eyes to heaven, the place of God. Possibly too the words carry the idea of the direction of prayer; originally, Christians did not pray in accordance with any geographical coordinates but turned directly to God.

The radically different posture and focus of attention brings with it a different kind of discourse as well. Prayer—intercession, for example, or a prayer which a representative, a liturgical spokesperson, utters on behalf of others—has a different character than a polemical discourse or an instruction to the disciples. In prayer contention disappears, as does discussion. In this respect the new kind of discourse falls into place quite naturally here, since it has been said in 16:25, 29-30, that all questions have now been answered and there are no more obscurities or enigmas. It is in fact a condition for prayer that people leave all problems aside and attain to an openness and accord in which what they have in common may find expression. In John's farewell prayer, this common center, which is the thing that matters in communal prayer, is the person of Jesus and his word. It is therefore surely no accident that Jesus himself speaks the prayer. It is from him that believers of every age must take their bearings. It is in him that they find their center, their normative point of reference, and therefore their own direction.

The salutation "Father" which recurs throughout the prayer (vv. 24, 5, 21, with "holy Father" in 11b and "just Father" in 25) is in keeping not only with the basic predicate for God in John but also with the tradition about the prayer of Jesus as found in other sources.[153] John may here be dependent on primitive Christian tradition, and specifically on a tradition that linked Jesus' special understanding of God with the apocalyptic conception of revelation;

194

it is such a tradition that we find in the prayer of jubilation (Matt. 11:25-27) from the discourses source.[154] The idea already existed prior to John that a special revelation is required in order to know God as Father and that this revelation is to be had only through Jesus, the Son. John probably took over this idea from oral tradition, but then made it the central theme of his theology of revelation.[155]

All this becomes immediately evident in the words that follow the salutation: "the hour has come" and "glorify your Son so that the Son may glorify you" (v. 1b). The reference to the "hour" having now come recalls the beginning of the last supper (13:1); there is no doubt that both texts refer to the same hour. Hour here is not an indication of chronological time. It describes rather the saving event of the death and resurrection of Jesus.[156] The important thing in John's eyes is the content of any given hour, and this content is determined in turn solely by what happens to Jesus. It is the death of Jesus as a redemptive death, the death of the Son of God and the Son of man, that makes the hour what it truly is, namely the hour of salvation for the cosmos and all of humanity. The hour therefore also introduces the eschatological turning point of the ages (eons) and consequently the permanent presence of salvation.

For this reason the hour is emphatically the hour of the glorification of Jesus[157] in which Jesus receives from the Father the recognition due him as Son of God. The honor which God thus gives Jesus is not however a mere external confirmation but consists in the acceptance of Jesus into the realm of divine brightness, light, and splendor. This is difficult to express in words, but art has managed to make it more meaningful to us by surrounding the enthroned Christ with the mandorla, the symbol of the godhead.

Since Jesus here asks the Father to "glorify" him, his journey into death is to be understood as an essential moment in that comprehensive dialogue between Father and Son that characterizes the life of Jesus and his entire earthly existence. In relation to the Father Jesus lives at every moment a life of dialogue. Even his death is to be seen as a divine work and not simply as something afflicted by blind, impious people, still less as an impersonal fate. The death of Jesus is indeed something he suffers, but at the same time it is completely active, an event to which Jesus gives himself without reserve.

In his death, moreover, his glorification by the Father is already beginning. Even here God the Father retains, in John's eyes, a final priority over Jesus the Son. This is connected with the fact that when all is said and done John does not have a purely speculative idea of God which is elaborated without reference to his revelation and therefore to his divine saving activity. Precisely as revealer Jesus remains linked to human history. If the glorification of Jesus by the Father and of the Father by Jesus takes place on the cross, this is an expression of the fact that here God is fully revealed by Jesus. For this reason, cross and resurrection are the climax of revelation. That is what John is talking about when he speaks of glorification.

Because of the stylistic inconsistency (the second-personal address is used in v. 1 and picked up again in v. 4, but vv. 2 and 3 objectivize the Son, speaking about him in the third person) verses 2 and 3 are regarded by some as a later insertion. In addition, verse 3 uses the language of explicit confession. But these are not cogent reasons for assuming that verse 3 must be a later addition. Here again the comparison with Matthew 11:25-27 is instructive, because in the latter passage there is a similar linking of a second-personal address in verses 25-26 with a shift to objectivizing language in verse 27. Furthermore, like John 17:3, Matthew 11:27 speaks of a "bestowal of authority" on the Son.

The glorification of Jesus is also the *confirmation of his divine authority*, which is described here as "authority over all flesh," that is, over the whole of humankind. While the concept of Jesus' authority in the synoptics seems to be connected chiefly with his miracles and in particular with the casting out of demons (cf. Mark 1:22, 27) or is presented as something unintelligible to outsiders and a subject of dispute,[158] in John authority is from the outset part of Jesus' endowment as Son of God and Messiah. Thus we read as early as 3:5, "The Father loves the Son and has put all things into his hands." As revealer Jesus is also the representative in the world of God's sovereign power. John probably took over the idea of Jesus' empowerment along with the Son of man christology. Thus 5:27 says, "And he (the Father) gave him authority to pass judgment, because he is the Son of man."

The bestowal of divine authority on the heavenly Son of man was already a common idea in Jewish apocalyptic. [159] The important thing, of course, is the change John introduces in applying the concept to Jesus, or, more accurately, under the influence of Jesus: Jesus, the Son of man has not received authority primarily in order to pass judgment, but "in order that he might give eternal life to all those whom you gave to him" (17:2b). The authority Jesus has is therefore primarily an authority in the interests of salvation, an authority to redeem and communicate eternal life, and only secondarily an authority to pass judgment.

There is here an unqualified priority of salvation over judgment, of the kind already expressed in 3:13-21. [160] Life and salvation, on the one side, and judgment on the other are not alternatives of equal weight; instead, the emphasis is on the salvation Jesus brings, while judgment is really only the accompanying shadow, the negative possibility with which people must reckon as long as human existence retains its fallibility. But this fallibility is constantly to be surmounted anew through faith!

Verse 2 says exactly the same thing as 3:13-21: Jesus has received full authority to communicate salvation. Even in this work, however, his abiding dependence on the Father finds expression: believers have been given to him by his Father (cf. also 6:37, 44). Throughout the saving events it is God who is carrying on his work, and this applies even to faith in Jesus.

In addition, the authority of Jesus in regard to salvation is universal; it extends, at least in principle, to all human beings. At the same time, however, believers do seem to constitute a special select group. It will be enough here to point out that John emphasizes both aspects, even though they cannot logically be subsumed under any obvious common denominator. He tells us that the authority of Jesus in regard to salvation is in fact universal in scope, extending to all human beings without exception. At the same time, however, he asserts that at all times only a limited number of individuals will explicitly reach out for the salvation Jesus offers and accept the word of revelation. What happens to the others lies beyond the range of our knowledge; it is a problem that must be left unresolved. Faith is therefore caught in tension: those who believe must hold fast to the idea and radical hope of the universal redemption of all humanity by Jesus Christ, but at the same time they cannot relinquish the concrete historical proclamation and faith as a personal confession, even while not passing judgment on those who do not (any longer) regard themselves as Christians. Despite their negative experiences believers may not surrender to a ghetto mentality.

"Eternal life" (Greek: *zoē aiōnios*) is, according to John, another name for the salvation that is linked to revelation.[161] "The Johannine Christ promises that those who believe in him will have *zoē* not simply as 'everlasting life' in the eschatological future but as a *present gift* bestowed on them even now in the course of their earthly lives."[162] The most frequently used idiom for expressing this fact is "to have life." The believer already shares now, in the present, in eternal life. That is why the First Letter of John can say:

> What was from the beginning,
> what we have heard, what we have seen with our own eyes,
> what we have gazed on and our hands have touched—
> we mean the Word (*Logos*) of life
> (yes, Life has appeared!)
> and we have seen it and we bear witness and proclaim to
> you the eternal life
> that was with the Father and has appeared to us—
> in short, what we have seen and heard,
> that we proclaim to you also,
> so that you too may have communion with us.
> And our communion is (communion)
> with the Father and with his Son Jesus Christ.
> And we write of this to you
> so that your joy may be complete (1 John 1:1-4).

The Johannine theology of life is grounded in God (theologically) and in Christ (christologically). Divine life alone is true, unconditional life, life without qualification and free of all death; only God possesses this kind of life. The world knows the desire for eternal life, but, apart from the desire, it is a world of death. Jesus is the divine *logos*, the word which was with God in the beginning and of which it is said that "in him was life, and the life was the light of men" (1:4). And this divine word of life "became flesh" (1:14) in order to give all a share in eternal life. The communication of life is therefore the most important salvational function of the Johannine Christ.

It thus becomes clear, in addition, that revelation and communication of life are immediately connected and form a single process, as verse 3 says, "Now this is eternal life: to know you, the only true God, and the one whom you sent, Jesus Christ." Knowledge of God and knowledge of Jesus Christ is the content of eternal life. There is no question here, of course, of knowledge that is theoretical and detached, but only of an acknowledgment or, better, a knowing that essentially includes interior participation and love, the element of profound upheaval that leads to faith. Verse 3 thus contains another concentrated Johannine short formula of the faith that sums up John's entire understanding of revelation. Here again, John stands within a broad Christian tradition when he makes *faith in God* and *faith in Christ* a single reality, as expressed, for example, in Paul's formula:

> But we have only one God, the Father, from whom the
>   universe (comes),
> and we (are ordered) to him,
> and one Lord Jesus Christ, through whom the universe (has
>   come to be),
> and we through him. (1 Cor. 8:6)

In the first member of the definition in verse 3, "to know you, the only true God," John is probably using the traditional idiom of the early Christian missionaries, but it is an idiom that goes even further back to the Jewish-Hellenistic preaching of the faith (cf. 1 Thess. 1:9-10). What we have in these words is the classic basic confession of biblical monotheism. The God of Israel is the one, true, living God as distinct from the many gods of the pagans (cf., e.g., Ps. 115:4-8) who of their nature are not gods at all but only "god-nonentities" (*elilim*). Primitive Christianity took over the Jewish proclamation of monotheistic religion. It too had to preach a strict monotheism, especially in the face of popular religion with its polytheistic inclinations. And yet it had to do this not in an abstract way, after the fashion in which the philosophically educated people of the day spoke of the unity of God, but in connection with the person of Jesus. For this reason, at a very early point, as Paul attests in 1 Corinthians 8:6, it became customary to set a confession of Christ alongside the confession of God and to link the two closely; the one

God and the eschatological revealer, Jesus Christ, belong together: ". . . and the one whom you sent, Jesus Christ."

Here we have the full name *Jesus Christ*, which occurs in this form only three times in the gospel of John, each time in a prominent place (1:17; 17:3; 20:31), and which here has attached to it the clause "whom you sent." Jesus is the one sent by God in a very precise sense.[163] To understand the Johannine concept of sending or mission, we must take as our point of departure the Jewish juridical principle "the envoy of a man is as the man himself."[164] This is a concept deeply rooted in the ancient practice of using emissaries, and it has perdured down to the present day. An ambassador is the representative of the government, standing in its place and being strictly bound by its directives. Thus in John too the concept of sending usually points to the authorization of Jesus by God. In virtue of his being sent Jesus has at his disposal a divine authority to reveal and save; so too, as revealer, he is God's representative in the world. Anyone who acknowledges him thereby acknowledges God; anyone who rejects him rejects God. For this reason, "all" should "honor the Son," that is, accept him fully for what he is, "as they honor the Father. He who does not honor the Son likewise does not honor the Father who sent him" (5:23).

John applies the notion of representation contained in the principle of mission, in order to describe Jesus' position in relation to God and in relation to the world. In his view, of course, the revealer and envoy of God, Jesus Christ, cannot be separated from God, and consequently true knowledge of God remains connected with the person of Jesus Christ. Once the eschatological revelation has been given in Jesus Christ there is no other way but this: *Per Christum ad Deum* (through Christ to God). The confessional idiom of verses 2 and 3, clearly different from the direct address proper to prayer, brings out once again the objective character of the Johannine understanding of revelation. But it is upon this acknowledgment of God and his revealer that the prayer and all it has to say is based.

The next verses, 4 and 5, return to the theme of glorification and go into it more fully with the help of two further ideas. Verse 4 looks back to the work of Jesus.[165] Jesus has already glorified the Father on earth—a first indication that John is looking at the earthly life of Jesus in its entirety as something already finished. The earthly activity of Jesus is here seen under the sign of *Soli Deo Gloria* (To God alone the glory), that is, of the glorification of God as providing the comprehensive meaning of Jesus' existence. Then John tells us in what the glorification of the Father by Jesus consists, namely in the fact that Jesus has "finished (accomplished) the work" which the Father had assigned him during his earthly life.

John speaks repeatedly of both the work (singular) and the works (plural) of Jesus. The plural works often refers to the miracles Jesus does, his "signs," as John calls them. The designation signs means that these works are to be understood as deeds of Jesus. They are not mere facts, simple occurrences. Instead, as works of Jesus they are at the same time works of God that become manifest in persons (9:3). This is to say that the particular sign-works have a wider context which is the activity of Jesus as revealer and savior. They bring out the meaning and power of the revelation after the manner of signs and symbols. As signs they point to Jesus for it is him and his purpose that they interpret. The point of these signs is not a sensational exhibition for its own sake, but rather to call attention to Jesus and stir faith in him.

The singular noun "work" looks rather to the activity of Jesus as a comprehensive and single totality. In 4:34 Jesus says, "My food is to do the will of him who sent me and to accomplish his work"; 5:36, on the other hand, says, "But I have a greater testimony than that of John, namely, *the works my Father has given me* to accomplish; these very works bear witness in my behalf that the Father sent me." The close relation of these two passages to 17:4 is obvious. Jesus accomplishes the Father's work; this is God's will for him, and it is the food on which he lives. To this extent the will of God is Jesus' central theme. In his eyes this divine will is not, of course, primarily an individual commandment to be carried out but the entire lifework of the revealer.

We must go a step further. The lifework of Jesus the revealer is not something extrinsic to him; it cannot be separated from the person of Jesus as an independent work or thing. If we make this kind of distinction between the work and the person of Jesus, we have not yet attained to a correct understanding of either. The work of Jesus does not stand over against him as does, for example, the work of a sculptor, poet, or philosopher. The work of these indi-

201

viduals becomes an independent entity, as it were, and leads a life of its own separate from its author. According to John, however, Jesus is identical with his work.

This becomes clear in the all-important phase of this work, namely, the passion, in which subject and object coincide in the person of Jesus. It is impossible to understand the passion as an external work or happening. No, *here Jesus is the work he accomplishes; he accomplishes or completes himself in relation to God.* When we speak of the "accomplishing" or "completing" (Greek: *teleioun*) of this work, the word itself reminds us of Jesus' final saying on the cross: "It is accomplished (or: completed)" (19:30). Now, if the very death of Jesus is placed under the sign of "It is accomplished," then, as we look back from it it becomes clear once again that the work of Jesus can only be his entire saving activity as embodied and concentrated in his person. It also becomes clear, finally, that Jesus and his entire life constitute a single work of God or revelation, and not simply a series of disparate communications about God. The issue, here again, is the overall theological understanding of Jesus.

At the same time, the relationship of Jesus to God is one of free exchange, of freely giving and freely receiving. Even the work Jesus accomplishes on earth is viewed as a gift. "Jesus received everything as a gift from the Father: not only his ability to accomplish but the actual accomplishment itself. But he also translated the gift into reality by bringing his redemptive work to full completion, as the Father had given him to do."[166]

For this reason Jesus also asks that the Father would glorify him, and this "in your presence," that is, in the divine world, "with the same glory I had in your presence before the world began" (v. 5). Here the idea of preexistence finds expression. There can hardly be any doubt that the evangelist is also reminding his readers of the prologue in which he says, "In the beginning, he, the Word [Greek: *logos*] was, and he, the Word, was with God, and he, the Word, was God. This was in the beginning with God" (1:1-2). And, further on, "And he, the Word, became flesh and dwelled among us, and we saw his glory, a glory such as belongs to the Only-begotten of the Father, full of grace and truth" (1:14).

John is convinced that Jesus is not to be comprehended in purely human categories or to be judged according to human standards. In the last analysis all criteria derived from the cosmos remain extrinsic, alien, and unsuited to the revealer. Jesus comes from the divine world; during his earthly life he continues to belong to that world, and it is to that world that he returns. Verse 24b will say that the eternal glory which Jesus had always shared by the Father's gift is nothing else than the eternal love between Father and Son: ". . . because you loved me since before the foundation of the world." The union of Jesus with the Father is thus not temporary and partial but radical and total; we can only use John's own language and say that it is an eternal union which has its ground not in time but before, above, and beyond all time.

The concept of preexistence gives the clearest possible expression to all this.[167] We need not further concern ourselves here with the prior forms taken by the idea of preexistence in the history of religions. Primitive Christianity found the thought pattern available and took it over in order to secure the divine revelatory character of the saving event and to express the radical union of Jesus and God. Since the saving event has its ground in God himself, it has no end. Consequently, the prayer of Jesus for his glorification by the Father likewise looks to the eternal continuance, the eternal future and abiding validity of the saving event. As saving event the death and resurrection of Jesus have eternal significance; they occurred once and for all. Therefore not only do they have a future, but the eternal future is already inaugurated in them.

The section 17:1-5 puts at the beginning of Jesus' farewell prayer the event of revelation and salvation as this (according to John) takes concrete form in the person of Jesus. To this extent Jesus himself, in his perpetual union with the Father, is the supporting ground, the abiding center, and the promise-filled future of eternal life.

Prayer for the Disciples
Left Behind in the World (17:6–19)

Jesus has accomplished the work or life-task appointed for him by God. But this work is not a self-enclosed isolated reality; rather, it was meant from the beginning to produce an effect or, in the idiom of John, it was to "bear fruit": "Amen, amen, I tell you, if the grain of wheat does not fall into the earth and die, it remains alone; but if it dies, it brings forth much fruit" (12:24). The most important fruit of the saving event, however, is *the establishment of Jesus' community of disciples, the Church.* John adverts to the fact that the revelation has not yet achieved its purpose in all human beings although it is addressed to all. But it has attained its goal among the disciples. Here the present time of the Johannine community and the past of Jesus and the first group of witnesses are again fused. In the first disciples of Jesus there had already occurred in an exemplary manner that which occurs in the community of every generation.

John does not, however, completely obliterate the historico-temporal distinction between the first and second generations. He holds fast to the truth that revelation and community also have a historical origin, an age of the founder and a generation contemporaneous with the founder, as well as a historical direction that may not be either ignored or reversed. The first generation disciples of Jesus are those who received the revelation directly from him, while later generations are those "who believe in me through their word" (v. 20b). To be sure, the essence of this faith is the same in both cases; there is no essential difference between the "immediate disciple" and the "disciple at second hand" (Kierkegaard) as far as faith in itself is concerned. In addition, there is the continuity of faith within the community of disciples. On the other hand, there is indeed a distinction that will be permanently valid, inasmuch as all later generations of disciples will remain dependent on the witness of the first disciples. In his own way, John takes this basic fact into account.

The revelation of God which Jesus brought has achieved its purpose in the group of the disciples. Jesus did not experience only failure. On the contrary, individuals came to him and, as his followers and in community with him, formed the first nucleus of the Christian community, the Church. John speaks of "those you gave me out of the world" (v. 6c), that is, he sees the establishment of the community as being a divine work. In his eyes, the Christian community is not an association brought into existence by human beings, but instead has its ultimate and permanent source in the action of God. It is a divine gift and not a human accomplishment that people should attain to faith in the revealer and through him to faith in God. Believers come out of the world, the cosmos. The latter is, on the one hand, the reservoir as it were that supplies the recruits for faith; on the other hand, everyone who believes leaves behind the cosmos with its prejudices and standards, and thus overcomes it and passes to the side of Jesus.

In the final analysis, the acceptance of the revelation of Jesus always has this character of freedom under grace; faith cannot be forced any more than love can. The Christian community too is founded on this basis of freedom under grace. Its existence in the world is a gift and from this point of view is completely insecure in worldly terms. Verse 6b expresses this aspect more clearly when Jesus expressly describes believers as *the Father's gift to him*. Inasmuch as they have accepted and kept the word of Jesus, they have also accepted God: ". . . and they have kept your word."

Here we have a constitutive element of the community's existence: the keeping of the word of God which is identical with the word of Jesus. It is this word that establishes the community of Jesus (the socializing function of proclamation), and it is also this word that assures the community's continued existence. To the extent that the disciples adhere to and keep the word of Jesus as the word of God, they also remain in communion with Jesus. This is especially true since Jesus in his very person as the word made flesh is God's all-important word to humanity. Furthermore, in accepting and keeping the word of Jesus the disciples have also grasped the content of the revelation of Jesus in its theological and christological context. They have recognized the divine origin of Jesus and his activity, that is, "that everything you gave me is from you."

The disciples have also come to see that they are involved in the passing on of the word. Here we have a distinctive aspect of the Johannine concept of tradition: the Father has given the word to the Son, the Son passes it on to the disciples, and the disciples in turn pass it on to later generations. It is important for the Johannine understanding of tradition that the passing on of the word in a tradition does not deprive it of any of its divine immediacy, since in every instance the Christ who is present stands behind the word and therefore encounters individuals in it. The tradition [i.e. handing on] of the word is always connected with the abiding presence of Christ, and this presence is in principle of greater importance than the tradition. Consequently, the person who accepts the word of Jesus as God's word stands within a tradition but cannot be enslaved to it; rather through it and in it he or she remains free. For via the word tradition opens the way to the immediate union of faith with Jesus himself: " . . . and they have accepted it and have truly realized that I came from you, and have believed that you sent me" (v. 8c). Knowledge on the basis of faith and belief that yields knowledge represent the wholly personal step that leads the individual into the graced freedom of communion with Jesus and thereby with God.

If the establishment of the community of Jesus' disciples is to be understood as a gift from God, as a gift of freedom under grace which is the fruit of God's action, then according to verses 9-19 the continued existence of the community is likewise to be traced to God's action. The community owes its ongoing existence to the intercession of Jesus and the support of God; in this sense the community has no autonomous or autarkic existence. As heavenly intercessor Jesus pleads for his disciples in the presence of God, but at the same time he is present and at work in the community. His prayer for the disciples is a sign that the entire event of which there is question here takes place within the space of graced freedom or, to put the same thing in other words, of divine love as disclosed once and for all by the work which is the revelation brought by Jesus. In this space Jesus and his disciples are fellows.

On this account Jesus is unable to pray "for the world"; in fact, the world is expressly excluded from his intercession. The "world" is the world that is imprisoned in unbelief, so that its exclusion from the intercession is consistent with what John has to say elsewhere about the world. Nonetheless, there is probably no statement in the gospel of John that opposes the unbelieving world and the community of disciples so sharply as this one does. We may indeed point out, with R. Bultmann,[168] that God's love, which is effectively at work in the Son, extends to the entire world (3:10) and that the world is in fact included in the intercession insofar as the prayer for the community has as one of its objects the winning over of the world (vv. 21, 23). Despite all this the statement remains a very harsh one. The world is here being defined radically as the realm of unbelief and damnation from which grace is absent and which not even the intercession of Jesus can help. True enough, the world is to "believe that you sent me" (v. 21) and to "recognize" God's love in this fact (v. 23); to this extent the farewell prayer does express a hope for the salvation of the world. Nevertheless we must ask how far John's thinking here is consistent with the spirit of Jesus as manifested in the commandment that we should love our enemies (Mat. 5:43-48; Luke 6:24-36).

A statement such as "I do not pray for the world . . ." is a warning to us that we may not uncritically absolutize even the statements of the gospels, but must attend carefully to their precise meaning in context. For us today at least it is no longer possible so easily to draw a clear line of demarcation between the unbelieving world and the community of Jesus' disciples. The statement must of course be understood in the light of the situation of the Johannine community which saw itself as a group of Jesus' friends set over against a hostile society. What we can retain from the passage is the idea that the Johannine Jesus prays for the preservation of the community from unbelief. The emphasis is on the dark background against which the community stands out by contrast. The intercession of Jesus therefore looks primarily to those whom the Father has given him. The community of disciples is seen as the possession of God and Jesus (v. 10). As such it shares in the glorification of Jesus. The community is the place where Jesus receives from faith the acknowledgment due him. This new situation of the community is the fruit of his glorification; in it his saving work continues and achieves completion ever anew.

The following verses locate the community of disciples in a positive way, and do it from ever new angles and vantage points. Negatively, in terms of separation from the world; positively, by showing the divine basis of the community. Verse 11 immediately takes up this second point. Jesus is no longer in the world, for he is on his way to the Father. But the disciples are in the world; in the time ahead the community will continue to have its place not outside the world but in the midst of it. However, the departure of Jesus means the establishment, outside the world, of the real ground of the community's existence, so that being in the world but not of the world will describe its special situation. This point will be taken up explicitly in verses 15 and 16 but it can already be glimpsed here in embryo. The community that Jesus is leaving behind in the world continues to be in need of the divine support that will "keep" it (v. 11b).

The salutation "holy Father" emphasizes God's holiness, the otherness that sets God's being apart from all that is non-divine and anti-divine. The anti-divine for John consists above all in unbelief and evil. Accordingly, the preservation of the community of disciples consists positively in keeping the community united to God, not letting it fall back under the control of the cosmic powers of evil, and confirming it in faith and love. In this verse special emphasis is laid for the first time on the unity of the community: " . . . that they may be one as we are one." The unity of the community should correspond to the unity between God and Jesus, the latter is the model for the former. The theme of unity will be taken up explicitly later (vv. 20-24).

Verse 12 reflects the departure situation in which Jesus is praying. As long as he was with his disciples on earth, he "kept" them, preserved them within the sphere of revelation, and even protected and guarded them so that none of them was lost except Judas, who is not named here but is described simply as the "son of perdition." But as the reference to the fulfillment of Scripture indicates, this perdition was, as it were, allowed for in the plan; it was no fault of Jesus that it occurred. The question of how the planned perdition of Judas, the fulfillment of the Scripture, and the judgment on Judas' action as sinful are to be interrelated is probably one that is not asked at this point. The point of the text is that the loss of Judas is not to be debited to Jesus; on the contrary, Jesus has carried out his task of preserving the disciples. A crucial point, however, is that now "another" must preserve the community. The community now needs another supporter, and it is in fact surprising that the Paraclete, the Holy Spirit is not mentioned here; the mention would be quite in place in view of what is being said.

An important point is that the departure of Jesus to the Father signifies the beginning of complete joy for the disciples;[169] the death and resurrection of Jesus mark the beginning of eschatological salvation for them, but this salvation is precisely the complete joy which the world does not give and cannot take away. "It is *his* joy which they are to share; i.e. they are not to receive the same *kind* of joy as his, but the very joy that he *has* is to be theirs; and this is so because their joy is grounded in his when the significance of his coming and going is borne home upon them, namely that it is the eschatological event."[170] In other words, since the community shares through faith in the eternal life of the risen Christ, by that fact it also shares in joy, for the presence of this eternal life is the ground of joy. If the ability to live a human life as such is already linked to joy, then eternal life certainly is.

The presence of salvation is guaranteed by the word of God, and Jesus has given this word to the disciples. But the word of God is the word that awakens to life and begets life, and that has already separated the community from the world. Consequently, it is only logical for verse 14b to assert that the disciples will encounter hatred from the world because they are no longer of the world, anymore than the revealer himself is. Believers share in the origin of the revealer. This, however, is not because of any natural ontological kinship with the revealer, as gnostic teaching maintained, but because through faith believers "are born of God" as the prologue puts it (1:13) or "from above through water and the Spirit" (cf. 3:1-6). The historical decision of faith gives believers a new origin from God, so that they are no longer of the world. And just as with the revealer in his time, so now the hatred of the world is leveled at them (cf. 15:18-19).

At the same time, however, the community is to put up with its being in the world (v. 15). Faith and the community's union with God do not mean that the community can live in a sheltered area, free from attack. As far as the world's hostility goes, the community remains vulnerable, insecure, and even at the mercy of death-dealing hatred. Security in God does not by any means imply a restored world in this life. What the community is to be preserved from is evil (or the evil one, i.e., the community is not to be at the mercy of the devil; both translations are grammatically possible). According to John the power of evil is marked above all by unbelief, lying, and hatred; in other words, by the kind of evil behavior that jeopardizes life itself. It is against this power that the community is to be protected, since this would cut it off from its divine source and thus destroy it. While Jesus himself has no ties with evil, evil does represent the one serious danger to the community, and therefore this petition seems especially necessary.

And yet it is true even here that the community, like Jesus, is not of the world but belongs on the side of God. In facing the attacks of the powers of evil it is not abandoned to itself and its own resources, for, if it were, it would in fact be doomed. The protection it enjoys is not due, however, to any efforts of the community. It has not located itself on God's side, quite the contrary: God in Jesus has put himself on its side. Therefore the community is also in need of sanctification, that is, of a continued assimilation to the being and ways of God: "Sanctify them in (or: through) the truth" (v. 17).

According to John truth is an essential attribute of God and his revelation, so that word of God and truth are one and the same. Truth is what one encounters and experiences through Jesus. John can therefore say, "If you remain in my word, you are truly my disciples; and you will know the truth, and the truth will set you free" (8:31-32). The reference here, of course, is not to a theoretical concept of truth. Truth is the divine reality itself as it reveals itself to people and goes out to them. Truth sanctifies just as it sets free. It changes and assimilates a person to the God of truth and love. The community of Jesus needs this kind of sanctification in every age because its members come out of the world, out of separation and alienation from God, and because they cannot themselves effect their assimilation to the God of truth and love. Sanctification or assimilation to God is a continuous process that never ends.

Despite its need of sanctification, the community shares in the mission of Jesus; this is the final statement of this section: "As you sent me into the world, so I have sent them into the world, and I sanctify myself for them so that they too may be sanctified in truth" (vv. 18-19). The sending of Jesus by the Father does not cease with his departure. Rather it continues in the sending of the community of disciples. John does not use the primitive Christian concept of *apostle* (the term occurs only once in this gospel—in 13:16—and there it has the very generic meaning of "one who is sent"). According to John, Jesus is the envoy of God in an exclusive and unqualified sense. The community can only bear witness that Jesus was sent by God, and understand its own mission as a continuation of the mission of Jesus. The concept *apostolic* here acquires a different and independent meaning: the community is apostolic because it has come into being entirely as a result of Jesus being sent by God; the mission of Jesus is, moreover, the enduring foundation of the community. It is this origin in Jesus that also constitutes the community as sent. The community is thus by its very nature intended and formed to be missionary; by continuing the mission of Jesus it also assumes Jesus' responsibility for the salvation of the world. The focus of the mission is and remains the world.

The ability of the community to continue the mission of Jesus to the world depends ultimately on Jesus sanctifying himself for his disciples. In this context the term sanctify acquires a new sense. It is here equivalent to "consecrate, present, offer sacrifice." As the formulaic "for them" suggests, we must see a reference here to the vicarious redemptive death of Jesus, his commitment of love to the end. The death of Jesus on the cross is thus understood as a consecrated death, a sacrificial death, that is at the same time a sanctification by the truth for the community. By means of the sacrificial death of Jesus the community is transported into the sphere of divine holiness. Against this background it is also clear that the community's mission to the world will always be carried on under the sign of sacrifice for the world, and that this last can include the surrender of earthly life. In John's eyes mission, witness to faith, and ability to believe are connected with the sacrifice and therefore the cross of Jesus.

Prayer for the Community (17:20–24)

Although the Christian community of every age has already been addressed along with the first generation (vv. 6ff.), it is only in verses 20-24 that the Church is expressly seen as extended in time: "I pray not only for these, but for all who believe in me through their word" (v. 20). The disciples of the first hour received the word from Jesus himself. In thus receiving it they acquired a share in his mission, as verse 18 shows. The word that entered the world through Jesus continues to be active. There will always be human beings who will attain to faith in Jesus through the testimony of his disciples. Consequently, there will be a constant repetition of the same pattern: the new disciples will become in turn the heralds of faith to the next generation. From this point of view the relationship between the first generation and the second generation is prototypical.

Verse 20 also expresses the fact that it is the living Christ himself who makes faith possible through the word of his disciples and the preaching of the Church. It will never be possible for the Church to take the place of Jesus. The Church's role is only to bear witness to what it has been given by Jesus; for John this means that the Church must bear witness to "the one true God and the one whom you sent, Jesus Christ" (v. 3). In the final analysis it is Jesus Christ whom we encounter in the Gospel. For, in John's understanding, the Gospel is simply Christ proclaiming himself through the mouths of his disciples.

Now it is certainly not accidental that at this point and with reference to the Church of all generations *the unity of believers* should be so emphatically set down as the primary concern: "that they all may be one, just as you, Father, are in me and I am in you, so they too may be one in us, in order that the world may believe that you sent me" (v. 21). The note of unity had already been sounded in verse 11: "that they all may be one." The "all" is to be given a temporal as well as a spatial extension and continuity. Through preaching and faith the spatio-temporal continuity of the community is established, as is its cohesion across the entire inhabited world.

Furthermore, when John focuses so emphatically on the unity of the community of disciples as being a unity of all believers, all Christians, he must have had good reasons for doing so. In all probability, this unity could no longer be taken entirely for granted in his day. It is possible that the farewell prayer of Jesus already reflects the picture of an ideal Church, according to which in the time of the first disciples this unity in the presence of Jesus had been an indubitable reality. At that time the sole exception was Judas, and his destiny had in fact been part of God's own plan (v. 12). Now, however, in the time of the evangelist, that is, in the second or most probably the third generation, the situation has changed.

As a matter of fact, the problem of the unity of the Church had played a role from the very outset, and, if we think about it, we will see, especially once the primitive community began to grow, it could not have been otherwise. The unity of the Church was not something that could be taken for granted; rather, it had to be achieved ever anew. It is evident that in the New Testament descriptions of the primitive Christian period the situation is heavily idealized and transfigured, as for example when we are told, "The community of believers was one in heart and soul. No one called anything he had his own, but they possessed all things in common" (Acts 4:32). When Luke writes this sort of thing, he is telling the Church of his own day how it should really be living. The flashback to the glorious beginnings provides ethical motivation for each present generation. The problem of the unity of the Church inevitably became morre urgent as new members kept coming into the Christian community, as communities multiplied, and as the factor of time and history made itself more keenly felt.

According to the Acts of the Apostles, the first tensions in the Christian community arose as social tensions in connection with the common possession of property (Acts 5:1-11: Ananias and Sapphira), then as tensions between the Hebrews and the Hellenists, that is, between the Aramaic-speaking sector of the original community, to which the earliest disciples of Jesus probably belonged, and the Greek-speaking sector which comprised chiefly Jews from the Diaspora who had converted to Christianity. These latter tensions probably did not have to do solely with the care of the poor but also involved basic theological questions of devotion to the law and, more generally, of belief in Jesus as Messiah with its possible consequences for the relationship to the community to Judaism (cf. Acts 6 and 7). As a result of the Apostle Paul's preaching still further tensions arose between the conservative-minded Jewish Christians, who wanted the Mosaic law to be binding on all Christians, and those who spoke for a mission to the pagans in which nothing was to be said about observing the law (Paul had meanwhile become the chief representative of this second group). On this subject the Apostolic Council (Acts 15:1-35; Gal. 2:1-10) succeeded in reaching a consensus and thus preserving the unity of the Church.

In the incident at Antioch (Gal. 2:11-21) in which Paul "opposed" Peter "to his face," there was almost an open break, a schism in the strict sense, between the Jewish Christian and the Gentile Christian parts of the community. We know, in addition, that in the community at Corinth factions arose at a very early stage which threatened the unity of the congregation from within: "Chloe's people tell me, brothers, that there is bickering and contention among you. I am referring to the fact that each of you is saying something different: 'I adhere to Paul!' 'I to Apollos!' 'I to Cephas!' Is Christ divided, then? Was Paul crucified for you? Or were you baptized in the name of Paul?" (1 Cor. 1:11-13). These examples could be multiplied.

The emergence of the Christian communities brought with it the problem of unity, that is, of their inner cohesion, their communion in life and teaching. The letters of Paul the Apostle to the communities show that from the beginning his efforts were devoted to preserving or restoring unity and, in addition, to strengthening the bonds of union between the separate communities. With the development of the early catholic or inclusive Church this problem inevitably became more pressing. The gospel of John evidently stands at the threshold of this development.

How did people attempt to grapple with the problem? Clearly, there were various possible approaches. Paul calls the disputing and divided Corinthians back onto the common ground of the one Gospel, the message of the cross (1 Cor. 1:17-31). According to Paul, the unity of the Church is not primarily a matter of organization or a sociological problem, but a spiritual reality (cf. especially 1 Cor. 12 and 13). If anyone wants to preserve unity, it can be done by reminding believers of the spiritual foundations of their Christian and ecclesial existence, and especially of the love that is more important than all the freely given gifts (the charisms) (1 Cor. 13). In the Letter to the Ephesians, which is not from Paul's hand but belongs to a later period (ca. A.D. 80), certain criteria of unity are already being listed: "Be humble, peaceful, and patient; support one another with love and endeavor to preserve the unity of the Spirit by means of the bond of peace. *One* body and *one* Spirit, just as you also received *one* and the same hope when you were called; *one* Lord, *one* faith, *one* baptism, *one* God and Father of all, who is above all and in all" (Eph. 4:3-6).

The idea of unity plays an especially important role in the letters of Bishop Ignatius of Antioch, who suffered martyrdom at Rome under Emperor Trajan in about A.D. 110. His conception of unity is of great interest because his letters are to be dated only a little after the gospel of John, and because he represents a direction that soon won out in the early Church and shows characteristic differences from John's conception of unity. This is how Ignatius exhorts his fellow bishop, Polycarp of Smyrna: "Be concerned about unity; there is nothing better than it" (*To Polycarp* 1,2). To the community at Ephesus he writes:

> Therefore you ought to walk together in accordance with the thinking of the bishop, as you are now doing. For your presbytery, which is justly renowned and worthy of God, is united to the bishop as the strings are to the harp. Thus by the accord of your sentiments and the harmony of your love you sing of Jesus Christ. Let each of you likewise become part of a choir, so that by the harmony of your mutual agreement you may take up God's melody in unison and with one voice sing to the Father through Jesus Christ, in order that he may hear you and acknowledge you as members of his Son on account of your good works. It is profitable for you, therefore, to live in blameless unity, in order that you may always participate in God.
>
> Now if I myself in so short a time entered into such a close relationship with your bishop, a relationship that is spiritual and not natural in character, how much more must I congratulate you on being so deeply united to him, just as the Church is with Jesus Christ and Jesus Christ with the Father, so that all things may be harmonious and one. (*To the Ephesians* 4, 1-5, 1)

And to the community at Philadelphia: "Therefore I did what is in my power as a human being created for unity. For where division reigns, God does not dwell. The Lord, of course, forgives all who repent, provided they return to the unity of God and to the senate of the bishop" (*To the Philadelphians* 8, 1).

As the texts show, Ignatius is thoroughly familiar with the idea of spiritual unity according to which the Church is linked to Jesus

Christ and Jesus Christ to the Father. Indeed, the God who promises unity is himself this very unity (*To the Trallians* 11, 2). What catches our attention, however, is the fact that for Ignatius unity with the bishop and his presbytery is set directly alongside the spiritual unity based on faith. Conversion to the unity of God and conversion to the senate of the bishop are one and the same thing to Ignatius (cf. the passages cited). In his view, the bishop, in union with the presbytery and the deacons, is the visible sign and at the same time the guarantor of the unity of the Church and consequently of the unity of all believers with Christ and God. In Ignatius, the *ecclesiastico-institutional factor* has acquired an importance for the understanding of unity that it did not previously have, at least to the same degree.

If we compare the texts of Ignatius with the Johannine statements in 17:20-24, the difference becomes clear: the institutional factor, consisting of the bishop and his presbytery, does not (yet?) play any clearly recognizable role in John. Instead, John bases the unity of the community directly on the divine model which is at the same time the ground of that unity: " . . . just as you, Father, are in me, and I am in you" (v. 21a). Here we meet once again the Johannine immanence formula which specifies the reciprocal relationship of the divine persons, Father and Son, as a reciprocal "being in," that is, as the most profound kind of communion and one that in the last analysis love alone can make possible (cf. v. 23).

This vital, reciprocal "being in" which is based on love is the spiritual ground for the unity of the community of Jesus' disciples. It follows that we must think of this latter unity as being similarly structured, that is, as a unity made possible by the divine love and reflecting, in however imperfect a way, the divine unity itself. In virtue of this unity the community will be a permanent witness to Jesus before the world: " . . . in order that the world may believe that you sent me" (v. 21b). The unity of the community is so astonishing and persuasive that it can bring the world to faith in Jesus. The converse is implied: Discord, hatred, and division in the community will cause the world not to believe and will confirm it in its unbelief.

Verse 22 adds a further detail: the community shares in the glory of Jesus. Jesus has bestowed on the community the divine light and splendor which he has received from the Father; he has passed it on to the community. Here again it is made clear that the unity of the community, which is a reflection in this world of the divine unity, is not a moral or organizational achievement of the community but wholly a gift from God. The community cannot of itself assure its own unity; only by its abiding union with Jesus can it obtain this unity and bear witness to it. This means, further, that as long as the community takes its bearings from Jesus, it need not be concerned about its unity. In this supposition the gift will never be lacking. For it is the exalted and now present Christ himself who is the center and ground of unity.

Unity, then, is the gift of the Christ who is present in the community. This means that the community does not at any point have its unity as a fixed possession but that it is rather on the way to unity, to perfect and complete unity: "I in them and you in me, so that they may be completely one, and the world may know that you sent me and that you love them as you love me" (v. 23). Perfect unity is thus the future that awaits the community; unity is something always ahead of it, just as its perfection in divine love is. In the final analysis, the unity of the Church, as John conceives it, is to be understood in eschatological terms. In any event, it is not unity as people ordinarily understand it, but rather a gift of the revealer and of revelation: it is a fruit of redemption. Therefore it cannot be coerced, even by ecclesiastical authorities.[171]

It is in keeping with Johannine eschatology that the unity of the community/Church can on the one hand be described as something already bestowed on it through the saving work of Jesus, and yet on the other hand as something future, the completion of which is still to come. According to John, unity is both a present gift and the constant goal of all believers. This state of affairs also reflects the fact that because the disciples are in the world their unity is constantly under attack and that as a unity which is visible to the world it is always in jeopardy and cannot be simply identified with perfect eschatological unity. R. Bultmann observes with justice:

> This unity is always called in question in the history of the community; there is always the danger that it will be for-

gotten or even denied. And whether the community remains true to its character, i.e. whether it remains the eschatological community in which the world is annulled, the community grounded in and preserved by the eschatological event and by nothing else, depends on the knowledge of this unity.[172]

If the unity of the community is to become a testimony to faith before the world, it must certainly have its visible side; given his presuppositions, John can hardly have thought of a completely invisible unity. But at this point the danger arises of ceasing to understand the unity of the Church in terms primarily of its spiritual ground and of revelation and of attempting to secure it chiefly by institutional means. That is the way which Ignatius of Antioch seems to have gone and which John for good reason avoided.

Verse 24 contains a petition for the perfection of the community, after verse 23b has already said that in the last analysis the one undivided love of God is the space in which the Christian community exists; here God's love for Jesus and his love for the disciples of Jesus is one and the same love. It follows that the perfection of the community can only take the form of its perfection in love. The community has its existence in the following of Jesus the revealer. And, as is repeatedly brought out in the farewell discourses, this following leads it along the way of Jesus to the clear vision of the divine glory. This vision is the totally secure and inalienable participation in the divine love that exists between Father and Son from all eternity. Thus the circle is closed.

Conclusion of the Prayer (17:25–26)

A further brief section brings the farewell prayer of Jesus to its end. This conclusion once again draws together all the essential motifs of the entire prayer, and at the same time makes it clear that in this prayer the true locus of the community of faith has been disclosed. This locus is the divine love from which Jesus the revealer came forth and to which he is now returning. His purpose was, and remains throughout the entire future, naught else but to disclose this sphere to believers and to lead them into it.

From among the various motifs and themes enunciated in the fare-well prayer of Jesus, we shall speak here only of the theme of unity (of the Church/churches).

The concept of unity is, of course, a many faceted one, and, even though it is so frequently invoked, it is anything but clear and unambiguous; consequently it is difficult to grasp.[173] The concept requires special attention when it refers to social entities, to groups, and thus to human beings. The unity of human groups depends on special conditions. We need only mention the danger of applying an abstract notion of unity to human groups or society and thus of failing to attend to the conditions required for a unity of persons. A distinction must be made between a purely organizational unity of multitudes and the unity of groups and social formations that have developed over a period of history. Finally, the unity of a community whose basis is faith poses a special problem of its own.

It is not only in the farewell prayer of Jesus that the idea of unity plays an important role in the fourth gospel. In the parabolic dis-course on the good shepherd we read, "I am the good shepherd, and I know my own and my own know me, just as the Father knows me and I know the Father, and I lay down my life for my sheep. I have still other sheep who do not belong to this fold; these too I must lead, and they will hear my voice, and there will be *one* fold, one shepherd" (10:14-16). According to this passage it is the task of Jesus as the good shepherd to bring people together into one fold, that is, into a single people of God. The other sheep here are distinguished from my own, that is, the disciples of Jesus. Thus on the one side there is the clearly delineated community of Jesus that is subject to him as true leader unto salvation, and, on the other side, the others, a term that undoubtedly includes all of humankind without exception and is unlimited in its comprehension. The mis-sion of Jesus extends to these others too; it is unconditionally universal.

The words of Jesus in 10:14-16 remind us of the evangelist's re-sponse to a remark of Caiphas, the high priest ("You are ignorant and do not understand that it is better for one man to die for the people than for the whole people to be destroyed"): "He said this, however, not of his own accord; rather, as high priest of that year, he prophesied that Jesus would die for the people, and not only for the (Jewish) people but in order that he might gather into unity the children of God scattered throughout the world" (11:49-52).

According to John, the person of Jesus, especially in his death that was motivated by committed love, is of absolutely vital importance when it comes to gathering humanity into the unity of the eschatological people of God. In this context, unity is conceived of in eschatological terms; it is the goal of God's saving activity, and as such it has an existence that is prior to all human endeavors in behalf of unity. But John is also convinced that in Jesus the decisive foundation for unity has already been laid. According to him, the unity of the community has its ground in the word and work of Jesus; seen from this point of view the unity is by no means something solely of the future but is already present in the community because of its union with Christ. For this reason we speak of the spiritual ground of unity. John gives expression to this idea when he speaks of the unity within the community of disciples as being proportionate to its unity with God the Father: " . . . my own know me, just as the Father knows me and I know the Father" (10:15); "that they may be one as we are one" (17:11); "that they all may be one, just as you, Father, are in me and I am in you, so they too may be one in us, in order that the world may believe that you sent me" (17:21).

Thus understood, the unity of the community, having as it does the divine unity of the Father and the Son as its ground and prototype, is evidently something far more than an organizational or sociological unity; it is not natural and human, but supernatural and divine. It is a unity that depends on faith, and therefore cannot be created by human commands and certainly not coerced. Even ecclesiastical officials cannot, as it were, enact the unity in question, for this would mean that they were attempting to be themselves the ground of unity. Unity must be won by prayer; that is, it must be received and accepted as a gift.

In the form of spiritual unity, however, and as the object of the eschatological promises of Jesus, the unity is prior even to the community of disciples. Thus, we may say with H. Schlier, "According to the New Testament the unity of the Church is always already given and not created solely by believers; it is a present and not merely future unity; it is a concrete historical unity and not simply an abstract ideal for the one people of God, which is the one body of Christ and the one temple of the Holy Spirit and which is to preserve and prove its unity in the united and unifying community of believers."[174] At the same time, however, we must note that according to John the divine unity of the Church has its abiding ground in God and Jesus Christ and that the empirical and historical factors in unity must be distinguished from this ground. The community must (this is the point of Jesus' petition) be *preserved* in unity. To this extent the contrast between abstract, ideal unity and concrete, historical unity does not do justice to what John is saying. For the spiritual unity in God and Jesus Christ is thoroughly real to faith and seriously meant, and the unity of the community is utterly dependent on this spiritual unity since the latter is not something created by the community.

On the other hand, this means, of course, that despite all human schisms and separations the unity of Christ's Church has never ceased to be a reality. If the unity of the Church is first and foremost a gift of God and Christ, a divine gift over which humans have no control, then we may not act at the human historical level of the Church and its denominations as though unity were a matter of human achievement and organization or even of ecclesiastical office. We shall return to this point. At bottom, all the denominations are and remain ordered to unity as thus understood, and they all share in this unity since in the root of their existence they are linked by faith to the divine unity and are not allowed to slip away from it.

If we reflect more fully on this point, we will see a new side to the movement for reunion, namely, that this reunion cannot be understood as a return to Rome under the supreme authority of the pope. No, the movement for reunion must be understood as first and foremost a quest of the denominations for the real spiritual ground of their existence and as an ever renewed movement toward this innermost center. The denominations must meet in Christ. Even the pope must sincerely participate in this quest and movement; he is not dispensed from it, since even he does not have unity at his disposal. At the same time, however, a certain justification attaches to the traditional Roman Catholic view that the unity of the

Church already exists and does not need to be restored by the denominations. The justification has its basis in the reference to the Church's authentically pregiven unity in God and Jesus Christ. Insofar as the pope bears witness to this unity and acknowledges himself to be its servant, his office is legitimate.

In addition, the gift of unity brings with it the task of preserving unity amid the concrete reality of history, of restoring it, bearing witness to it, and so on. Here again we are reminded of Pascal's words, "Thou wouldst not be seeking Me, hadst thou not found Me." The work of the denominations for unity can therefore only be understood as being the ever renewed quest of the one ground of unity that is already given in God and Jesus Christ, in order thereby to be united and brought together ever anew. The crucial problems, of course, are to be found on the empirical and historical side. And in this area it is becoming clear to us today that calls for unity which are based solely on dogma will not solve the problem of the one Church and many denominations.

Even if Rome is correct, as we said above, in pointing to a unity that already exists and does not have to be restored at a later date, it would nonetheless be misleading for it to act as though it had played no part in the division of the Church but had always been the *una sancta, catholica et apostolica ecclesia* (one holy, catholic and apostolic Church) in its historical and concrete fullness. By reason of its own not inconsiderable share in the guilt the Roman Catholic Church has become a particular, denominational church, and in its present form no longer reflects the total fullness of Christianity. The fullness of Christianity finds expression today only in all the Christian groups together.

The one Church that thanks to God's grace has never ceased to be exists in a historically pluralistic world of peoples, cultures, periods, epochs, and so on. As a social formation composed of human beings it is also subject to certain laws governing the things of this world and applying to all the large-scale groups that can be described and interpreted with the help of sociological categories. Finally, with regard precisely to its concrete historical existence, the one Church is not only Christ continued and the body of Christ but also the Church of sinners, in part because of its entanglement in secular dealings and disputes of every kind. As long as the doctrine of the

Church or ecclesiology is concerned only with theologico-dogmatic statements and fails to take into consideration the sociologico-historical side of the Church with all its admittedly difficult and often unpleasant problems, those who cultivate it are engaged in a cover-up operation and imprisoned in a false consciousness.

Even in regard to its unity the Church finds itself caught up in the eschatologico-historical tension between the already and the not yet. Unity, therefore, is an ever new task. It is a hoped for goal, and consequently the perfection of unity can, from the eschatological viewpoint, only be the work of God himself as brought to completion. If we keep this truth before us, the existence of the many denominations takes on a new significance. What these many churches represent is not only an apostasy from the one true Church but also a more complete historical manifestation and development of the fullness of Christianity. In considering this aspect of the matter we should not forget that the apostasy of the early Church from the Gospel of Jesus was often enough the forerunner of new divisions and therefore may not be viewed in an exclusively one-sided way. Even in reference to the multiplicity of denominations we must accustom ourselves to speak of a *felix culpa*, a "fortunate sin."

The historical approach is thus a major and indeed indispensable aid in understanding eschatologico-historical unity. Modern sociological and socio-psychological findings likewise provide rich resources for a better understanding of schism and heresies and of their motives, origin and development, than the dogmatic aspect alone can supply. In this way it is possible to move beyond an understanding of Church unity that is infected by authoritarian thinking.

We saw earlier how in Ignatius of Antioch the emphasis in the conception of unity shifts strongly to institutional factors, and especially to the role of the bishop. The monarchical bishop was now regarded chiefly as guarantor of unity, and this view entailed certain consequences of course. These can be found clearly expressed in the work *On the Unity of the Catholic Church* by Cyprian (ca. 200-28), bishop of Carthage.[175] The formulas set down in this book were to be extremely important in the future.

Cyprian interprets the saying on Peter the rock in Matthew 16:18-19 ("You are Peter and on this rock I will build my Church") as referring to unity. The Lord "established by His own authority a source for that oneness having its origin in *one* man alone. No doubt the other Apostles were all that Peter was, endowed with equal dignity and power, but the start comes from him alone, in order to show that the Church of Christ is *unique*" (ch. 4). How is it possible, then, for a person to adhere to the faith if he does not adhere to the unity?

It is the task primarily of the bishops to safeguard this unity: "Now this oneness we must hold to firmly and insist on—especially we who are bishops and exercise authority in the Church—so as to demonstrate that the episcopal power is one and undivided too" (ch. 5). Those who jeopardize or even destroy the unity of the Church commit adultery in a spiritual sense, says Cyprian.

> Whoever breaks with the Church and enters on an adulterous union (by joining a heretical or schismatic group) cuts himself off from the promises made to the Church; and he who turns his back on the Church of Christ will not come to the rewards of Christ: he is an alien, a worldling, an enemy (*alienus est, profanus est, hostis est*). You cannot have God for your Father if you no longer have the Church for your mother. If there was any escape for one who was outside the ark of Noah, there will be as much for anyone who is found to be outside the Church. The Lord warns us when He says: *"He that is not with me is against me, and he that gathereth not with me, scattereth."* Whoever breaks the peace and harmony of Christ acts against Christ; whoever gathers elsewhere than in the Church, scatters the Church of Christ. . . . If a man does not keep this unity, he is not keeping the law of God; he has broken faith with the Father and the Son, he is cut off from life and salvation. (ch. 6)

This sixth chapter of Cyprian's *On the Unity of the Catholic Church* supplies formulas that were to mould the Catholic understanding of the Church for centuries and to some extent still mould it today. The Church is the institution for salvation apart from which no one can reach God. No one can have God for his Father who does not have the Church for his mother. And then there is the well-known *Extra ecclesiam nulla salus* (Outside the Church no salvation), which appears here in rhetorical dress in the image of the ark of Noah. Just as no one could be rescued from the flood if he was outside the ark of Noah, so no one can be saved who is outside the Church.

Similarly, anyone who leaves the Church becomes an alien (*alienus*). Cyprian repeatedly demands that no one have any further contact of any kind with such a person: "Whoever is separated from the Church must be avoided and fled from" (ch. 17). Such a person becomes *profanus*, that is, one who is outside the sacred precincts. Profane or worldly is the opposite of holy (*sacer*) and in the present context means lacking in salvation, lost, or, in an ecclesiastical sense, outlawed. According to an even stronger term, he becomes a *hostis*, and enemy to whom love is refused.

We also find in Cyprian the supposition that a person who leaves the Church or jeopardizes the unity of the Church cannot possibly have any positive reasons for doing so, but only bad ones. "Let no one think that good men can leave the Church; it is not the grain that the wind carries away, nor the solidly rooted tree that the storm blows down: it is the empty chaff that is swept away by the storm, the weakling trees that are overturned by the blast of the whirlwind" (ch. 9). A good person cannot leave the Church; it is always and only the wicked, the empty chaff that do so.

All these moral judgments were to become deeply embedded in the ecclesial consciousness and to leave their mark right down to the present day. Even if Christians who have separated from the Church, that is, from the inclusive Church represented by the bishop, should die as martyrs, it would be of no avail to them. Even such a death does not purge "the irremissible sin of schism." Whoever is not in the Church cannot be an authentic martyr. For those there is likewise no communion with God. And even if they be burned or thrown to wild beasts just like the real martyrs, this is only a punishment for infidelity and an end to recklessness. "Such a man may be put to death; crowned he cannot be. If he calls himself a Christian, the devil also often calls himself the Christ, and is a liar" (ch. 14). The apostate is thus utterly defamed.

It is possible to understand to some extent how the bishop of a third-century community could think in this fashiion and define the Church, the *catholica ecclesia*, with the bishop at its head, as the place of salvation which people might on no account abandon if they wished to be saved. It is also understandable that unity should be especially precious to such a bishop, for in the background can be glimpsed very concrete pastoral concerns. Nonetheless the establishment of such clearcut boundaries and the verdicts passed are disturbing, even if we allow for the rhetorical and juridical development of the thought and for the juridical mentality (which plays an even more important role). In our day we must also take into consideration the historical effects these formulas have had; we must come to grips with them and clear the ground of them, for they are our Catholic past (a past that extends right down to the present). Only a mind that is theologically naive can still make these formulas its own.

Where precisely is the problem with Cyprian? It is to be located in the assurance, so incredible to our way of thinking, with which the boundaries of the Church are taken as determining what is possible or impossible for God? Cyprian even dares to say, "The grievous irremissible sin of schism is not purged even by a violent death" (ch. 14). Schism, an offense against unity, is here interpreted as an unforgivable sin; unity, on the other hand, has become an absolute value for its own sake. These views undoubtedly made possible an unusually effective social control.

Cyrpian's formulas also proved extremely dangerous in the course of the Church's history. They became slogans under the egis of which all outsiders, deviants, etc., were to be either destroyed or brought to reason. The church frequently used them as justification for a maternal despotism according to which union with God depended on it. All who wished to have God for their Father had to have the Church for their mother.

Above all, there was the formula about the "only true Church" (*Extra ecclesiam nulla salus*) with its claim to be sole adminstrator of revealed truth and salvation. People today make every effort to interpret this "venerable axiom" (de Lubac) in such a way as to give it an unobjectionable meaning by emphasizing the positive sense of the negative formula: Salvation comes through the Church and through it alone. But Cyprian and later theology did not give it such a positive meaning! The formula is in fact not a carefully weighed theological statement of an objective state of affairs; it is a *battle slogan*, just as the whole of Cyprian's *On the Unity of the Catholic*

Church is an exhortatory and polemical pamphlet. It utters drastic threats about the damnation to be incurred by all "divisive spirits." This is precisely the key objection to these formulas about the "one true Church" and "no salvation outside the Church": they are polemical slogans meant to imbue Christians with an anxiety about salvation and to exercise a holy coercion by threatening people with damnation. Once we realize this, we can no longer adopt either these formulas or the mentality behind them.

Unity and Multiplicity or Plurality: This problem can be solved only if the vital tension between unity and plurality is accepted and made fruitful for the future. This means that a monolithic understanding of Church unity with its centralizing, totalitarian, and uniformist tendencies blocks the way to the genuine communion of churches and must therefore be eliminated.

It is profitable for us at this point to think back once again to the primitive and early Christian beginnings. The New Testament witnesses still reflect a real plurality of confessional forms, patterns of thought, and varying community practices. Our gospels contain four quite distinct pictures of Jesus that cannot be fused into a single harmonious picture. If we add Paul and his theology as well as the other New Testament writers, it becomes clear that in the founding age of the Church there were quite disparate christologies, quite disparate ways of understanding and confessing Jesus, quite disparate Christianities.

The Christianity of Paul and his communities in the mission has a quite different stamp in many respects from the Christianity of Matthew or Mark or Luke or John. Different again is the Christianity of the Letter of James or the Letter to the Hebrews. Or we may think of the differences between Jewish Christianity and Hellenistic Christianity; the distinction between these two was hardly less than between Catholics and Protestants today. With the help of several decades of research exegetes have learned to see the differences more clearly than they used to. Primitive Christianity already showed a multiplicity of Christianities that manifested considerable differences according to their social and spiritual milieus, even if we cannot yet speak of confessions in the post-Reformation sense. The early Church happily resisted the temptation to combine the four gospels into a single harmonized gospel. The attempt was made indeed in the second century by Tatian, a Syrian, but without official success; unofficially, his *Harmony* enjoyed great popularity.

If such notable differences existed, is it at all possible to speak of the unity of the New Testament? Of course, there is such a unity! But it is not an extrinsic, superficial unity or even the verbal unity of a dogmatic formula. In the final analysis, the unity is given by the figure of Jesus, about whom the writings tell us. But the one Jesus is variously mirrored in the four gospels, in Paul, and so on, just as light breaks down into various colors. It is a well-known fact that light itself, light as such, cannot be painted; only the various colors can be painted—and yet there does exist the one light which makes the colors possible. No single color, moreover, can claim to be the fullness of light.

This comparison is a helpful one. Unity exists, but it is difficult to grasp in any direct way. Or, to put it differently, unity is had only in and with the plurality of the various confessions and theologies. Only from the second century on do people begin to take unity as meaning chiefly *uniformity*. The emphasis is now on a standardized organization of the various local churches and on uniform practices for all the churches. In this process the conflict with the heresies of the early Church played an important role. As the overall development of the inclusive Catholic Church proceeded, the concept of unity required that the possibility of a plurality of approaches and distinctive forms be suppressed; this was truer in the Roman-Latin West than in the Greek East. The new and strongly uniformist Latin conception of unity that now became predominant was incompatible with any plurality; in this it differed from what we find in the East which is still familiar with a plurality of confessions, images of Jesus, and forms of Christianity. The difficulty, especially in Roman Catholicism, is that people have now become so accustomed to the Latin conception of unity with its uniformism that they cannot conceive of unity except as taught in the Latin Church, despite the loss it entails for the fullness of Christianity.

In any case, pluralism cannot be wholly eliminated. Anyone who thinks historically cannot fail to see that the Western-Latin Roman Church has in the course of its history undergone a particularist development of its own, just as much as have the churches of the East, Constantinople, Russia, Armenia, and so on. From a historical viewpoint, therefore, it is impossible without reservations to predicate a genuine, universalist catholicism of the Latin Church. Until the modest beginnings of the regional conferences of bishops after the Second Vatican Council, Rome constantly endeavored to impose the Latin ecclesiastical system and understanding of Christianity on all Christian peoples and groups, on the grounds that it alone represented the fullness of Catholicism. In fact, the endeavor meant suppressing a true and authentic catholicity.

As judged by the historian, then, the universality of Rome and the Latin Church is a claim that will not stand up against the historical evidence. What is correct and true in the claim is that the idea of "one, holy, catholic, and apostolic Church" was retained at all and did not perish. The Roman-Latin Church, however, must itself rediscover authentic catholicity and give the plurality of churches the place due to it. This has been true especially since the great Western Reformation of the sixteenth century. The Counter-Reformation brought an enormous narrowing of vision to Roman Catholicism and a loss of Christian universality. In this period the Roman Catholic Church became itself a denomination; this development lasted until the end of the nineteenth century. Initially, the First Vatican Council only reinforced the trend. It is only since the two World Wars that a contrary ecumenical movement has gotten under way. As far as Roman Catholicism is concerned, this movement found its first tangible expression in the *Decree on Ecumenism* of the Second Vatican Council.

How can the churches make effective and give visible historical expression to the unity they ever already have in God and Jesus Christ? The first step would be a self-critical reflection on the New Testament evidence. There is now a consensus in all the Christian churches that the Bible is the normative foundation. In addition, since the end of the Second World War exegesis has become an interconfessional discipline; biblical exegesis and biblical theology are thus a factor making for communion in all the Christian churches. The need is to reflect on the foundation we share and to accept the critical challenges which it raises for us. Even the pope and the ecclesiastical magisterium must allow the New Testament to ask them critical questions.

In the New Testament truth is something personal: it is the reality of God as it encounters persons in Jesus Christ. The formulas of faith praise and extol this reality, but the reality cannot be wholly captured in any formula. The churches, therefore, may not make it a condition for the attainment of unity with one another that the other churches must formally accept all confessions. At this point, confidence in the transcedent truth of Christ must be so great that earlier formulations will be in good measure simply dropped.

In the area of social service community has proved to be already existent at many levels. Only the tiresome concept of office stands in the way of intercommunion. Many theologians in the various denominations are agreed that this need not be the case. The argument that intercommunion can only be the crown and conclusion, the great celebration at the end, when all questions have been answered, represents an unhistorical perfectionism. It is like making an appointment for doomsday, for when will there be no more theological questions to ask?! Here we might well ask with Hillel, the great Jewish rabbi, "If not now, then when?"

As we have seen, unity always remains a task and a goal. In this world even the unity of the Church will always be only provisional, incomplete, open-ended. If it is not to be understood in a totalitarian way, then neither should it be understood in perfectionist terms. The real issue is the relatively few but important and central matters regarding which people should and even can reach a consensus. The real issue is also honest dialogue that is ready to reach a consensus not only with the other church but also with the others within one's own church. This dialogue requires patience; it is a lengthy process. But now the churches are, in fact, on the move.

NOTES

Works Frequently Cited:

Blank, J. *Krisis: Untersuchungen zur johanneischen Christologie und Eschatologie* (Freiburg, 1964).
Bultmann, R. *The Gospel of John: A Commentary*, tr. by G. R. Beasley-Murray, R. W. N. Hoare and J. K. Riches (Philadelphia, 1971).
Käsemann, E. *The Testament of Jesus according to John 17: A Study of the Gospel of John in the Light of Chapter 17*, tr. by G. Krodel (Philadelphia, 1968).
Schnackenburg, R. *Das Johannesevangelium* (Herders Theologischer Kommentar zum Neuen Testament 4), 3 vols. (Freiburg, 1965, 1971, 1975). English translation of vols. 1 and 2: *The Gospel according to St. John* (New York-London, 1968, 1979).
Schulz, S. *Das Evangelium nach Johannes* (Das Neue Testament deutsch 4; Göttingen, 1972¹² = Berlin, 1975).
Strathmann, H. *Das Evangelium nach Johannes* (Das Neue Testament deutsch 4; Göttingen, 1951⁶, 1968¹¹).

Abbreviations

CCL   *Corpus Christianorum, Series Latina* (Turnhout, 1953ff.).

LTK²   *Lexikon für Theologie und Kirche.* New ed. by J. Höfer and K. Rahner (Freiburg, 1957-65).

PL   *Patrologia Latina.* Ed. by J. P. Migne (Paris, 1844-64).

RAC   *Reallexikon für Antike und Christentum.* Ed. by Th. Klauser (Stuttgart, 1950ff.).

RGG³   *Die Religion in Geschichte und Gegenwart.* 3rd ed. by K. Galling (Tübingen, 1956-62).

TDNT   *Theological Dictionary of the New Testament*. Ed. by G. Kittel,
            tr. by G. Bromiley (Grand Rapids, 1964-74).

NOTES

1 Käsemann, p. 1.

2 For these I refer the reader chiefly to the detailed discussion in Schnackenburg's extensive commentary, I:11-217. See also the various introductions to the New Testament.

3 On this problem cf. S. Kierkegaard, *Philosophical Fragments* and *Concluding Unscientific Postscript*.

4 H. Schürmann, *Der Abendmahlsbericht Lukas 22, 7-38 als Gottesdien-
   stordnung, Gemeindeordnung, Lebensordnung* (Paderborn, 1957), p.
   95. Also in Schürmann's *Ursprung und Gestalt* (Düsseldorf, 1970), p.
   150.

5 In Jewish literature cf. also the *Testaments of the Twelve Patriarchs*.
   In its oldest parts, which from a theological viewpoint are closely connected with the circles in which the Qumran texts originated, the composition belongs to around 100 B.C. But the text seems to have
   undergone a Christian revision. It is possible that John was familiar with
   the tradition of the *Testaments of the Twelve Patriarchs*. Nonetheless,
   the significance of such farewell discourses is best illustrated by the
   example of Deuteronomy.

6 On this, see G. von Rad's introduction in *Deuteronomy: A Commentary*,
   tr. by D. Barton (Philadelphia, 1966), pp. 11-30. Among contemporary
   students of the Old Testament there is no longer any doubt that the
   collection of laws in Deuteronomy belongs, as a code, to a much later
   time, namely the period of King Josiah (609-539 B.C.) and that the
   collection is probably identical with the Book of the Law which was
   found in the temple (cf. 2 Kings 22:3-13). The story that serves as a
   framework for the collection may have originated even later and probably comes from the deuteronomist school.

7 Von Rad, *Deuteronomy*, p. 28.

8 Cf. Blank, pp. 109ff.

9 On the whole problem, cf. Blank, especially pp. 281ff.

10 On this point see the important Excursus 5, "The 'Son of Man' in the Fourth Gospel," in Schnackenburg, I:529-42. According to Schnackenburg, "John is giving a new interpretation to existing primitive Christian tradition" (p. 538).

11 The new (German) ecumenical translation of the New Testament also has "supporter" (i.e. *Beistand* in German). The older translation, "consoler," has a venerable tradition behind it but is philologically indefensible.

12 If the "supporter" is understood to be the "spirit of truth," the informed reader will be reminded of certain parallels in the Qumran literature, but he will also perceive the differences. John shows no signs of the kind of dualism found in the teaching of Qumran on the "two spirits" (*Rule*, 1QS 3, 13-4, 26), in which the spirits of truth and perversity are in opposition from the beginning of creation to the end. The most important difference, however, is the radical linking, in John, of the "spirit of truth" with Jesus. The "truth" which the Spirit renders accessible and to which he "leads in" the believer, etc., is the truth of Jesus and of the Jesus-revelation, nothing else.

13 F. Mussner is right, therefore, in describing the gospel of John as "an explanatory anamnesis of the life of Jesus" (*The Historical Jesus in the Gospel of St. John*, tr. by W. J. O'Hara [Quaestiones Disputatae 19; New York, 1967], p. 44).

14 Suetonius, *Caligula* 26: "Caligula did not show any greater respect or generosity in dealing with the Senate. He forced senators on whom the highest honors had been bestowed to run several thousand paces in their togas alongside his chariot or to don aprons, like slaves, and stand behind his couch at table, or at his feet, to wait on him."

15 So Bultmann, p. 469 and n. 1.

16 Ibid., pp. 478-79.

17 Cf. H. J. Kraus, *Die Psalmen* 1 (Neukirchen, 1960, 1961[2] = Berlin, 1972), p. 314.

18 "I am" is the "revelation formula"; cf. Schnackenburg, 2:59-80, Excursus 8.

19 Cf. J. Blinzler, "Judas Iskarioth," *LTK*[2] 5:1152-54.

20 Cf. above on 13:18-20.

21 On this point cf. Schnackenburg, 1:97-100.

22 "Son of man," a title of majesty, originates in Jewish apocalyptic where

it designates the heavenly "man" who will appear in the final age (cf. Dan. 7; Ethiopian Enoch, ch. 37-71). In the Jewish apocalyptic tradition some links are already established between the "Son of man" and the concept of Messiah; on this problem cf. S. Mowinckel, *He That Cometh* (Oxford, 1956), pp. 346-50. Probably in dependence on authentic Son of man sayings of Jesus himself, the primitive Church took over the title and made it a christological title of majesty for Jesus; cf. F. Hahn, *The Titles of Jesus in Christology*, tr. by H. Knight and G. Ogg (Cleveland, 1969), pp. 15-67.

The significance of this application is that the primitive Church was thereby assigning a redemptive and eschatological significance to the person and destiny (cross and resurrection) of Jesus.

23 Schnackenburg, 1:529-42, Excursus 5: "The 'Son of Man' in the Fourth Gospel."

24 In apocalyptic literature "glory" is predicated of the Son of man as a sign that he belongs to the divine realm.

25 Contemporary scholars are even of the opinion that the composition of the canonical gospels, the collection and commitment to writing of the tradition about Jesus, and the organization of this tradition into a history of Jesus such as we see first in Mark, were all a reaction to the etherealization of the historical Jesus in various pneumatico-enthusiastic movements.

26 *Adversus haereses* III, 2, 3.

27 Bultmann, p. 600.

28 Behind the phrase lies a mythological representation that is known to us from Jewish apocalyptic (Enoch 41, 2; Slavonic Enoch 61, 2-3) but also from gnostic thought (cf. references in Bultmann, p. 601, n. 1).

29 Cf. A. Schlatter, *Der Evangelist Johannes* (Stuttgart, 1930), p. 292: "We are hardly true to John if we identify the Father's house with heaven. The departure of Jesus to make a place for the disciples is indeed an ascension, but the introduction of the disciples into God's house will take place only at the parousia. The 'Father's house' and the 'kingdom of God' are not to be separated from one another. The word 'house' corresponds to the name 'Father,' the word 'kingdom' to the name 'God.' " In these comments Schlatter does not really grasp what John is saying, but he does put his finger on the precise problem. The fourth evangelist, with his christologically grounded eschatology, is here taking

the principle at work in the idea that salvation is already present in Christ, and drawing the logical conclusion from it.

30 Cf. Acts 9:2; 16:17; 18:25, 26; 19:9, 23; 22:3; 24:14, 22.

31 On the whole problem, cf. Schnackenburg, 2:58-80, Excursus 8, with further bibliography.

32 Ibid. 2:69.

33 This interpretation is in keeping with the fact that the Old Testament "I am" formula was already a cultic revelation formula; cf. W. Zimmerli, "Ich bin Jahwe," in *Gottes Offenbarung* (Munich, 1963), pp. 11-40.

34 Here is a principle that, in the Christian perspective on revelation, necessarily leads to a critique of religion, and in the course of history has in fact led to such a critique over and over again.

35 Bultmann, p. 605.

36 On this cf. Schnackenburg, 2:268-81, Excursus 10: "The Johannine Concept of Truth," with bibliography.

37 On this cf. F. Mussner, *ZOE: Die Anschauung vom "Leben" im vierten Evangelium* (Munich, 1952).

37 On this cf. F. Mussner, *ZOE: Die Anschauung vom "Leben" im vierten Evangelium* (Munich, 1952).

38 Cf. R. Borig, *Der wahre Weinstock* (Munich, 1967), pp. 199-236.

39 It was to such formulations that the later trinitarian theology of the early Church and the Church fathers appealed. But John was not yet thinking of such theological interpretations. For him the immanence formula is situated wholly within the concept of revelation.

40 For the Johannine understanding of the concepts "work," "works," and "to work," cf. the voluminous book of J. Reidl, *Das Heilswerk Jesu nach Johannes* (Freiburg, 1973)

41 Ibid. p. 285.

42 According to Bultmann, the word "greater" refers to the post-Easter preaching of the community. This preaching can be called "greater" because the activity of Jesus was limited in time and still incomplete; it had not yet fulfilled its intention. The "completion" of which Bultmann is speaking has to do with the word of revelation "in its continual newness on every occasion when it is present" and not with supplementing or

surpassing Jesus' work in a quantitative way (Bultmann, op. cit., pp. 610-11).

43 On the whole subject cf. the article "Gebet," in *RGG*[3] 2:1209-44; the citation is from col. 1230, VI.

44 P. L. Berger, "Soziologische Betrachtungen über die Zukunft der Religion," in O. Schatz (ed.), *Hat die Religion Zukunft?* (Graz, 1971), pp. 67-68).

45 We must doubtless admit that these questions are quite legitimate in relation to many pseudo-devotional formulas and rituals of prayer; even prayer, and especially the language of prayer, should be subjected to a critique that is based on Scripture.

46 Bultmann, p. 612.

47 Cf. 8:51, 52, 55; 14:15, 21, 23, 24; 15:10, 20; 17:6; 1 John 2:3, 4, 5.

48 Cf. 8:42; 14:15, 21, 23, 24, 28; 21:15, 16.

49 So Bultmann, p. 612.

50 Ibid., p. 615.

51 Cf. Blank, pp. 323-24.

52 We must therefore regard *pneuma* as a "theo-anthropological term"; cf. H. W. Wolff, *Anthropology of the Old Testament*, tr. by M. Kohl (Philadelphia, 1974), p. 32.

53 Cf. above, pp. 16-17.

54 Bultmann, p. 619.

55 Cf. Blank, p. 70, n. 61.

56 In this context, it is interesting to note that in the middle of the second century Montanus, founder of the Montanist (Phrygian) heresy, claimed to be himself the promised Paraclete and thus attributed to Spirit-filled prophecy a revelatory function that transcended the revelation given in Jesus. Abbot Joachim of Fiore was to do the same in the Middle Ages. Cf. "Montanismus," *RGG*[3] 4:1117-18. John, however, clearly represents the tendency to link all Christian teaching to the word of Jesus.

57 Cf. 2:17, 22; 12:16; 15:20; 16:4.

58 Cf. G. R. Schmidt, in *Handbuch der Religionspädagogik* 2 (Gütersloh, 1974), p. 25.

59 On this point cf. especially E. Gilson, *The Christian Philosophy of St. Augustine*, tr. by L. E. M. Lynch (New York, 1960), chap. 5, sec. 1: "The Inner Master," where numerous citations are given.

60 Cf. Bultmann, pp. 625-31, where he attempts to reconstruct the original sequence of verses; in our exposition we keep to the traditional order of the text.

61 Cf. G. von Rad and W. Foerster, *"eirēnē, " TDNT* 2:400-17. The quotation in the next sentence is from p. 402.

62 The later dogma of Chalcedon sought to restate these ideas in its doctrine of the "two natures." The reader of the Bible will probably prefer the more open, less dogmatic formulation.

63 On this and related problems cf. Blank, pp. 218ff.

64 Cf. I. Kant, *Zum ewigen Frieden: Ein philosophischer Entwurf* (Königsberg, 1795); translated as *Perpetual Peace* by L. W. Beck in *Critique of Practical Reason and Other Writings in Moral Philosophy* (Chicago, 1949).

65 *Tractatus in Evangelium Joannis* 77, 3-4 (*PL* 35:1833-34; *CCL* 36:521-22).

66 Chapter 5 of Part II is entitled: "The Fostering of Peace and the Promotion of a Community of Nations." The quotation is from no. 77, in W. M. Abbott, S. J. (ed.), *The Documents of Vatican II* (New York, 1966), p. 290.

67 On the Johannine "I am" formula cf. R. Borig, *Der wahre Weinstock;* E. Schweizer, *Ego eimi: Die religionsgeschichtliche Herkunft und theologische Bedeutung der johanneischen Bildreden* (Göttingen, 1965²).

68 Following Schweizer (*Ego eimi*, pp. 40ff., 68, 79), R. Bultmann has been the chief proponent of the view that the vine in chapter 15 must be traced back to the myth of the tree of life. The most important support for this hypothesis comes from the texts of the so-called "Mandeans," a baptist sect which still exists today on the lower Euphrates and Tigris and whose origins reach back to the early Judaic and early Christian period. Their religious mythology still shows clearly gnostic traits; cf. C. Colpe, "Mandäer," *RGG*³ 14:709-12. Bultmann writes: *"The vine is the tree of life. . . .* Just as the myth has dreams of a water of life and of a bread of life, so it has of a tree of life. But what is dream there is reality here: *egō eimi";* thus, according to Bultmann (pp. 530-31), John is making Jesus say, "I am the true tree of life."

69 For example, Isaiah's well-known Song of the Vineyard (5:1-7), or Jer. 2:21: "I planted you a choice vine, wholly of pure seed. How then have you turned degenerate and become a wild vine?" Cf. also Ezek. 15:1-6; 19:10-14; Ps. 80:9-15.

70 According to the account given by the Jewish historian Flavius Josephus, there was over the gate (the *hekal*) to the sanctuary proper in the Jerusalem temple a golden vine with clusters of grapes hanging from it (*Jewish War* V, 210; *Antiquities of the Jewish People* XV, 395). Tacitus, *Histories* V, 5, likewise reports that there was a golden vine in the temple at Jerusalem. O. Michel and O. Bauernfeind note that "vine, grapes, and cup were among the oldest symbols used by the Jews. In the New Testament period these were frequently placed at grave-sites and on ossuaries and coins; they were not lacking even on the coins issued by the procurators, who thus adapted themselves to Jewish ideas, and on coins from the time of the first and second rebellions. Later on, these symbols made their appearance chiefly in synagogues" (in their edition of Flavius Josephus, *De Bello Judaico—Der jüdische Krieg* 2/1 [Darmstadt, 1963], pp. 253-54, n. 77).

71 Borig, *Der wahre Weinstock*, p. 97.

72 Cf. John 14:6, and J. Blank, "Der johanneiasche Wahrheitsbergriff," *Biblische Zeitschrift* 7 (1963), pp. 163-73.

73 Borig, p. 33.

74 Ibid., p. 97.

75 This means that there is no room for a Eucharistic interpretation of the passage on the vine, nor certainly for an interpretation that would relate the passage to Church law; cf. e.g., K. Mörsdorf, "Kirchengewalt," *LTK*[2] 6:218-21, espec. 220.

76 As verse 5 shows, there is an inclusion here.

77 Cf., e.g., Ps. 1; but cf. also Matt. 3:8, 10; 7:16-20; 12:33.

78 Bultmann, p. 533, n. 4.

79 Cf. Borig, pp. 48-49.

80 Ibid., pp. 199-236.

81 Thus Borig, p. 59.

82 Thus Bultmann, pp. 539-40.

83 Cf. above on 14:3.

84 "Asia Minor . . . constituted *the* Christian country *kat'exochēn* during the pre-Constantine era" (A. von Harnack, *The Mission and Expansion of The Church in the First Three Centuries*, tr. by J. Moffatt [New York, 1908], 2:182).

85 Pliny the Younger, *Epistulae* X, 96, tr. by W. Melmoth and W. M. L. Hutchinson (Cambridge, Mass., 1915), 2:403, 405. Hetairies were brotherhoods, associations, private clubs.

86 Cf. J. Blank, "Der historische Jesus und die Kirche," in *Jesus von Nazareth: Geschichte und Relevanz* (Freiburg, 1972), pp. 122-50.

87 Cf. 16:20, 21, 22, 24; 17:13; 20:20.

88 Cf. 13:34-35 and the interpretation above.

89 Cf. 10:11, 15, 17, 18; 13:37-38; 1 John 3:16. The expression is a semitism; cf. H. L. Strack and P. Billerbeck, *Kommentar zum Neuen Testament aus Talmud und Midrasch*, 2:537.

90 Bultmann, p. 547.

91 Cf. Mark 13:9-13 par. Matt. 24:9-14; Luke 21:12-19; Matt. 5:11-13 par. Luke 6:22-23.

92 Here again, therefore, there is no need of harking back to gnostic models, contrary to Bultmann, p. 548. There may, however, have been some terminological borrowings.

93 On the problem of the persecution of Christians in antiquity cf. J. J. Vogt, "Christenverfolgung, I, historisch. Bewertung durch Heiden und Christen," *RAC* 3:1159-1208; H. Lost, "Christenverfolgung II, juristisch," *RAC* 3:1208-28; J. Moreau, *Die Christenverfolgung im Römischen Reich* (Berlin, 1961).

94 Cf. 8:23; 15:19; 17:14, 16; 18:36; 1 John 2:16; 4:5.

95 Cf. also 12:37-50; Schnackenburg, 2:513ff.

96 Bultmann, p. 551.

97 Cf. Blank, *Krisis*, pp. 198ff.

98 Cf. N. Brox, *Zeuge und Märtyrer* (Munich, 1961); idem, *Der Glaube als Zeugnis* (Munich, 1966).

99 Cf. the Babylonian Talmud, Tractate Berakoth, 28b 29; "Rabban Gamaliel II," *Encyclopaedia Judaica* (Jerusalem, 1971), 7:296-98.

100 Tr. by P. Riessler, *Altjüdisches Schrifttum ausserhalb der Bibel* (Augsburg, 1928), p. 9.

101 Strack-Billerbeck, 4:330-31.

102 Cf. P. Stockmeier, *Glaube und Religion in der frühen Kirche* (Freiburg, 1975), pp. 81ff.

103 The decree *Cunctos populos*, tr. in H. Bettenson (ed.), *Documents of the Christian Church* (2nd ed.; New York, 1963), p. 31.

104 On this problem cf. M. Simon, *Verus Israel: Etudes sur les relations entre chrétiens et juifs dans l'empire romain* (2nd ed.; Paris, 1964).

105 Ibid., pp. 264-66.

106 On this cf. Blank, *Krisis*, pp. 332-39.

107 Bultmann, p. 563.

108 Ibid., p. 566.

109 The Greek word *pneuma*, like the Hebrew *ruah* and the Latin *spiritus*, means both "breath of wind" and "spirit." The term "gentle breath of the wind (Spirit)" (*Geistbraus*) is from Martin Buber.

110 Bultmann, p. 615.

111 Cf. ibid., pp. 560-61.

112 We may also remark in passing that the traditional natural/supernatural schema is hardly adapted for grasping the objective meaning here. This schema, especially in its concept of supernature, leads to the mistaken idea that religion is a superstructure and thus to the formation of a static dualism, when in fact it is types of existential behavior that are the issue.

113 Cf. Acts 2:17-18; 19:6, 21:9; Rom. 12:6; 1 Cor. 12:10; 13:2, 8; 14:6, 22; 1 Thess. 5:20; Eph. 2:20; 3:5; 4:11.

114 Cf. especially on 14:18-20 above.

115 M. Werner, *The Formation of Christian Dogma: The Historical Study of Its Problem*, tr. by S. G. F. Brandon (New York, 1957; Boston: Beacon Paperbacks, 1965), p. 44 (paperback edition).

116 Cf. Blank, *Krisis*, pp. 53-108.

117 Bultmann, p. 577.

118 Pesiqta Rabbati 36/162a, in H. L. Strack and P. Billerbeck, *Kommentar zum Neuen Testament aus Talmud und Midrasch* 4/2 (Munich, 1924), p. 982 (italics added). Cf. also P. Volz, *Die Eschatologie der jüdischen Gemeinde im neutestamentlichen Zeitalter* (Tübingen, 1934), pp. 147-49.

119 Bultmann, p. 581.

120 Cf. R. Schnackenburg, *God's Rule and Kingdom*, tr. by J. Murray (New York, 1963), pp. 195-214; idem, "Naherwartung," *LTK* 7:777-79.

121 Cf. Insel-Ausgabe (Leipzig, 1939), pp. 428-30.

122 Bultmann, p. 589.

123 Cf. Amos 5:16-20; Joel 2:1-11; Zech. 12:1-11. On this subject cf. G. von Rad, *Old Testament Theology*, tr. by D. M. G. Stalker, 2 (New York, 1965), pp. 119-25; Volz, op. cit., p. 93.

124 Cf. Mark 12:32; Matt. 7:22; 24:38; Luke 6:23; then Paul especially: 1 Cor. 1:8; 3:13; 5:5; 2 Cor. 1:14; Phil. 1:6; Rom. 13:12-13.

125 Bultmann, p. 583.

126 Cf. F. Hauck, "paroimia," *TDNT* 5:854-56.

127 Cf. H. Schlier, "parrhēsia," *TDNT* 5:871-86.

128 Hauck, p. 854.

129 As H. Schlier, pp. 871-75, explains.

130 Acts 2:29; 4:13, 29, 31; 28:31.

131 Cf. 7:4, 13, 26; 10:24; 11:14, 54; 16:25, 29.

132 Bultmann, p. 587.

133 Cf. 1:12; 11:52; 1 John 3:1, 2, 10; 5:20.

134 Cf. E. Coreth, "Frage," *Handbuch philosophischer Grundbegriffe* 2 (Munich, 1973), pp. 485-93.

135 *Pensées*, fr. 202 (Brunschvicg), tr. by H. F. Stewart, *Pascal's Pensées* (New York, 1950), p. 151.

136 Karl Marx, *Toward the Critique of Hegel's Philosophy of Law*, in L. D. Easton and K. H. Guddat (eds. and trs.), *Writings of the Young Marx on Philosophy and Society* (New York, 1967), p. 250.

137 Ibid.

138 *Pensées*, fr. 139 (Bruschvicg), tr. Stewart, p. 59.

139 Pascal, *The Mystery of Jesus*, tr. Stewart, p. 369.

140 So Strathmann, *Johannes*, p. 229.

141 Schulz, *Johannes*, p. 208.

142 Ibid.

143 Bultmann, p. 593.

144 Volz, *Die Eschatologie der jüdischen Gemeinde*, p. 147.

145 Cf. also Rev. 2:17, 26; 3:5, 21.

146 Eusebius, *History of the Church* X, 2, 1-2; tr. by G. A. Williamson, *Eusebius: History of the Church* (Baltimore, 1965), p. 382.

147 Leo the Great, *Sermo* 82, 1; text in *PL* 54:422-23.

148 The source of this account is the diary of Fray Celso Gargia, in R. and E. Grün (eds.), *Die Erorberung von Peru: Pizarro und andere Conquistadoren, 1526-1712* (Tübingen-Basel, 1973).

149 Ibid., pp. 47-54.

150 Käsemann, p. 3; cf. W. Thüsing, *Herrlichkeit und Einheit: Eine Auslegung des Hohenpriesterlichen Gebets* (Düsseldorf, 1961).

151 Bultmann has the following division: Introduction (13:1); The Petition for Glorification (17:1-5); The Intercession for the Community (17:6-26), this last being in turn divided into: (1) The Founding of the Community (17:6-8); (2) The Petition for the Preservation and Sanctification of the Community (17:9-19); (3) The Petition for the Oneness of the Community (17:20-23); (4) The Petition for the Perfecting of the Believers (17:24-26). In thus dividing the prayer, he sees correctly that verses 6-26 belong closely together and overlap in their general themes. As a matter of fact it is not possible in John to make a clean distinction between the first disciples of the earthly Jesus and the community of believers. Nonetheless we must take into account the fact that John does distinguish at least verbally between the first and the later community of disciples, and does so, it is clear, in order to give his presentation a certain degree of clear temporal and historical distance. But this means that he is fully conscious of the problem of a historical difference between the first and the later disciples. This fact deserves attention even if in John's solution to the problem the contours are blurred.

152 Bultmann, p. 486, with the justification on p. 489.

153 Cf. Matt. 11:25 par. Luke 10:21; but also Mark 14:36 par. Matt. 26:39b; Luke 22:42.

154 On this theme cf. P. Hoffmann, *Studien zur Theologie der Logienquelle* (Münster, 1972), pp. 102-42.

155 This conception of revelation has its roots in early Jewish apocalyptic; John, of course, has given it a radical reinterpretation along christo-logical lines.

156 On this cf. Blank, *Krisis*, pp. 135ff.

157 Cf. above on 13:31-32.

158 Cf. the pericope on the "question of authority": Mark 11:27-33 par. Matt. 21:23-27; Luke 20:1-8.

159 Cf. especially Dan. 7:9-14, 22, 26, 27; Ethiopian Enoch 45, 3; 46, 1-6; 49, 2-4; 61, 8-9; 62, 1-3; and cf. Blank, *Krisis*, p. 89, n. 125, and pp. 120ff.

160 Cf. Blank, *Krisis*, pp. 75ff.

161 Cf. F. Mussner, *ZOE: Die Anschauung von "Leben" im vierten Evangelium* (Munich, 1952).

162 Ibid. p. 144. Cf. 3:36; 5:24; 6:47, 53, 54; 8:12, also I John 3:15; 5:12, 13.

163 Cf. Blank, *Krisis*, p. 70, especially n. 61; also Reidl, *Das Heilswerk Jesu*, pp. 57ff.

164 Cf. Strack-Billerbeck, 3:2.

165 On this cf. especially Reidl, pp. 81-186.

166 Reidl, p. 92. Reidl has rightly directed special attention to the fact that the glorification, according to John, is reciprocal and is therefore, in the final analysis, the expression of the love that exists between Jesus and the Father; cf. pp. 118-19.

167 On this cf. Schnackenburg, 1:494-506, Excursus 2: "Pre-existence."

168 Bultmann, p. 500.

169 Cf. also 15:11; 16:20, 21, 22, 24.

170 Bultmann, p. 507.

171 "It is rather the case that if we can isolate unity from the being of the community (as a community of faith) and describe it as its *raison d'être*, then it can be regarded as an essential characteristic of the community only in so far as it is eschatological" (Bultmann, p. 517).

172 Ibid.

173 Cf. K. Rahner, "Einheit," *LTK* 3:749-50, and M. Zahn, "Einheit," *Handbuch philosophischer Grundbegriffe* 2:320-37. According to Rahner, the concept of unity is "analogous as is the concept of being; it comprises in a unique way both unitive comprehensiveness and distinguishing differences, the removal of distinction . . . and the positing of it." A proper understanding of unity requires us to realize that multiplicity and distinction are not contradictory to unity but on the contrary must be seen and thought together with it. Or as Zahn puts it, "We speak for example of a unit of currency, but also of the unity of a work of art, of a nation, of personality and the individual, of the organism and life, of time, space, and action, as well as of the unity of being itself. In addition to different concepts of unity that are distinguished by their relations to different kinds of *objects*, the concept is also differentiated by the application of other viewpoints. Thus different concepts of unity emerge when unity is thought of as a source or as a (still to be attained) goal; when it represents the common dependence that holds a multiplicity together or as an order that exists of and for itself" (p. 321).

174 H. Schlier, "Einheit der Kirche, I," *LTK*² 3:754.

175 The following passages are from *Cyprian: De Lapsis and De Ecclesiae Catholicae Unitate*, ed. and tr. by M. Bévenot, S. J. (Oxford, 1971), pp. 63, 65, 67-69, 85, and 79 (italics added).